# Ontology Pipeline®

## A Framework for Knowledge Engineering

JESSICA TALISMAN

Technics Publications
SEDONA, ARIZONA

TECHNICS PUBLICATIONS

115 Linda Vista, Sedona, AZ 86336 USA

https://www.TechnicsPub.com

Edited by Steve Hoberman

Cover design by Dylan Werner



First Printing 2026



ISBN, print ed. 9798898161392
ISBN, Kindle ed. 9798898161408
ISBN, PDF ed. 9798898161415

Library of Congress Control Number: 2026945272

*For my children, Colby and Gus, and my life partner, Dave, who have been with me every step of this journey.*

# Endorsements

Jessica makes the dense world of knowledge engineering accessible without sacrificing depth. She walks you from controlled vocabularies to knowledge graphs as one clear, buildable progression, grounded in real examples and honest warnings about common traps and mistakes. Her library science background is the book's secret weapon, bringing hard-won discipline to the messy realities of data and AI. What I value most is that she never loses sight of the people - she is precise about the skills, roles, and judgment that make ontologies and knowledge graphs truly valuable. Her passion shows on every page and is contagious – a must read for everyone who is really serious about making AI work!

**Tiankai Feng, Author of Humanizing Data Strategy & Humanizing AI Strategy**

*What I most appreciate about this book is the way Jessica makes explicit many of the implicit assumptions that experienced knowledge engineering practitioners often don't even realize they're making. That's what makes this book such a valuable guide for anyone looking to accelerate their journey into knowledge engineering. Her library science background brings an important and often overlooked perspective to knowledge engineering, and it's one of the reasons she's able to make those implicit assumptions so clear. For anyone looking for a detailed, holistic, and standards-based guide to ontology development and semantic technologies, this book is an outstanding resource.*

**Juan Sequeda, PhD, Principal Data Strategist and Researcher, ServiceNow**

One of the biggest shifts happening in our industry is that enterprise data management is expanding into enterprise knowledge management. AI is accelerating that transition because it depends on more than well-managed data. It depends upon context, shared meaning, trusted relationships, and the ability to organize the vast stores of unstructured knowledge that exist across every large enterprise. As AI becomes the primary interface to enterprise information, knowledge management will become the foundation that unlocks *trustworthy AI at scale.*

*Jessica Talisman demonstrates that the future of enterprise AI will be determined not simply by the sophistication of our models, but by the quality of the knowledge we make available to them. Ontology Pipeline provides data leaders with a practical blueprint for operationalizing that knowledge as governed enterprise infrastructure. CDOs looking beyond today's AI hype and toward the capabilities that will differentiate their organizations will find this to be an important contribution to the evolution of data leadership.*

**Malcolm Hawker Chief Data Officer, Profisee**

*This is the guide that engineers need to ground their generative AI systems in knowledge, expertise, organizational standards, and context. This book carries readers from motivating philosophy and theory all the way to practical, brass tacks implementation of ontology pipelines as an organizational process and technical reality.*

**Matthew Housely, PhD Author of Fundamentals of Data Engineering**

*Far too often, enterprises treat their language as any other living language. But to use enterprise language powerfully, it must be formalized. That is the methodology Jessica Talisman puts forward. In the words of the author: Start where your language already lives.*

**Ole Olesen-Bagneux, PhD - VP, Chief Evangelist, Actian**

*As someone who consistently sees organizations struggle to scale large language and multimodal models, I highly recommend Jessica Talisman's The Ontology Pipeline for its pragmatic framework that bridges library science and modern data architecture to solve the semantic crisis in artificial intelligence. The book demystifies the journey from simple controlled vocabularies to complex knowledge graphs, showing that explicit ontological commitments are the essential 'semantic rails' needed to move large language models beyond statistical guessing. Whether you are on a team building Retrieval-Augmented Generation (RAG) systems or autonomous agents, or someone just starting out, this book brings a practical roadmap and systems thinking for creating a shared understanding between humans and machines to achieve reliable, trustworthy AI.*

**Michelle Yi, Founder and Former IBM**

*Semantic work dies in the budget conversation because nobody can price it. Jessica fixes that by making the invisible parts explicit, from provenance tracking on day one to competency questions that scope the graph and a staffing model per architecture pattern, so you can tell a CFO what you are buying and when it pays back. I have watched enough AI programs collapse for want of agreed meaning to know this is the missing manual.*

**Amy Raygada, Principal Data & AI Strategist, Thoughtworks**

*The ontology has taken the stage front and center in an age where text is at the forefront. But ontologies are – of necessity – complicated. Let Jessica Talisman help lead you through the maze of ontologies and guide you through the obstacles that await you as you explore the intricacies of the world of ontologies. Read Jessica's book to get you on the ontology train.*

**Bill Inmon**

*Jessica's book is a masterclass in Ontologies. She simplifies complex concepts, and makes them actionable for practitioners building the foundation for AI: context in their organisations.*

**Prukulpa Sankar Cofounder, Atlan**

*Jessica Talisman's Ontology Pipeline turns semantic knowledge management from a dark art into a pragmatic guide that adds trust to traditional applications and AI agents alike. She brings precision to enterprise AI by clearing the "probabilistic fog." The Ontology Pipeline is a working method, not a manifesto.*

**Sanjeev Mohan, Founder SanjMo and Former Gartner**

# Acknowledgments

Thank you to my reviewers, Bill Inmon, Malcolm Hawker, Juan Sequeda, Prukulpa Sankar, Ole Olesen-Bagneux, Matthew Housley, Amy Raygada, Michelle Yi, and Sanjeev Mohan. All of you have raised the bar and challenged my thinking, helping clarify my words and ideas.

Joanna Miller, my friend and Director of Operations, for keeping things real and supporting me along the way.

My Substack subscribers, who followed me through this writing journey and gave valuable feedback along the way. Without the collective you, this wouldn't have been possible.

My ontology and knowledge graph friends, thank you for continuing to advance the field. Katariina Kari, Veronika Heimsbakk, Tony Seale, Charles Ivie, Ora Lassila, Tara Raafat, Andrew Padilla, Larry Swanson, and Margaret Warren. Your creative energy and brilliance light the spark for innovation.

For the countless librarians who have stood for knowledge and the importance of provenance, building, maintaining, and fighting for knowledge over centuries of civilization and human thought. You continue to inspire me every day, with your courage and passion.

The Knowledge Graph Academy and my partners in education. Daisy Barnes, Tony Seale, Katariina Kari, Callum Hornblower and Veronika Heimsbakk. And to the Academy students and graduates, for teaching while learning and learning while teaching.

My deceased father, Mark Talisman, my mother, Jill Talisman, and my brother, Raphael Talisman. Knowledge was the center of our world. Books and libraries, museums and travel.

# Contents

# Foreword

Most people who work with graph technologies lack a precise understanding of terms such as *ontology*, *semantics*, *taxonomy*, and *knowledge graphs.* Even so, there have been useful definitions of these terms in place for at least three decades—just never put together in one place alongside the practices that make them work. As Jessica Talisman states, "Ontologies solve a problem most engineers were never taught to see."

Fixing that gap would require an expert librarian willing to pull together the references and citations required—which is exactly what Jessica has done. Reading the *Ontology Pipeline* feels like having an expert at your side during a workshop on a real business problem, walking your team through how to grapple with your organization's context and semantics. It reads like a storyboard: clear sequencing, a consistent tone that's competent, encouraging, and useful throughout. I've worked in this field for years, and while reading drafts, I've lost track of how many times I've scrambled back to my active projects to make notes on fixing things, based on Jessica's advice—what to change and why. Pro tip: the section on competency questions is pure gold.

Each stage of the book sets up the next, providing you with a repeatable, measurable process. The guidance is clear, well-researched, and carefully cited, making it accessible to anyone who wants to go deeper. And it comes from real experience—Jessica has guided this kind of work at the US Department of Justice, Amazon, Adobe, and many other organizations working on important use cases.

*Shared context* across an organization is a hard problem that never holds still. Language and understanding evolve as people collaborate—any healthy business should expect that. But *misunderstood context* is also a common root cause for costly errors, competitive disadvantage, service disruptions, customer churn, legal exposure, and employee frustration. Ignore at your own peril. Conversely, handle it well and this becomes a great way to distinguish your team.

* * *

**Scene 1:** I introduced Jessica as a speaker at Connected Data London several years ago. Her talk was one of the best in the track—she addressed questions attendees and other speakers had been arguing about, explained carefully and clearly, suggested helpful learning resources, then punctuated with a mic drop: "People in the tech industry are arguing over matters librarians have had to handle for 3,000 years." From clay tablets to card catalogs to the web, through the rise of data science and now the global scramble to adopt AI, librarians and library science have repeatedly come to the rescue for some of the thorniest problems.

**Scene 2:** Over the following months, a flurry of inspiring articles from Jessica kept surfacing online. Clearly something bigger was in the works—this book. I followed carefully and started recommending articles.

**Scene 3:** At a conference in UC Santa Cruz in 2025, I was standing next to Jessica when my CEO called: "We need to get an expert to help us with metadata definitions, how the results of our product align with [a large ontology]. Know anyone?"

Yes, in fact. Jessica and I talked long and far on the subject, beginning a project together. We brought her in as a consultant to define a small SKOS taxonomy for describing the semantics of our product's results. We wanted to align with controlled vocabularies and ontologies such as NIEM, FollowTheMoney, Beneficial Ownership Data Standard, WorldCat, and others. We asked Jessica to write an article describing our project and how to use it.

**Scene 4:** Months later, my CEO called again: "I keep getting questions about ontology. Do we have anything written?" I sent him Jessica's article. "Oh, this is perfect!"

To be clear, I'm not trying to be harsh on our CEO, who happens to be a brilliant, intelligent leader, plus a really fine person, and a friend. The point is that once your leadership starts hearing "ontology" and "semantic layer" from customers and partners, you'll be having the same conversation. Get a jump start and do your team a favor: apply what's in this book, and buy them copies.

* * *

Corporate and public-sector teams have lived with murky, ambiguous context for a long time. Sales defines "customer" one way, Support uses another, and their dashboards never agree. The usual fix is ad hoc: endless meetings to align on meaning. But those stakes just went up, as Jessica makes clear:

"Agentic AI systems that make decisions and take actions need unambiguous understanding of their operational domains."

As AI tooling moves into production ever so rapidly, an organization without clearly defined context will see those tools generating garbage at speed. GenAI tools will rapidly generate large numbers of conflicting, potentially buggy results, incurring high costs and causing significant confusion. Your most experienced people will end up spending their time reviewing AI output rather than leading their teams. If you're thinking of "AI" as synonymous with "automation," this is a game where you're already upside down and clearly won't win.

Of course, many organizations are reluctant to invest in efforts to define their business context. But many will discover that their competitors or adversaries have already done so, and gained an advantage from it. That's not something to ignore. It's where the investment needs to start, with the practices detailed in this book.

Paco Nathan
Senzing

# Introduction

Roughly 55 percent of the data enterprises collect is "dark"—stored but never analyzed or put to use—and for some sources, such as sensor data, that figure climbs toward 90 percent.[1] The bottleneck is rarely storage or compute. It is meaning; most organizations cannot reliably tell a machine what their data is about. A semantic knowledge management system (SKMS) is the framework that provides the missing layer—an organized structure of concepts, definitions, and relationships that lets both people and machines interpret information consistently and act on it with confidence. This book is about how to build one, stage by stage.

Organized, structured, and semi-structured SKMSs are rapidly emerging as essential for achieving highly performant large language models (LLMs) and AI systems. Many technologists either view SKMSs as overly simplistic (limited to text labels or annotations) or as too labor-intensive to justify investment. In response to this confusion, there has been an overreliance on out-of-the-box public taxonomies, such as the Google Product Taxonomy, resulting in homogenous knowledge ecosystems. This cookie-cutter approach fails to meet the needs of a domain or business.

Failure to model and represent an organization's unique aspects and attributes is evident in AI implementation failures and challenges in deriving context and meaning from knowledge management systems, such as knowledge graphs.

*A semantic knowledge system requires investment in both people and tools, but does not need to be limited to simple annotations or labor-intensive human efforts.*

The construction and maintenance of a SKMS often operate as a black box due to a lack of existing frameworks and workflows, making it difficult for businesses to determine the exact scale of investment in both the short- and long-term. Additionally, direct returns on investment can be challenging to measure, as the benefits of a SKMS tend to be secondary and primarily reflected in

[1] *The State of Dark Data,* Splunk, 2019, www.splunk.com/en_us/form/the-state-of-dark-data.html; "What Is Dark Data?" *IBM,* 2 Apr. 2026, www.ibm.com/think/topics/dark-data.

the success of RAG implementations, entity management systems, and information retrieval metrics.

A formal SKMS program can be scoped, scaled, and positioned as both a product and a unique domain of expertise by structuring knowledge management stages and phases with logical sequences and workflows. Establishing a robust and dynamic knowledge management program enables organizations to invest in this infrastructure with greater confidence, hiring people and leveraging machines to refine data and information systems while guiding the construction and maintenance of semantically rich ecosystems.

---

## Enter the librarians

The Library and Information Science domain provides principled, logical methods and frameworks for organizing and structuring data into information, which becomes knowledge when made accessible to all users (human and machine). Librarians have codified these methodologies and strategies to manage complex information ecosystems, thereby enhancing the accuracy and reliability of information retrieval. Having successfully leveraged machine learning (ML) and artificial intelligence (AI) as workflow and cataloging tools for over a decade, the library science domain offers repeatable methodologies for building scalable and extensible SKMSs that drive accuracy and reliability in AI systems.

A quick distinction before we proceed:

---

*Data are raw, uninterpreted facts, values with no context attached.*
*Information is data placed in a context that answers a question.*
*Knowledge is information understood well enough to act on.*

---

Think of the number "50." On its own, it is data, a value that could mean anything. Told that it is the balance in your checking account, we have information: the number now answers a question. And knowing that a $50 balance will not cover an $80 bill, so the purchase has to wait, is knowledge, information put to work to guide a decision. Librarians specialize in moving material up this ladder:

turning scattered facts into organized information, and organized information into shared knowledge.

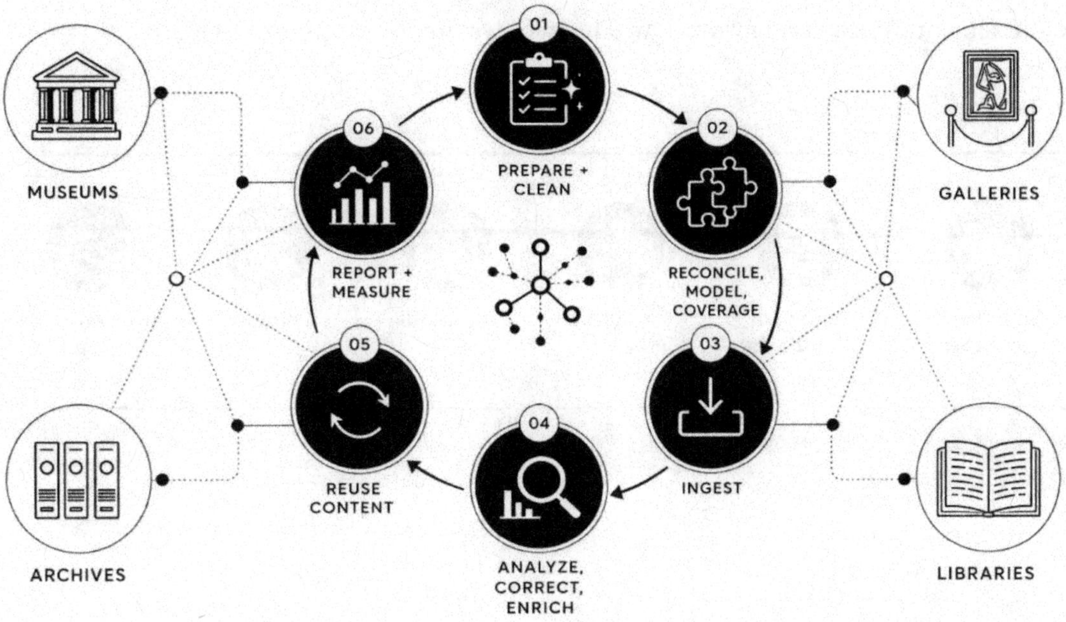


Figure 1: Library science data preparation for AI Systems. Derived from Fuzheado (https://commons.wikimedia.org/w/index.php?curid=128955050 https://www.ontotext.com/blog/vladimir-alexiev-ontology-semantic-enrichment-linked-data).

Technology domains can learn from librarians by prioritizing knowledge management workflows and processes to support reliable, resilient SKMSs, thereby positioning these systems as valuable investments for businesses.

---

## The Ontology Pipeline

This introduction is a map, not the territory. It outlines every stage of the Ontology Pipeline: controlled vocabulary, taxonomy, metadata schema, thesaurus, ontology, and knowledge graph, but defines each only briefly. Every one of these terms has its own chapter, with full definitions, worked examples and construction steps. If a term feels dense in this section, know that the details are coming.

The Ontology Pipeline is derived from librarians' workflows. It offers a systematic methodology for constructing a SKMS. The pipeline consists of iterative building blocks, with each phase preparing for the next stage of building. This iterative process incorporates data cleaning and preparation tasks into the semantic engineering workflow. The iterative processes appear in Figure 2.

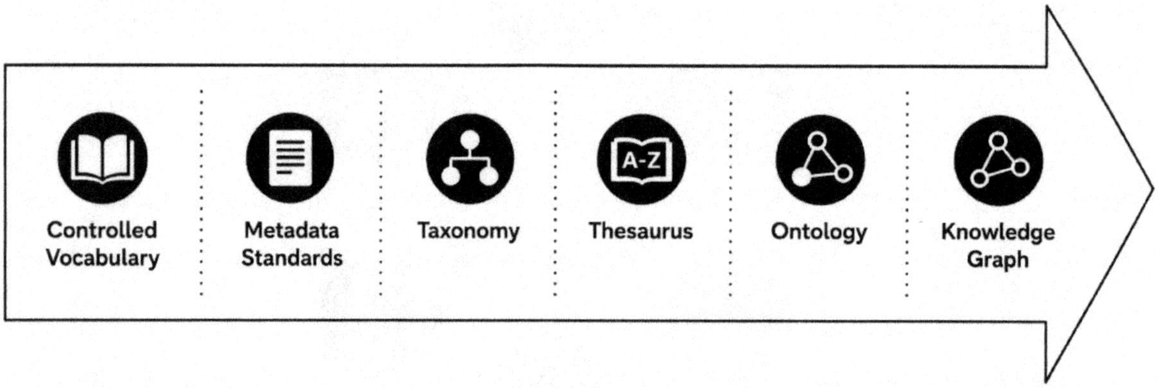


Figure 2: The Ontology Pipeline. Derived from ANSI Z39.19 (https://www.niso.org/publications/ansiniso-z3919-2005-r2010).

Figure 2 captures the pipeline at a glance, where each stage prepares the material for the next. A controlled vocabulary establishes clean, disambiguated terms. Metadata standards describe what those terms are about. A taxonomy arranges the terms into a broad-to-narrow hierarchy with concepts organized into parent-child relations. A thesaurus enriches that hierarchy with equivalent, associative, and matching relations using a lightweight upper ontology. An ontology then adds formal classes, properties, and logical relations so machines can reason over the model. Finally, a knowledge graph populates the ontology with real instance data, producing a queryable web of meaning. Each term is introduced only briefly here; each has its own chapter ahead.

---

*The Ontology Pipeline is designed to codify a framework for the architecture and construction of semantic knowledge management systems.*

---

This tangible workflow and process enable a more accurate estimation of investment requirements, both human and machine. Without the Ontology Pipeline, organizations struggle to understand the levels of effort and investment required, let alone how to derive metrics to measure benefits, system performance, and returns on investment.

Leaders and stakeholders gain greater visibility into a semantic system's requirements when the business understands the system's components. With clear goals and outcomes in sight, organizations can build and maintain a SKMS with confidence, knowing these investments are crucial to supporting data infrastructure, data transformation, and AI initiatives.

---

## Controlled vocabulary

A controlled vocabulary is a curated, finite list of preferred terms—each disambiguated and defined—that an organization agrees to use consistently when describing its data and information. What makes it "controlled" is the discipline: one preferred label per concept, explicit handling of synonyms, and a governed process for adding or retiring terms.

It helps to distinguish it from three things it is often confused with. A general vocabulary is simply the words people happen to use, with no control over duplicates, synonyms, or scope. A data governance glossary defines business terms for human readers but usually is not structured for machine use or bound to a single preferred label. A data dictionary documents the fields, types and constraints of a specific database—it describes how data is stored, not what concepts exist in the domain.

A controlled vocabulary sits above all three: it is the shared, machine-ready set of concepts to which the other artifacts point back. A controlled vocabulary is also the raw material from which we shape a taxonomy and thesaurus. It is the foundation from which we can determine how best to structure a hierarchy, placing vocabulary terms in parent-child relations within a taxonomy, and, for a thesaurus, how to determine which terms remain preferred and which are curated as alternative labels or aliases. For example, a museum requires every object's medium to be chosen from a fixed list—"oil paint," "watercolor," "tempera"—so that a search for "watercolor" reliably surfaces every watercolor in the collection, even if the original donor called it something else.

A controlled vocabulary is the general term used to describe a flat list of terms, a taxonomy, or a thesaurus. In the context of the Ontology Pipeline, a controlled vocabulary is a flat authoritative list of disambiguated, defined terms. Variants or alternative labels may or may not be present in a controlled vocabulary.

A controlled vocabulary is the first building block in constructing a SKMS. It works in tandem with data cleaning and preparation tasks. As part of the vocabulary construction and refinement workflow, data must be deduplicated, merged, and defined to create a clean, disambiguated vocabulary fit for its purpose.

Deduplication involves reconciling synonymous terms to clarify the vocabulary. Best practices include defining each term or concept in the controlled vocabulary list, ensuring all users and stakeholders share a common understanding of the chosen terms. For example, Figure 3, illustrates that *Mission to Planet Earth* has a definition in NASA's controlled vocabulary index. The indicator UF means "Use For", and MTPE is the abbreviated acronym for *Mission to Planet Earth.* This illustrates how duplicates, near duplicates, and synonyms can be resolved when architecting a controlled vocabulary. A controlled vocabulary is the first step toward creating unified domain vocabularies, fostering alignment across people and machine systems while supporting a shared and common understanding.

**Mission to Planet Earth**
*(added April 1995)*

DEF A NASA initated program that uses both space and ground based measurement systems to provide the scientific basis for understanding global change.

UF *MTPE*

GS programs
NASA programs
. . **Mission to Planet Earth**

RT climate change
Earth Observing System (EOS)
geophysics
global warming
∞ missions
remote sensing
scientific visualization

Figure 3: Controlled vocabulary (https://ntrs.nasa.gov/citations/20000026924).

## *Metadata standards*

Now that we have controlled vocabularies, we develop *metadata standards* to encode the common understanding or "aboutness" of data and information. A metadata standard is a requirement intended to establish a common understanding of the meaning or semantics of the data, ensuring its proper use and interpretation by its owners and users. To achieve this common understanding, a number of characteristics or attributes of the data have to be defined, also known as metadata (https://en.wikipedia.org/wiki/Metadata_standard).

Metadata standards provide schema-based control for databases and information systems. Metadata elements define the fields that are needed to describe data and information assets. These elements are categorized by their characteristics: *STRUCTURAL* (for machine readability), *DESCRIPTIVE* (for context), and *ADMINISTRATIVE* (for asset maintenance and lineage). For example, a STRUCTURAL element might be the page sequence of a scanned book or the file format of an asset such as a PDF or spreadsheet—information a machine needs to render or process it. A DESCRIPTIVE element might be the title, author, or subject keywords that tell a person or system what the asset is about. An ADMINISTRATIVE element might be the creation date, rights statement, or preservation format that governs how the asset is maintained over its lifecycle.

While these are the most common types of metadata elements, practitioners and stakeholders have expanded these categories to include subject areas such as social or provenance metadata. Regardless of the types of metadata elements, each must be well-defined, with clear direction on what each element type is designed to handle.

With well-defined metadata standards, each metadata element is prepared to accept controlled vocabulary values. A metadata standard can support various workflows and data streams, often serving as the foundational architecture for entity value systems and concept models. The controlled vocabulary provides the controlled or allowable values to pair with metadata elements. By implementing a metadata standard, a natural framework emerges for entity reconciliation, vocabulary management, and schema-based validation matrices to enforce vocabulary control and semantics. Additionally, metadata standards provide valuable insight into extended vocabulary needs, helping scope future requirements in subsequent steps of the Ontology Pipeline.

In Figure 4, the metadata element TITLE has the value of *Mad Men Season 5: Plot Predictions*. The metadata element TYPE specifies article, indicating the content type. By normalizing the metadata element and its expected allowable values, the metadata standard and controlled vocabulary work together to describe the asset, providing context and meaning.

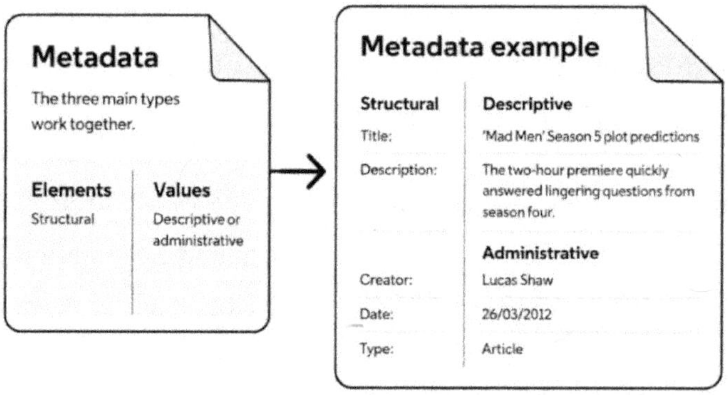


Figure 4: Metadata standard example.

---

## Taxonomy

A taxonomy is a hierarchical classification or categorization system in which all the terms belong to a single hierarchical structure and have parent/child or broader/narrower relationships to other terms. Taxonomies allow for classification according to a predetermined system.

The creation of controlled vocabularies and metadata schemas is often overlooked in the rush to build taxonomies. Without proper data hygiene—resolving synonyms and duplicate concepts, as we do when building controlled vocabularies and metadata schemas—a taxonomy can be difficult to build and quickly becomes unwieldy.

*A taxonomy takes the controlled vocabulary and transforms it into a hierarchical structure.*

This marks the beginning of building relationships between concepts, paving the way for a more mature, ontology-rich system. These relationships serve as helpful classification structures for machine learning algorithms to assist with front-end navigation and organize assets. Additionally, taxonomies are often used in tagging and annotation systems.

Figure 5 shows two examples. *Levels* is the simple form: a two-level taxonomy where Level is the parent and Beginner, Intermediate, and Expert are the child concepts. Adobe Experience Manager is the fuller example: a three-level taxonomy taken from a working system. The top concept, level one, is *Adobe Experience Manager*, with Administration and Security as level two, or its child concepts. Nested beneath *Administration* are level three concepts, representing more granular concepts such as *Access Control* and *Access Rights.* Each term is a child of the one above, so reading down a branch takes you from the platform to a platform feature, finally ending in the specific capabilities of the platform.

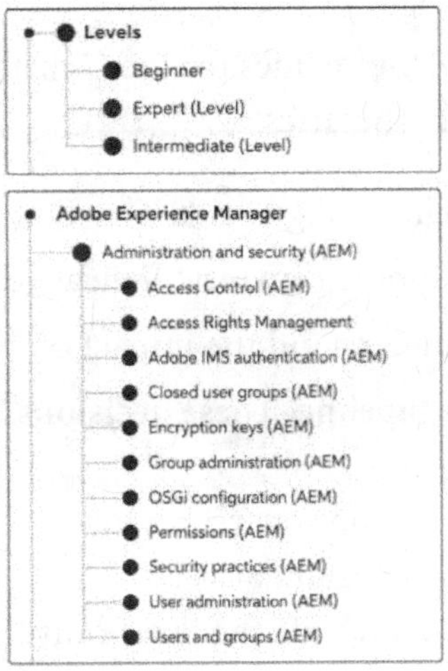


Figure 5: Taxonomy example.

Taxonomies are often built and maintained in spreadsheets. However, managing and scaling a taxonomy in a spreadsheet format can become unwieldy. Additionally, a spreadsheet-based taxonomy often lacks the machine-readable, semantic encoding structure necessary to support a fully developed SKMS.

To build a resilient taxonomy that is both human and machine-readable and optimized for AI systems, it is best to invest in a semantic middleware tool, such as Graphwise or TopQuadrant. This allows an emerging taxonomy to be structured using an upper ontology, such as Simple Knowledge Organization System (SKOS), and aligned with standards that inform the middleware validation matrices, which check for structural integrity and help resolve issues such as recursive loops and relationship clashes. While seemingly innocuous, the introduction of faulty logic, even within a base-structure-like taxonomy, can lead to the proliferation of errors throughout SKMS. Therefore, construct a taxonomy according to ISOs and ontology logic, with validation matrices in place, to ensure the soundness of the taxonomic structure.

Taxonomy guidelines and validation usually include basic ontological reasoning based upon standards, including:

1. ISO 25964-1, Information and documentation—Thesauri and interoperability with other vocabularies.
2. ISO 25964-2, Information and documentation—Thesauri and interoperability with other vocabularies—Part 2: Interoperability with other vocabularies.
3. RDF (ontology) validation.
4. ANSI/NISO Z39.19 (R2010) Guidelines for the Construction, Format, and Management of Monolingual Controlled Vocabularies.

In turn, these standards and guidelines align with The Ontology Pipeline, documenting similar architectures and frameworks to support semantic logical reasoning, ontology construction, and validation matrices. It is critical to understand the impact of design decisions during the taxonomy build and management phase of the pipeline. These decisions include:

- How many levels should the taxonomy represent?
- What is the determined level of granularity?
- Will localization be enabled alongside the taxonomy?
- Will the controlled vocabulary be deprecated or remain in use when the taxonomy is deployed?
- How will new concepts and terms be integrated into the taxonomy?

Building and structuring the taxonomy using ontological reasoning and in accordance with standards and guidelines will ensure it is ready for the next phase of the Ontology Pipeline workflow.

---

## Thesaurus

A thesaurus is a controlled vocabulary that adds relationships between concepts—not only the broader/narrower hierarchy of a taxonomy, but also associative ("related") and equivalence ("use / use-for") relations. Where a taxonomy tells you where a concept sits, a thesaurus also tells you which concepts are interchangeable and which are meaningfully connected. A thesaurus will also include alternative labels and hidden labels, a method for including all of the other expressions used for any given term. Alternative labels include synonyms and acronyms while hidden labels are used for deprecated terms or terms used for search that should not be part of the published thesaurus.

An RDF taxonomy delivers immense value by defining meaning that is both human and machine readable. Terms become concepts and each concept carries an identifier, its alternative labels, a definition and rich context in the form of documentation properties. I always structure taxonomies to evolve into thesauri because it is the crucial first step toward building a semantic, ontology-based knowledge management system.

A thesaurus handles ambiguity by forming associative relationships between terms, going beyond the parent-child relationships within a hierarchy. A thesaurus further encodes these structures, often using a lightweight, mid-level ontology such as SKOS-XL or the Simple Knowledge Ontology System. Much like a traditional thesaurus used to discover near terms or synonymous concepts in vocabulary management, an ontologically encoded thesaurus matures a controlled vocabulary, metadata standard, and taxonomy to support resolution at scale, while enforcing the logical reasoning embedded within ontologies. In Figure 6, you will see *BT* (broader term), *SYN* (synonym), *NT* (narrower term), and *RT* (related term). A thesaurus architected with ontologies and a machine-readable encoding structure supports interoperability and is highly useful for helping both machines and humans understand context and meaning. With context and meaning, a thesaurus establishes semantic reasoning and primitive knowledge management, making it ready for the next step in the Ontology Pipeline.

```
Cloud platforms
    SYN cloud provider
    NT Amazon Virtual Private Cloud
    NT Predix software
    NT IBM Cloud
    NT Amazon Web Services
    NT Microsoft Azure
    NT Google Cloud Platform
    NT Immuta
    NT Orbitera
    NT Heroku
    NT Oracle Cloud Platform
    NT vMware vSphere
    NT Alibaba Cloud
    NT Google App Engine
    NT Dell Technologies Cloud
    NT Mirantis Cloud Platform
    NT Amazon Elastic Compute Cloud
    NT Azure Cloud Services
    NT OpenStack
    NT SAP Cloud Platform
    NT AWS Lambda
    BT Platforms
    RT Cloud computing
V-Ray
    SYN VRay
    SYN Vismat
    SYN Vray
    SYN Vray Software
    SYN v ray
    BT Creative tools
UiPath
    SYN uipath rpa awareness
    SYN uipath studio
    BT Business tools
Robotic process automation
    SYN rpa
    BT Machine learning & artificial intelligence
    BT Business processes
Mixed reality
    SYN Hybrid reality
    SYN Intereality
    SYN Interreality
    SYN MR
    BT Creative
```

Figure 6: Thesaurus example.

## Ontology

An ontology is a formal, machine-readable model of a domain that defines classes of things, the properties that describe them, and the logical rules governing how they relate. Where a thesaurus records relationships between terms, an ontology encodes axioms a reasoner can act on to infer new facts. Having followed the iterative stages of the Ontology Pipeline, data and information are now primed and ready for the ontology build. With a basic ontological structure in place to describe vocabulary control, the taxonomy hierarchy, and the thesaurus, we can now add domain ontologies and standard, open ontologies to further expose direct and indirect relations and nuanced, descriptive contexts.

Ontologies enhance vocabularies by describing and contextualizing relationships between concepts, and by introducing logical reasoning. By assigning classes, properties, relations, and attributes, ontologies establish rule bases that define how concepts behave in the wild, ensuring a level of coherence within complex information systems.

*Machines love ontologies* because of their high-fidelity disambiguation and description, which bring clarity to machine understanding for tasks such as information retrieval, entity management, concept discovery, and RAG implementations for AI systems.

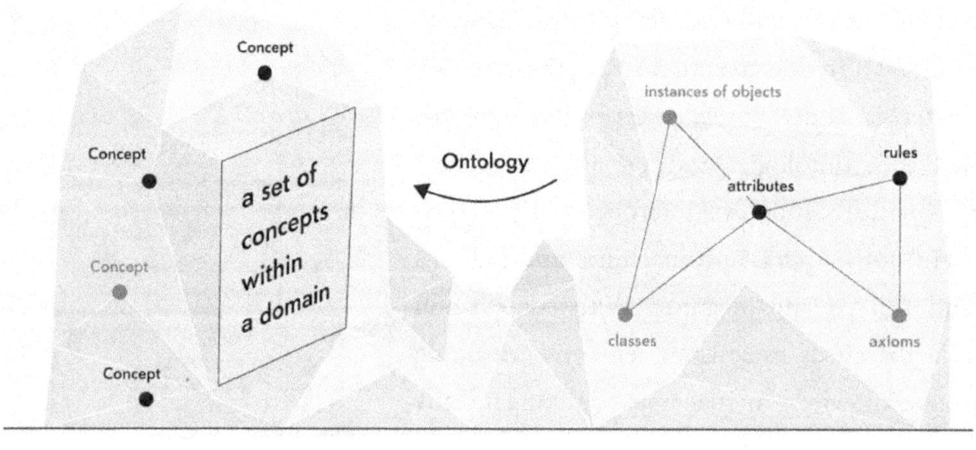


Figure 7: Ontology structure (https://www.ontotext.com/knowledgehub/fundamentals/what-are-ontologies/).

Ontology construction can be very difficult without established controlled vocabularies, metadata standards, taxonomies, and thesauri, as the underlying data and information structures lack integrity and may suffer from data quality issues. It is nearly impossible to build an ontology with messy, undefined vocabularies because introducing logic becomes extremely difficult when the underlying data itself is not logically structured.

*Building ontologies is like writing a story that defines domains, complex systems, and the relationships among all the characters, places, things, and concepts.*

---

## Knowledge graph

Finally, we arrive at knowledge graphs, the current Rosetta Stone of a SKMS and the Ontology Pipeline's visualization layer. The last step in the Ontology Pipeline involves synthesizing the four building blocks to culminate in a knowledge graph, which is essentially a knowledge management tool. Knowledge graphs are an assemblage of controlled vocabularies, metadata schemas, taxonomies, thesauri, and ontologies. The Ontology Pipeline naturally presents a layered knowledge graph, making it easier to troubleshoot broken logic while providing the control planes necessary to scale and extend the graph.

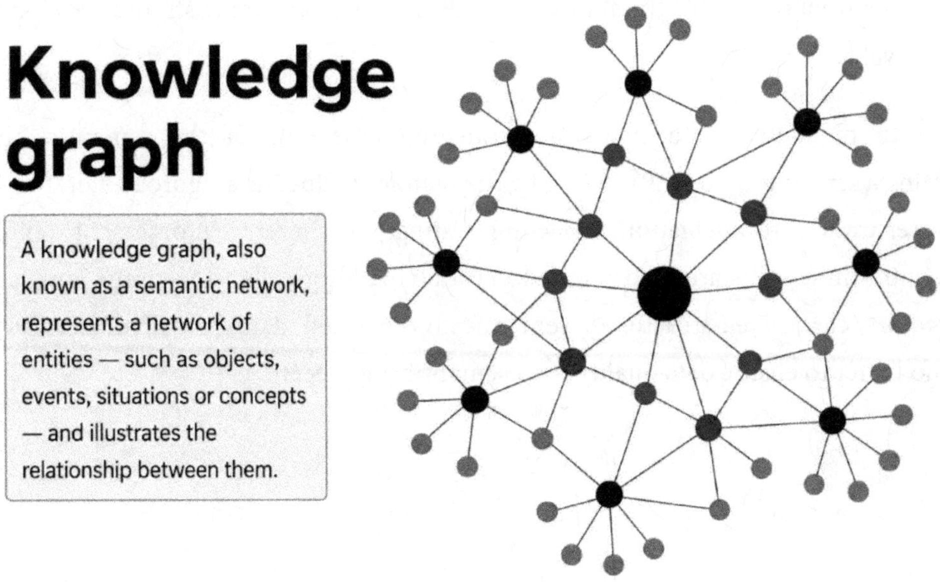


Figure 8: Knowledge graph explanation.

Knowledge graphs represent the synthesis of all stages of the knowledge modeling process, now visualized through clear, graphical representations. Because knowledge management can be complex, the visualization serves as an organizational language and communication interface, creating opportunities for teaching and learning across a domain and within the organization.

Knowledge graphs allow stakeholders, users, and contributors to interact and query a SKMS, demystifying the value proposition of semantics and surfacing knowledge as a first-class citizen. They use query languages such as SPARQL and SHACL, enabling the precise discovery of data and information across the graph. The only dependencies are the logical reasoning rules introduced by the encoded system. A knowledge graph is highly flexible, with its limitations defined by the complexity of the logical rule bases and data encoded within.

## The Ontology Pipeline: A semantic knowledge management framework

By building a SKMS using the logical steps outlined in the Ontology Pipeline framework, organizations can document time, effort, and cost estimates to secure funding and organizational support for future iterations and maintenance. As many organizations struggle to justify investment in a SKMS, a proven, repeatable framework enables them to estimate costs and develop metrics to demonstrate value.

It's crucial to highlight the ancillary and integrated benefits of the semantic build when implementing a semantic system. By following the Ontology Pipeline's rigorous, iterative process—cleaning, preparation, reconciliation, modeling, testing, enrichment, enforcement, reporting, and measurement—these steps are incorporated naturally. Additionally, since large language models (LLMs) require clean, well-structured, semantically enriched data to deliver accurate, reliable results, who better to ensure data quality than semantic engineers?

CHAPTER 1

# Controlled Vocabularies

A controlled vocabulary is a curated collection of terms and concepts used consistently across an organization. Unlike natural language, where multiple words can mean the same thing and the same word can mean different things, a controlled vocabulary establishes preferred terms, defines relationships between concepts, and creates a shared understanding of what words mean in your specific context. You're organizing, pruning, and cultivating the terminology already in use within your organization.

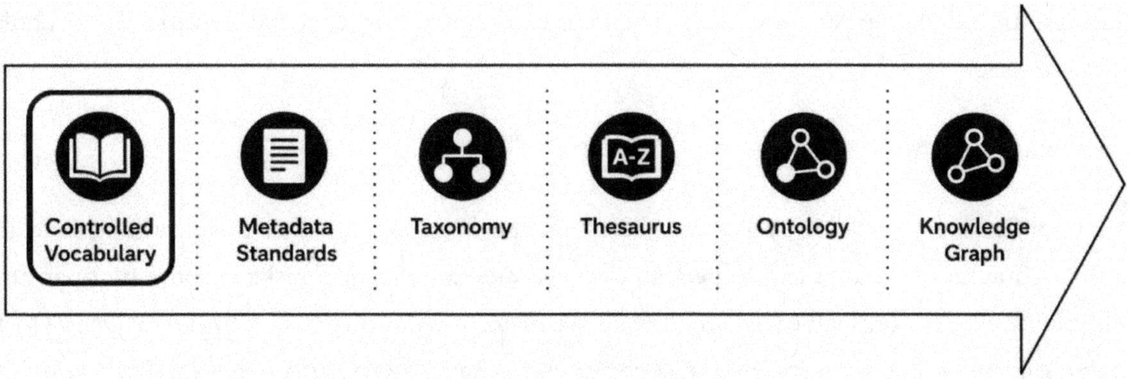


Figure 9: The Ontology Pipeline framework.

A controlled vocabulary is the first step in building a semantic knowledge ecosystem, as detailed by the Ontology Pipeline framework in Figure 9. For many organizations, simply establishing operationalized controlled vocabularies delivers immense benefit, with or without artificial intelligence entering the equation. Let's dive into controlled vocabularies, exploring their benefits and the process of building them.

A controlled vocabulary is the simplest, most reliable agreement a team can make about language. It is a curated, finite list of approved terms, each with one intended meaning and a few rules for how those terms appear. You keep a preferred label—say "Tee shirt"—for every concept and capture the everyday variants that should map to it, such as "t-shirt" or "tshirt." You add a short scope note to pin down meaning, give the term a stable identifier so systems can reference it even if the wording changes, and define light usage guidance like capitalization or singular/plural. The result is consistency: the same idea is called the same thing across content, tools, and teams.

---

## Consistency pays off

That consistency pays off quickly. In content platforms and CMSs, it means editors tag with the same words, making searches more precise and recommendations less noisy. In product catalogs, it eliminates duplicate labels ("tee shirt," "t-shirt," "tshirt") that fracture analytics and confuse customers. In customer support and CRM, uniform reasons for contact and resolution types turn messy tickets into clean data that leaders can trust. Compliance programs benefit from predictable markings for sensitive or regulated content. And when organizations exchange data—across business units or with partners—everyone avoids endless mapping exercises because the vocabulary is the contract.

*Synonym Ring, ANSI Z39.19*

AI amplifies these gains. Models learn faster and perform better when their training data isn't splintered across near-duplicate labels. Extraction and classification tasks become more accurate when outputs are constrained to an allowed set of terms; the model is nudged to "snap" to the canonical label rather than invent a new phrasing. Retrieval-augmented generation and search get sharper when prompts, filters, and facets use stable identifiers and agreed-upon terms.

Evaluation also improves because metrics are comparable over time: you are always measuring "the same thing" rather than a moving target of synonyms and typos. Even disambiguation becomes easier, because scope notes and usage guidance give both humans and machines a North Star for meaning.

## Simple Precision and Recall for Metrics

$$\text{Precision Ratio} = \frac{\text{Number of relevant documents retrieved}}{\text{Total number of documents retrieved}}$$

$$\text{Recall Ratio} = \frac{\text{Number of relevant documents retrieved}}{\text{Total number of relevant documents in system}}$$

Figure 10: Simple precision and recall for metrics.

## What a controlled vocabulary is not

It helps to clarify what a controlled vocabulary is not. It is not the place where you model the world or encode rich semantics. Other artifacts—taxonomies, thesauri, and ontologies—go beyond a controlled vocabulary by introducing additional structure, cross-term relationships, or formal rules. A controlled vocabulary deliberately stays small and pragmatic: it is the approved set of words and the governance that keeps them stable. Here, we focus on that baseline and leave those other tools aside.

## How to build a controlled vocabulary

### *Define purpose and scope*

Building a controlled vocabulary follows a straightforward path. Start by defining purpose and scope. Decide what decisions the vocabulary should support—search, tagging, analytics, routing—and name what is out of scope, so the effort does not sprawl. Then, collect candidate terms from the language you already have from site content, search logs, customer tickets, product names, SEO lists, and interviews. Real usage surfaces the concepts people need.

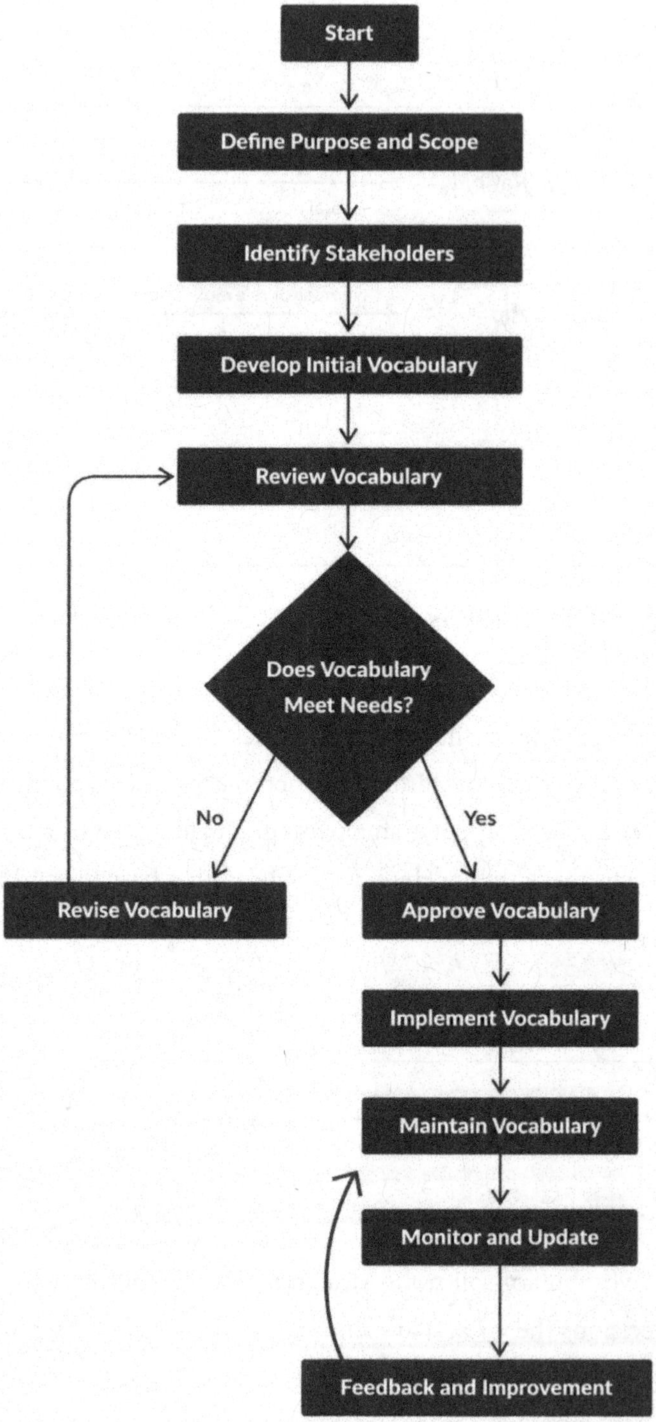


Figure 11: Controlled vocabulary build process.

## *The Word hunt: Concept discovery and reconciliation*

You need to discover your vocabulary before you can control it. Organizations rarely start from scratch; terminology is already embedded in countless systems and documents. The challenge is extracting candidate concepts systematically. Your first concept mining efforts will focus on the systems that already contain terminology.

---

*Start where your language already lives.*

---

Pull terms from the metadata your systems already emit, and the tagging structures people use. Export tag values, categories, and free-text labels from content platforms and CMSs; harvest document titles, library names, and custom properties from SharePoint; scan page titles, labels, and space names in Confluence; look at issue types, components, custom field values, and labels in Jira; and mine repository names, topics, issue labels, and pull-request titles in GitHub.

Add search queries, autocomplete logs, and customer ticket subjects to capture the phrases users type rather than the ones teams prefer. Treat all this as raw evidence of concepts, not final answers, and expect noise: misspellings, near-duplicates, and idiosyncratic jargon.

Data catalogs, database reference tables, metadata repositories, and collaboration platform taxonomies and vocabularies are four of the primary sources you should consider your "first stop" for discovering vocabulary.

Let's look at each of these in turn so you can learn how to maximize your vocabulary discovery efforts.

### Data catalogs

Data catalogs are goldmines of organizational vocabulary. They contain table names, column names, dataset descriptions, and business glossaries. Extract these systematically, paying attention to naming conventions and patterns. A column named `cust_acq_dt` tells you that your organization uses abbreviations for "customer acquisition date."

Note though that the label 'cust_acq_dt', while meaningful within an organization, lacks true semantics. The naming convention "cust_acq_dt" is often referred to as abbreviated or truncated naming and is commonly used in database schemas and legacy systems. It's a form of snake_case (using underscores to separate words) combined with heavy abbreviation. The label isn't semantic because it sacrifices readability for brevity:
"cust" instead of "customer".
"acq" instead of "acquisition".
"dt" instead of "date".

A semantic label is self-documenting and immediately understandable without context, like customer_acquisition_date or, even better in some contexts, customerAcquisitionDate (camelCase) or CustomerAcquisitionDate (PascalCase). It is recommended that a semantic label in a controlled vocabulary be formatted in sentence case or title case if a formal noun. Best practices favor semantic, self-documenting names, since storage is cheap and code readability/maintainability is more valuable than saving a few characters.

**Database reference tables**

Database reference tables are fabulous sources for terms and concepts. Look for lookup tables with codes and descriptions—these are controlled vocabulary concepts hiding in plain sight. A 'product_status' reference table with values like "ACTIVE," "DISCONTINUED," "PENDING" represents decisions someone has already made about how to categorize products.

**Metadata repositories**

Metadata repositories, such as data dictionaries, business glossaries, and enterprise architecture tools, contain concepts and, sometimes, formal definitions and relationships among them. These are authoritative sources that can anchor your vocabulary if you leverage metadata to support interoperability and integration patterns.

**Collaboration platform taxonomies and vocabularies**

Collaboration platform taxonomies and vocabularies, such as those in GitHub, Confluence, and SharePoint, contain rich organizational structures that reveal how your teams naturally categorize knowledge. GitHub repositories use topics, labels, and organizational hierarchies that reflect how engineering teams think about projects, technologies, and domains. Repository names, branch naming conventions, and issue labels form an emergent taxonomy of technical concepts. Confluence spaces and page hierarchies show how documentation is organized, with page titles, labels, and space categories revealing business and technical terminology. SharePoint sites, document libraries, and metadata columns expose how different teams structure their information—folder hierarchies often represent functional or process-oriented taxonomies that have evolved organically. These common collaboration platforms also contain invitation trees—the structural relationships among spaces, repositories, and sites that show how knowledge domains connect and subdivide. A parent Confluence space for "Product development" might contain child spaces for "Mobile apps," "Web platform," and "API services," revealing both terminology and conceptual relationships. Mining these invitation trees through APIs or via manual CSV downloads provides a ready-made hierarchical structure that reflects actual usage patterns.

The tags and labels users apply to content across these platforms are particularly valuable because they represent folksonomy, the vocabulary people organically use when categorizing their own work. While not as controlled as formal taxonomies, these crowdsourced tags reveal synonyms, variations, and emerging concepts that formal vocabularies might miss. Extract these tags and folksonomies, analyze tag frequency and co-occurrence, and use them to validate or enhance your controlled vocabulary with concepts that reflect how people work.

Keep in mind that databases and data warehouses often hide de facto vocabularies in lookup tables, enumerations, and reference data such as product types, reason codes, line-of-business names, device categories, and region lists. Extract distinct values, count frequencies, and examine co-occurrences to see which terms truly carry meaning in the work. Pair this with qualitative sampling: Read a slice of tickets, specs, and commit messages to understand context and boundaries for each candidate term.

## Corpus analysis: Learning from actual usage

While structured systems tell you what *should* be used, analyzing actual content reveals what *is* being used. Document analysis is part of corpus analysis and involves scanning reports, specifications, policies, and other organizational documents to identify frequently occurring terms and phrases. A simple frequency analysis reveals which concepts matter most to your organization. If terms and concepts occur with a high frequency, they are likely to be welcome candidates for a controlled vocabulary. Set a frequency threshold so you gather terms with a frequency of at least XX, as part of a document analysis strategy for candidate concept harvesting.

### *Natural Language Processing*

Natural Language Processing (NLP) takes this further. Modern NLP techniques can extract named entities (people, places, organizations, products), identify noun phrases that represent concepts, recognize multiword or compound terms that function as single concepts, detect acronyms and their expansions, and find synonymous terms through distributional similarity. Tools like spaCy, NLTK, or cloud-based NLP services can process thousands of documents to surface terminology patterns. Pay special attention to noun phrases that appear frequently in similar contexts—these are likely important organizational concepts.

### *User search queries*

User search queries in search and query logs reveal how people look for information. Search logs from your intranet, document management system, or data catalog show the vocabulary gap between what users think and what your systems understand. These query logs might highlight common internal biases—when internal perceptions of concept importance or meaning do not align with external customer search logs. User search queries account for internal, domain systems in addition to search logs sourced from external sources. Mediating the balance of sources is critical for the integrity of any vocabulary.

### *Stakeholder interviews*

Stakeholder interviews remain invaluable. Subject matter experts carry domain knowledge that doesn't exist in any system. Ask them about the terms they use daily, the distinctions that matter in their work, and the concepts that newcomers struggle to understand. Often, taxonomists, ontologists, and metadata professionals use tools such as card sorting and tree testing to gather stakeholder input and deconstruct language and vocabularies.

Stakeholders are the people who use terms and concepts in context and are important sources of input for validating vocabulary concepts, such as which label should be preferred and which concepts should exist as alternative labels. Stakeholders are also helpful for understanding the relationships among concepts, relative to workflows, and for helping form definitions for concepts.

---

## Existing standards

Existing standards in your industry provide ready-made vocabularies. Why reinvent terms for financial instruments, medical procedures, or chemical compounds when international standards already exist? Leverage industry ontologies, classification systems, and standards as starting points. Some interesting standards of note:

- **SNOMED CT**: Terminology and standard for exchange of clinical health information.
- **NIST-NICE Framework**: Skills, roles, and general workforce competencies.
- **ESCO**: European skills, competences, qualifications and occupations.
- **Google Product Taxonomy**: For online commerce.
- **EU AI Taxonomy**: Structured hierarchy of concepts describing AI systems.

There are tons of open SKOS vocabularies on the open web that are very useful for modeling domains and defining concepts. I've included some of these in the Resources section at the end of this book.

---

## Application schemas

Application schemas contain field names, dropdown options, and validation rules that represent vocabulary decisions. An expense management system's list of expense categories is a controlled vocabulary for spending types. You'll inevitably discover the same concepts from multiple sources but expressed differently. This is where the real work begins: tracking provenance and understanding where a candidate concept comes from and its intended use in the source system. Because context relies upon provenance, document where each term came from before merging anything.

## Provenance matters

Create a simple system to track provenance and context. This can be as simple as reading columns in a spreadsheet to document the necessary provenance information. This documentation is critical because it helps inform disambiguation needs and settings. Using the example below, it is very likely that Customer acquisition cost has a unique definition, meaning, and context, and that its use as a concept will be specific to the finance side of the business.

- **Candidate concept**: Customer acquisition cost.
- **Source**: Finance Data Warehouse.
- **System**: Oracle ERP.
- **Date Extracted:** 2025-10-15.
- **Authority**: Finance Department.
- **Definition Source**: CFO Policy Document 2023-06.

By collecting basic provenance, future semantic work such as maturing a controlled vocabulary into a taxonomy or modeling the future ontology will also be easier, as the source, system, and authority for concepts are at the ready, adding the essential context needed for vocabulary design decisions.

Provenance also matters because it helps resolve conflicts, such as which definition is authoritative or whether there should be two disambiguated concepts for context-specific representations. Provenance also lays a foundational governance element, documenting the source and system for any term or concept and answering the question, "Who owns this term?"

Documenting provenance enables traceability, allowing us to detail where a term is actually used. Finally, provenance supports impact analysis, so we are eyes wide open as to what breaks if we change this term.

## Resolving duplicates

You need a resolution strategy when the same concept appears with different names across sources. Exact duplicates are easy—same term, same meaning. Just consolidate and retain all provenance records. When we start to account for synonyms, acronyms, and misspellings, we are required to choose a preferred term if following the SKOS data model logic.

To build a robust controlled vocabulary, appoint one preferred term and as many alternative terms as necessary, accounting for all the ways a preferred term can manifest. Alternative labels can include synonyms, acronyms, and misspellings. This is where we start modeling coverage or enriching coverage models. Coverage models ensure that we capture as many expressions as possible for each item in our systems.

When making these decisions and modeling semantics, consider official policy or regulatory requirements, the frequency of use across the organization, term semantic quality (such as clarity), alignment with industry standards, and technical versus business language preferences. For example, if you find "Customer acquisition cost," "CAC," "Cost to Acquire," and "New Customer Cost" across different systems, you might choose "Customer acquisition cost" as the preferred label because it's clear, complete, and widely understood.

---

## Handling homonyms

Handling homonyms (the same term with different meanings) is trickier. A "customer" might mean different things to Sales (potential buyers), Finance (accounts receivable), and Support (service recipients). Don't force them to reconcile when the base (contextual definition of each instance) is unique. Create distinct concepts with context qualifiers: "Customer (Sales prospect)," "Customer (Account)," "Customer (Support case)." Doing this ensures concepts are disambiguated and their context is inferred.

---

## Partial overlaps

Partial overlaps represent concepts that are similar but not identical. "Employee" and "Staff member" might seem synonymous, but in some organizations, contractors are staff members, not employees. Clarify the boundaries through careful definition.

1. The bandage was wound around the wound.
2. The farm was used to produce produce.
3. The dump was so full it had to refuse more refuse.
4. We must polish the Polish furniture.
5. He could lead if he would get the lead out.
6. The soldier decided to desert his dessert in the desert.
7. Since there was no time like the present,
   he thought it was time to present the present.
8. A bass was painted on the head of the bass drum.
9. When shot at, the dove dove into the bushes.
10. I did not object to the object.
11. The insurance was invalid for the invalid.
12. There was a row among the oarsmen on how to row.
13. They were too close to the door to close it.
14. The buck does funny things when does are present.
15. A seamstress and a sewer fell down into a sewer line.
16. To help with planting, the farmer taught his sow to sow.
17. The wind was too strong to wind the sail.
18. After a number of injections my jaw got number.
19. Upon seeing the tear in the painting I shed a tear.
20. I had to subject the subject to a series of tests.
21. How can I intimate this to my most intimate friend?...

Loy Machedo
*loymachedo.com | loymachedo.tv*

Figure 12: 21 reasons why English is hard to learn.

Consider the circular synonym problem illustrated by variations like "cuisinart," "cuizinart," "food processor," "blender," "kitchenaid," and "kitchen aid." These terms have overlapping but distinct meanings: Some are brand names, some are product types, some are misspellings. Your controlled vocabulary must decide whether "Cuisinart" is a preferred term for the brand, with "food processor" as a separate concept for the product type. Map these relationships explicitly, designating terms according to their preferred utilities.

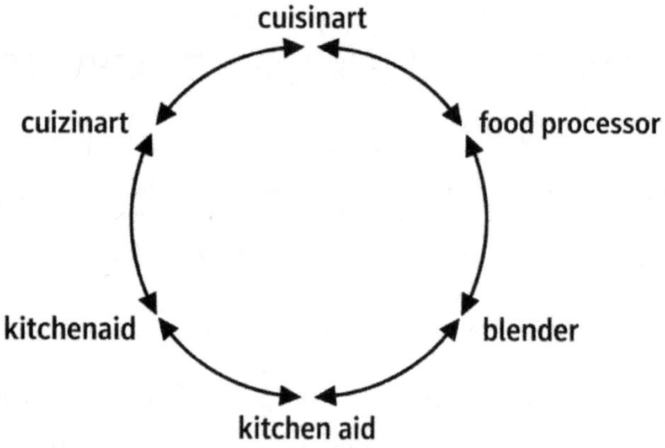


Figure 13: The circular synonym problem.

## Definitions: Giving terms a precise meaning

A controlled vocabulary without definitions is just a list of words, and is only semantic to humans by way of text labels. Definitions transform terms into concepts with precise boundaries. The controlled vocabulary concepts, along with their associated definitions and altLabels, must then be encoded using metadata schemas and ontologies to provide semantics for machines. This is why SKOS is so powerful for modeling concepts and controlled vocabularies. We are leveraging a W3C-compliant data model standard and technically, an OWL FULL ontology.

## Writing effective definitions

Let's take a slight detour here before digging into the nuts and bolts of definitions. Effective definitions provide rich descriptive context, enabling genuine understanding for machines and humans. Within the realms of cognitive and learning science principles, well-crafted definitions embed context clues to guide interpretation through four key mechanisms: synonyms that offer alternative expressions, antonyms that establish boundaries through contrast, explanations that unpack complex concepts into comprehensible components, and examples that ground abstract ideas in concrete instances. These contextual elements transform definitions into dynamic, purpose-built, context-rich nuggets that actively facilitate comprehension and semantic processing.

## Context clues

Embed context clues to make a good definition a great definition. Context clues are part of teaching reading competencies to humans. Clues are textual hints, embedded within surrounding words, sentences, or paragraphs that enable readers to decode unfamiliar terms without consulting external references. By providing definitions, synonyms, antonyms, or illustrative examples, these linguistic signals guide readers toward understanding new vocabulary through inference rather than interruption. This decoding strategy forms a cornerstone of effective reading comprehension, empowering readers to maintain flow and grasp meaning efficiently as they navigate through complex texts. This may seem like a big "So what? What does this have to do with semantics?" But think for a minute what we are doing when we engineer context. We are engineering context clues to guide LLMs through a quagmire of text, code, and infrastructure workflows. A SKOS-controlled vocabulary is a context clue framework. We structure our vocabularies to encode machine-readable, interoperable, context-rich data with context clues. Each concept imbues context via synonyms (altlabels and hiddenLabels), antonyms (a custom class label can capture this characteristic), explanation (the concept itself, definitions, and linked data authority files), and example (definitions and other documentation properties such as skos: example and skos: scopeNote).

| **Type** | **Context Clue** |
|---|---|
| **Synonym** | A word, morpheme, or phrase that has the same or nearly the same meaning as another word in the same language.<br><br>My opponent's argument is ***fallacious,*** misleading—plain wrong. |
| **Antonym** | A word that means the opposite, or nearly the opposite, of another word.<br><br>Although some men are ***loquacious,*** others hardly talk at all. |
| **Explanation** | When the unknown word is explained in a sentence, or in a sentence immediately preceding.<br><br>The patient is so ***somnolent*** that she requires medication to help her stay awake for more than a short time. |
| **Example** | Samples of a word or words, used contextually in a sentence.<br><br>***Celestial bodies,*** such as the sun, moon, and stars, are governed by predictable laws. |

Table 1: Context examples.

SKOS, being an RDF-based vocabulary, can be rendered in any RDF serialization format. This can be presented to LLMs and machines in RDF/XML, Turtle, JSON-LD, RDF/A, and a few other formats. This means that by building a SKOS vocabulary with proper text definitions, you are engineering context. Context engineering with SKOS means taking the time to formalize text definitions that are rich in context clues. This may seem like extra effort, but I promise that well-formed definitions will go a long way toward stitching the context fabric that is valuable for humans and machines.

## Back to definitions

SKOS definitions provide direct explanations of concepts, using context clues to provide explicit meaning, like how a textbook defines a term. These context clues allow LLMs to understand that a "customer," defined as "an individual or organization that purchases goods or services," refers to a buyer relationship rather than other potential meanings, such as "customs officer" or "customizer."

Definitions do not work with the concept preferred label alone. We are building each concept to exist as a robust concept record. Remember, alternative labels in SKOS function as synonyms, which become restatement context clues for machines and humans. By teaching AI systems to learn that when they encounter "client," "buyer," "purchaser," or "patron" in text, these are semantic variations of the same concept represented by the preferred label "customer."

This semantic concept enrichment enables better entity recognition and disambiguation across diverse vocabularies. The combination of preferred labels with their alternatives and definitions creates a rich semantic fingerprint that helps LLMs recognize concepts through pattern matching. When an AI system encounters text about "purchasing," "buying," or "commercial transactions," these encoded contextual semantics provide the inference clues needed to correctly identify and link to the "customer" concept, even when the exact preferred label isn't present in the text.

### *Genus-differentia*

To form reliable, descriptive definitions, start with the Genus-Differentia Structure for any given concept. This means determining the broader category (genus) and then specifying what distinguishes this concept (differentia) from its genus. "Customer acquisition cost is a financial metric that measures the total cost of acquiring a new customer, including marketing and sales expenses." This is an especially helpful approach because Genus-Differentia helps define concepts in context and serves as pre-work for future taxonomies, thesauri, and ontologies. Take note of potential future relations that will not be accounted for directly in controlled vocabularies.

### *Circularity*

Next, avoid circularity. Don't define terms using the terms themselves. "Customer churn is when customers churn" tells us nothing. Add detail and define in-context usage or context relevant to systems. Use simple language, also known as plain language. Definitions should clarify, not obscure. Avoid jargon in definitions unless the act of defining is to define jargon. Simple, descriptive language goes a long way, especially when definitions also serve to disambiguate concepts.

### *Scope and boundaries*

Specify scope and boundaries by detailing what a concept definition includes and excludes. For example, "Employee includes full-time and part-time staff with formal employment contracts. It excludes contractors, consultants, and temporary workers." Detail the intended coverage of the concept by explicitly stating the scope and boundaries within the definition, thereby helping users and machines understand how best to make sense of a concept, its intended use, and semantics.

### *Provide context clues*

Enrich definitions by providing context clues for each definition. While the context can also be documented as part of a documentation property, such as SKOS: scope note, adding richer context and usage guidance to a definition is helpful, as this effort also helps establish scope and boundaries for concepts.

I personally like to document organizational and domain context as part of the definition during the controlled vocabulary building stage, and to separate the usage guidance into a scope note field only at the taxonomy building phase. This is only for simplicity's sake, to avoid introducing multiple schema fields while curating candidate concepts.

### *Authority files and linked data*

Finally, go the extra mile with authority files. Link authority files that lend confidence and validity to concept definitions. I like to call this "touching grass" for concepts. Authority files may be HTTP or HTTPS URIs that can be encoded as "SKOS: exactMatch." A form of linked data, the authority file can be an internal, reliable source used to define a concept or an external source.

Linking to an external authority file, such as DBpedia, provides a canonical, globally unique identifier for the concept "customer," ensuring that systems referring to this URI are talking about the same concept, regardless of local variations in terminology or language. Sources like DBpedia have ontological backbones and serve as knowledge graph architectures.

Authority files sourced from ontology-bolstered sources such as DBpedia, VIAF, the Getty, and Wikidata, supply machine-readable, standardized definitions, multilingual labels, and related concepts (broader/narrower/related terms). Creating a shared understanding via authority files prevents semantic drift and reduces ambiguity across different applications and datasets. By referencing DBpedia's rich contextual information, including the concept's relationships to other entities, historical usage, and domain-specific variations, systems can inherit validated semantic knowledge without having to redefine or maintain this conceptual framework independently.

### *Definition sources*

Document where definitions come from. This step is critical for operationalizing vocabularies and for gathering data about concept constraints and guidelines. Typical definition sources include regulatory requirements, industry standards, internal policies, subject matter expert input, documentation of common usage within the organization, and authority files. When sources conflict, make choices based on authority, applicability, and historical usage of concepts. A regulatory definition usually trumps internal preference and the languages of brand and marketing. You may always create a custom class concept to represent the "display label" or front matter if marketing and branding insist on an ambiguous concept name that does not match the more widely known meaning of a thing.

---

## Creating consistency through normalization

Because discovered concepts will always be rooted in different source systems and potentially an array of technologies, candidate concepts will present with a variety of different formats, cases, and structures. The normalization of formats, cases, and structures creates consistency, supports interoperability, and supports machine readability.

The goal is *NOT* to overhaul all source systems to comply with the new vocabulary structure and format—that would be impractical. *Normalize the vocabulary* and prepare by documenting where data transformations may be necessary to fully leverage and operationalize the well-defined, structured vocabulary concepts.

For example, the Simple Knowledge Organization System (SKOS) and the World Wide Web Consortium (W3C) recommend using the international ISO 8601 standard for the unambiguous representation of dates and times. Obviously, if implementing a SKOS model, all date and time formats and structures must be presented in ISO 8601 format. This is because a record dated "03/04/2026" is ambiguous and unreliable across systems: Does this format communicate March 4 or April 3? With ISO 8601, the same date is unambiguous: "2026-03-04" for the date, or "2026-03-04T14:30:00Z" when the time and time zone matter. A SKOS model requires this format; "3/4/26," "March 4th," and "Q1 2026" are not acceptable substitutes.

This is a requirement of the SKOS data model; it is not optional. Follow the prescribed data formats and structure as defined by the W3C to build a resilient and reliable system and identify where transformers will be necessary to derive bidirectional value from the controlled vocabulary.

### *Syntactic normalization*

Establish conventions for syntax and vocabulary style. I normally build a style guide to accompany the release of my vocabularies, taxonomies, thesauri, and ontologies. Style guides are great governing artifacts, useful for adopting and using vocabulary. Syntax should detail decisions such as:

- **Capitalization**: Title Case, lowercase, or UPPERCASE?
- **Abbreviations**: Spell out or use standard abbreviations?
- **Punctuation**: Hyphens, spaces, or camelCase for multi-word concepts?
- **Singular vs. Plural**: Use the singular form unless the concept is inherently plural.
- **Word Order**: "Cost, Customer Acquisition" or "Customer Acquisition Cost".

Choose conventions that align with how users think and search, and with metrics such as term frequency in search logs and existing data assets.

### *Synonyms*

Group synonymous terms under a preferred label. The preferred label (prefLabel) is the primary term used throughout the organization. This is what appears in official documentation, reports, and formal communication. The alternate labels (altLabel) are synonyms, acronyms, abbreviations, and variations that users might search for or encounter. These redirect to the preferred label. For example:

- **prefLabel**: Customer acquisition cost.
- **altLabel**: CAC, Cost to Acquire, Customer Acquisition Expense, New customer cost.

### *Display labels for user interfaces*

Sometimes, the preferred label isn't ideal due to UI constraints, or the most data-driven, logical concept label is shot down by branding and marketing. This is where creating a custom concept class like "Display Label" settles all feuds. A display label can be anything, really, and it behaves as front matter.

When faced with ambiguous or random concept labels that lack integrity, such as the word "Freeform" used to describe a platform feature, accept the term for what it is and relegate it to the "Display Label" field. The preferred label should be less ambiguous, say, "Freeform panel." Disambiguate and add context with alternative labels and a nice, rich definition.

For "Freeform panel":

- **prefLabel**: Freeform panel.
- **displayLabel:** Freeform.
- **altLabel**: Free form, freeform, freeform panels, free form panels.

Display labels maintain clarity while accommodating practical constraints and organizational politics. Display labels have saved me hours of pain by satiating creative naming conventions for the front-end while preserving semantic integrity on the backend.

I allow myself the grace of a display label, which one may think is NOT part of a controlled vocabulary. But since brand and marketing tend to have a very heavy hand in naming things with flair, one must consider how best to support the business while maintaining semantic integrity.

## Infrastructure for thinking

A controlled vocabulary is an infrastructure for thinking. It makes implicit knowledge explicit, transforms confusion into clarity, and turns the chaos of organizational language into a structured asset. Because AI systems increasingly mediate how we interact with information, clear, consistent, well-defined terminology is essential for humans and machines alike to understand what we're talking about.

The terminology already exists in your organization. It may be scattered, inconsistent, and ambiguous, but the concepts are there and ripe for organizing, and we've already identified and discussed the sources for mining them. A controlled vocabulary allows organizations to take control of context and meaning and transform well-defined vocabularies into strategic assets that make everyone—and every system—work better. Start small, but start today. Your future self, your colleagues, and your AI systems will thank you.

## Beyond the probabilistic fog

We've established controlled vocabularies as the foundational building block of SKMS and explored their role in creating disambiguated, structured language for both human and machine comprehension.

*As organizations deploy AI at scale, controlled vocabularies have emerged from their traditional role in library science to become critical infrastructure for AI reliability, accuracy, and governance.*

The promise of AI systems—particularly Large Language Models (LLMs)—has collided with a harsh reality: without structured semantic foundations, these systems produce inconsistent results, hallucinate facts, and fail to maintain domain-specific precision. Controlled vocabularies provide the semantic foundations necessary for reliable, accurate AI.

When organizations rush to implement AI systems without controlled vocabularies, they're essentially asking their most sophisticated, black box technology to operate in a semantic wilderness. Large language models, for all their statistical prowess, fundamentally operate on probability distributions—they predict what word should come next based on observed patterns. Without controlled vocabularies providing definitional anchors and semantic boundaries, these systems drift into what I call probabilistic fog, where plausible-sounding outputs distract us from detecting fundamental misunderstandings of domain concepts.

The most obvious use cases for controlled vocabularies involve reducing hallucinations and improving accuracy for metrics. However, the loftier mission for controlled vocabularies is to transform human-computer interactions into semantically grounded reasoning systems that can distinguish between "bank" as a financial institution and "bank" as a river's edge, not through statistical correlation, but through explicit semantic disambiguation.

To manage this known problem, large encyclopedic sources such as Wikipedia and DBpedia link disambiguation pages to manage semantics, at scale, highlighting the importance of semantics and disambiguation for large information retrieval systems and knowledge bases. By creating dedicated pages to reconcile homophones and heteronyms, disambiguation is handled through controlled vocabularies with ontology backbones and linked data.

If you want ready examples of how knowledge is managed at scale through controlled vocabularies, semantics, and SKOS, look no further than systems such as Babelnet.org, the Getty, SNOMED CT, ESCO, AGROVOC, Unified Astronomy Thesaurus, Research Vocabularies Australia, NASA, and the Library of Congress. Controlled vocabularies serve as the scaffolding for many commonly used systems, many of which you have interacted with and perhaps have appreciated for their robust information retrieval abilities.

---

## Statistical learning and domain precision

Modern commercial AI systems excel at finding patterns across massive datasets, but patterns do not make meaning. When a language model encounters specialized terminology—whether medical, legal, or enterprise-specific—it relies on sparse, ambiguous, or contradictory contextual clues.

Consider how an AI system might process "cell division" without controlled vocabulary guidance. In biology, "cell division" refers to cellular mitosis or meiosis. In telecommunications, it might reference network architecture. In organizational contexts, it could mean departmental restructuring. The model's response depends entirely on which patterns dominated its training data, not on understanding the actual domain context of the query. This is exactly why modeling and defining the context and meaning of domains are necessary for domain-specific, AI-infused systems.

This is where controlled vocabularies prove valuable, providing clarity and disambiguation for AI systems. Controlled vocabularies solve for fundamental mismatches by providing what training data cannot: authoritative, unambiguous definitions that establish conceptual boundaries. They transform an AI-relegated task from "Guess the most statistically probable meaning" to "Reference the established definition for this context."

*This bifurcation in approach, from probabilistic inference to semantic reference, represents a fundamental difference in AI system architectures for enterprise use.*

## Disambiguation at scale

The disambiguation power of controlled vocabularies extends far beyond word disambiguation or homonym reconciliation. In enterprise environments, terminology evolves through organizational silos, creating layers of semantic confusion that compound when fed into AI systems. Marketing might call something "customer engagement," while Sales refers to "lead nurturing," and Customer Success speaks of "account management"—all potentially referring to overlapping or identical processes.

Now, you might be thinking, "What if the same concept has multiple contextual meanings within a team or department?" It's not uncommon for a single, unique term to shapeshift depending on use and context. A controlled vocabulary can capture the nuances through definitions. In addition to definitions, if the same term has multiple contextual meanings, you can add a disambiguation setting in the form of a qualifier encased in simple parentheticals. This low-tech implementation places the actual context of a specific concept by capturing the context in (parentheses).

**Plates (Engineering)**

**Plates (Tableware)**

**Balls (Parties)**

**Balls (Sporting goods)**

Figure 14: Ambiguity example. (The Library of Congress).

Parenthetical qualifiers serve as a critical mechanism for disambiguating homographs in controlled vocabularies, functioning as contextual glosses that specify the domain of meaning to which a term belongs. According to ANSI Z39.19, Guidelines for the Construction, Format, and Management of Monolingual Controlled Vocabularies, qualifiers should be enclosed in parentheses and treated as integral parts of the term itself. However, their use should be minimized whenever possible due to the complications they introduce in filing and retrieval systems.

When parenthetical qualifiers become cumbersome, several alternatives keep concepts disambiguated. You can carry the distinction in a scope note (skos:scopeNote) rather than in the label itself; you can model the two senses as separate concepts with distinct URIs, so the disambiguation lives in the identifier instead of the display text; or you can use a self-disambiguating compound term ("River bank," "Financial institution"). In practice, distinct URIs plus scope notes scale best, because the machine-readable identity does the work and the parenthetical is reserved for the human-facing label only when it genuinely aids retrieval.

The standard establishes that all homographs require qualification even when one appears in its primary sense, as in the case of "Cranes (Birds)" and "Cranes (Construction equipment)," coexisting within the same vocabulary. Qualifiers should ideally consist of a single, unambiguous word—often a broader, parent term—and must be standardized consistently throughout the vocabulary to avoid confusion between variant forms like "biology" and "bioscience."

Compound terms are recommended to minimize the use of parenthetical qualifiers when natural language usage permits. For example, a rich compound term like "Phonograph records" might be better than "Records (Phonograph)," thereby reserving parenthetical qualification strictly for disambiguation rather than for representing the true semantics of concepts or attributes. Applying qualifiers ensures that controlled vocabularies maintain semantic precision while supporting cross-domain interoperability in multidisciplinary retrieval environments. AI appreciates this form of disambiguation, as the effort is explicit and encoded (if using SKOS) as part of the concept's format.

Forensic dermatology
*not* Dermatology (Forensics)

Automobile racing
*not* Racing (Automobiles)

Figure 15: Compound terms example (The Library of Congress).

Further, when you transform your flat list-controlled vocabulary into a taxonomy (hierarchy), you will add more context through categorization and parent-child relations. Once transformed into a hierarchy, the parent-child relations among concepts embolden your maturing controlled vocabulary to support inference. The defined relationships enable inference engines and AI to automatically deduce new information from the existing data. For example, if Concept A is skos:broader than Concept B, and Concept B is skos:broader than Concept C, an inference engine can deduce that Concept A is also skos:broader than Concept C.

*A controlled vocabulary can supply a lot of contexts and meaning, but is limited in its semantic expressivity when modeled as a flat list.*

## Next-level data hygiene

Systems quickly become unwieldy without proper data hygiene, which is performed by resolving synonyms and duplicate concepts through controlled vocabularies. Deduplication includes reconciling synonymous terms to clarify vocabulary, with best practices requiring definitions for each term or concept to ensure all users and stakeholders arrive at the same meaning for chosen vocabulary. This principle becomes exponentially more critical in AI contexts. Each unresolved synonym, each ambiguous term, and each undefined acronym become a potential failure point where the AI might confidently generate incorrect interpretations.

When controlled vocabularies are properly implemented, they create what I term "semantic rails" for AI systems. These rails guide the model's interpretations along established conceptual paths, minimizing the kind of creative misinterpretation that leads to hallucinations. The vocabulary doesn't constrain the AI's ability to generate novel combinations or insights; rather, it ensures those insights are built from solid definitional foundations.

---

## SKOS: Meaning for AI systems

The Simple Knowledge Organization System (SKOS) provides a framework for reconciling synonyms and acronyms while establishing parent-child relations, alternative labels, hidden labels, and related concepts. SKOS provides a strategy and framework for creating machine-translatable semantic structures that AI systems can leverage for contextual understanding.

When an AI system trained on SKOS-encoded vocabularies encounters a concept, it consumes concepts with defined relationships, synonyms, misspellings, and acronyms as alternative labels, linked data, and definitions. Instead of inferring that "ML" might mean "machine learning" based on surrounding words, the system can reference the controlled vocabulary to confirm this interpretation—or recognize when "ML" means "milliliter" in a different domain context.

SKOS modeling is a critical foundation for developing more complex ontologies, as it's impossible to model messy, undefined, or unrefined data. This foundation provides the semantic stability necessary for reliable reasoning in AI systems. Each concept becomes a fixed point of meaning that the AI can reference, reducing the computational uncertainty that leads to errors.

## From RAG to riches: Production AI

The practical benefits of controlled vocabularies manifest most clearly in Retrieval Augmented Generation (RAG) implementations. Research indicates that organizations implementing advanced RAG techniques with semantic search can achieve significant improvements in retrieval precision.

A 2025 Microsoft Research paper on Ontology-Grounded Retrieval-Augmented Generation demonstrated significant AI reliability improvements: a 55% increase in recall of accurate facts, 40% improvement in response correctness across four different LLMs, 30% faster attribution of responses to context, and 27% boost in fact-based reasoning accuracy. A 2025 meta-analysis assessed evaluation approaches from 582 research papers. Researchers reported that optimizing retrieval precision can improve cost efficiency by up to 50% through reducing token consumption during LLM inference, as measured by Retrieval Precision ROI (Return on Investment).[2][3][4]

While larger context windows have pushed RAG out of the AI limelight, RAG is still recommended as a stable context layer for AI architectures. RAG is still a stable force, especially in large organizations and for enterprises building complex workflows. And controlled vocabularies combined with RAG greatly enhance AI performance.

### *Consistent prompt engineering*

When prompt templates reference controlled vocabulary terms, they produce more consistent, predictable outputs across different model versions and use cases. The vocabulary serves as a semantic contract between the prompt engineer and the model, so that the user and the LLM are operating together from the same concepts and their meanings. Words have meaning, and a simple, controlled vocabulary can help establish a machine-human-defined vocabulary.

---

[2] Sharma, Kartik, et al. "OG-RAG: Ontology-Grounded Retrieval-Augmented Generation for Large Language Models." *arXiv*, 12 Dec. 2024, arxiv.org/abs/2412.15235.

[3] Brown, Andrew, et al. "A Systematic Literature Review of Retrieval-Augmented Generation: Techniques, Metrics, and Challenges." *Big Data and Cognitive Computing*, vol. 9, no. 12, 2025, article 320. *MDPI*, https://doi.org/10.3390/bdcc9120320.

[4] Gan, Aoran, et al. "Retrieval Augmented Generation Evaluation in the Era of Large Language Models: A Comprehensive Survey." *arXiv*, 21 Apr. 2025, arxiv.org/abs/2504.14891.

A controlled vocabulary serves as a bedrock for prompt engineering, guiding the language used in prompts and providing stable reference points. Ideally, an organization has prompt libraries, where prompts are classified using a controlled vocabulary for easy discovery and retrieval. If you haven't thought of organizing prompts into prompt libraries, now is the time to do so. Know where and when prompts are executed and in what contexts, to measure prompt stability and performance over time.

### *Reduced training data requirements*

Models fine-tuned with controlled vocabulary structures require significantly less domain-specific training data to achieve production-ready accuracy. The vocabulary structures the conceptual space, allowing the model to learn relationships rather than having to infer them from examples. For vector-based semantic systems, use controlled vocabularies to guide the categorization of vectors, thereby expanding existing controlled vocabularies. As a vocabulary is enriched with new concepts, synonyms, and acronyms, model fine tuning will enable AI reliability as domain context becomes more dialed in and explicit.

### *Explainable AI outputs*

When AI systems reference controlled vocabularies in their reasoning chains, their outputs become inherently more explainable. Stakeholders can trace how the system moved from input concepts through vocabulary-defined relationships to reach its conclusions. Controlled vocabularies can reduce the "black box effect," lending transparency to reasoning chains, as semantic patterns emerge to support AI explainability.

### *Cross-system interoperability*

Controlled vocabularies ensure consistency while allowing for system-specific extensions. This becomes crucial when AI systems need to communicate with legacy databases, enterprise applications, or external APIs. The vocabulary provides the semantic bridge that enables meaningful data exchange.

## The context engineering revolution

Building a robust context engineering practice means treating context as an intentional arrangement of domain-specific information and knowledge, enabling AI to synthesize responses reliably. Controlled vocabularies are the foundational layer of this intentional arrangement. They establish the semantic coordinates that allow AI systems to navigate complex information spaces without losing their bearings.

Consider how a medical AI assistant processes a query about "respiratory failure." Without controlled vocabularies, the system might conflate acute respiratory distress syndrome, chronic respiratory failure, and respiratory arrest—all distinct conditions requiring different interventions. With proper vocabulary implementation, following standards such as SNOMED CT or ICD-10, the AI can maintain these critical distinctions while understanding their relationships within the broader respiratory system taxonomy.

> *The quality and precision of the "context" AI systems receive has become the single biggest determinant of whether they perform reliably or hallucinate spectacularly.*

Context, in and of itself, goes beyond simple prompt tweaking when it comes to LLMs. Context is optimized when controlled vocabularies and ontologies explicitly structure context as encoded relationships and meaning, surfacing disambiguated facts and ensuring the AI always sees the right information at the right moment.

## The guidance: ANSI/NISO Z39.19

ANSI/NISO Z39.19 (R2010) Guidelines for the Construction, Format, and Management of Monolingual Controlled Vocabularies provides the methodological framework that ensures vocabularies are constructed with sufficient rigor for AI applications. The guidelines encode decades of information science wisdom about how to structure meaning for computational processing.

ANSI Z39.19 and SKOS are companions. Z39.19 is the rule base, while SKOS is the machine-readable, encoded data model—two halves of a whole. Encoded in SKOS, the guidelines emphasize the use of documentation properties, semantic elements that become critical for AI systems. Think of documentation properties as context nuggets that stay connected to the concepts they reference.

When a controlled vocabulary entry includes a definition for "customer" as "any individual or entity that has completed at least one transaction within the past 24 months," the AI system gains precise operational boundaries for the concept. This prevents the kind of scope creep that occurs when models trained on general text apply consumer-focused definitions to B2B contexts or vice versa.

Building and structuring vocabularies using ontological reasoning and in accordance with standards and guidelines ensures that semantic systems are prepared for AI integration. These standards align with the Ontology Pipeline, documenting similar architectures and frameworks to support semantic logical reasoning, ontology construction, and validation matrices.

---

## The governance imperative

Controlled vocabularies for AI aren't static; they're living systems requiring active governance. Language norms shift because societies shift, and vocabularies must evolve accordingly while maintaining semantic consistency. The World Health Organization (WHO) issued naming best practices in 2015 to avoid place-based or stigmatizing disease names, a move that directly affects ontology modeling, dataset columns, and downstream analytics. Controlled vocabulary governance structures include:

- **Semantic change management**: Version control for vocabulary updates, with impact analysis on dependent AI models.
- **Term discovery and concept approvals**: Workflows and interfaces for stakeholders and customers to propose new terms and to develop decision-making matrices for integrating terms into controlled vocabularies.
- **Cross-functional vocabulary committees**: Representatives from data science, domain experts, and business stakeholders who collectively own vocabulary evolution.

- **Automated consistency checking**: Systems that detect when AI outputs suggest the vocabulary may need updating or when new terms emerge in organizational use.
- **Feedback loops**: Mechanisms for AI systems to signal when they encounter terms outside the controlled vocabulary, feeding back into vocabulary maintenance workflows.

As ontologist consultant Jenn Bridgens noted in response to my work,

> *"Many don't realize that taxonomies, controlled vocabularies, and the like are living organisms and must be tended as if they were a garden."*

This organic metaphor captures how controlled vocabularies require continuous cultivation to remain effective for AI systems.

---

## Vocabularies for autonomous AI

Controlled vocabularies become even more critical as AI systems evolve toward greater autonomy. Agentic AI systems that make decisions and take actions need an unambiguous understanding of their operational domains. A procurement AI agent must distinguish between "purchase order," "purchase requisition," and "purchase agreement"—distinctions that carry legal and financial implications.

Glossaries, catalogs, metadata, controlled vocabularies, taxonomies, thesauri, ontologies, and knowledge graphs form rich semantic systems that provide the scaffolding for autonomous AI operations. Without this scaffolding, autonomous systems risk making decisions based on statistical correlations rather than semantic understanding—a recipe for costly errors.

Knowledge graphs represent the synthesis of all stages of the knowledge modeling process. The Ontology Pipeline naturally presents a layered knowledge graph, making it easier to troubleshoot broken logic while providing the control planes necessary to scale and extend the graph for AI applications.

## The semantic foundation for trustworthy AI

The integration of controlled vocabularies into AI systems represents a fundamental shift from probabilistic approximation to semantic precision. Organizations that invest in this semantic foundation build AI systems that can be trusted with critical business decisions, explain their reasoning in domain-appropriate terms, and evolve alongside organizational knowledge.

Controlled vocabularies lend semantic clarity to AI systems. As Ernst & Young describes, AI-ready data is "information that is easily combined to form business knowledge. These knowledge assets are used to enhance enterprise AI models, improving AI inference."[1]

Alienation (Philosophy)

Alienation (Rhetoric)

Alienation (Social psychology)

Alienation (Theology)

Figure 16: Semantic issue (The Library of Congress).

| Concept Category | Acceptable Preferred Term | Entry Terms (Synonyms) | Prohibited Preferred Term | Rationale |
|---|---|---|---|---|
| **Cloud Infrastructure** | Cloud Infrastructure | "Cloud Infra"; "Public Cloud" | Public Clouds Infrastructure | ☑ Acceptable uses singular, sentence-case and has synonyms.<br>✗ Prohibited uses plural incorrectly. |
| **User Authentication** | User Authentication | "Auth"; "Login Process" | Auth of Users! | ☑ Acceptable is a clear noun phrase.<br>✗ Prohibited includes punctuation and a verb-like structure. |
| **Data Retention Policy** | Data Retention Policy | Data Retention Policy | "Retention Policy"; "Data Archival" | ☑ Acceptable is concise.<br>✗ Prohibited is redundant and confusing. |

Table 2: Examples of acceptable vs. prohibited cases.

Organizations that will thrive in the AI era aren't necessarily those with the largest models or the most data. They're the ones who have invested in semantic discipline to ensure their AI systems understand the patterns in their data and the meaning behind them. Organizations that continue to separate semantic concerns from AI implementation, or those that ignore semantics altogether, will continue to struggle with reliability, accuracy, and velocity.

**★Rule:**

- How to handle overly complex terms with taxonomy modeling:
  1. "Load Balancing" (broader).
  2. "Cloud Load Balancing" (narrower).
  3. "Real Time Cloud Load Balancing" (narrower).

- Terms exceeding four words should be reviewed for possible splitting into broader and narrower concepts.
- !! ***Example Not Acceptable:*** "Real-Time Adaptive Cloud Load Balancing Framework"

**Improper Use of Punctuation & Styling**

**★Rule:**

- Do not include colons, semicolons, or parentheses in preferred term labels.
- Avoid question marks, exclamation points, or unnatural capitalization (e.g., "BEST Practices").
- No markup (HTML tags, Markdown syntax) within term labels.

Figure 17: Overly complex compound terms.

## Workflow and governance

Decide how new terms get in before rolling out your style guide. Set acceptance criteria grounded in evidence: frequency in logs, regulatory need, business priority, or demonstrated user confusion. Pilot the vocabulary in the real workflow—have editors tag content, run sample searches, or classify a ticket backlog—and watch what happens. Measure precision and recall, note where editors hesitate, and capture the error patterns that suggest a missing term or an unclear scope note.

Finally, put lightweight governance in place. Specify who can request changes, who approves them, how often you review, and how you version and deprecate terms. Publish the vocabulary where people and systems actually work: inside the CMS, as a selectable list in tagging tools, as a lookup table in the data warehouse, and as a reference set for model outputs. Then, maintain it. Monitor usage, retire what no one uses, and evolve labels when the business or the audience changes—without breaking the identifiers that downstream systems depend on.

**Change Requests & Issue Tracking**

★**Rule:**
**Requestor:**
- name
- Adobe alias
- team

**Example**: Jane Doe, @jane_doe, Marketing

- Proposed Term(s), Definition(s), and Relationships (BT, NT, RT)
- Rationale

**Example**: Addition of new AI Model Lifecycle concept for upcoming product launch

- !! All proposed updates must be submitted via a standardized Change Request Form through our ExL Tag Request Service.
- !! Upon approval, schedule changes for the next vocabulary release cycle.
- !! Upon rejection, provide rationale and suggestions for revision.
- !! A proposed term may be added as an altLabel if it is a synonym or acronym for an existing term.

**Deprecation & Retirement**

★**Rule:**
- Mark Status = Deprecated in the record.
- Insert a "USE" or BT/NT link to the replacement term (e.g., "Deprecated: 'VM Type' USE 'Instance Type'").
- Record the Date of Deprecation and Reason in metadata.
- When a term is no longer needed or is superseded, do not delete deprecated terms immediately; instead retain them for historical tagging, legacy data migration, and AI model training data.

**Validation & Consistency**

★**Rule:**
- No cycles exist in the hierarchy graph.
- Each preferred term has at least one definition.
- No duplicate preferred labels (case-insensitive).
- Entry terms (Display Label or Alternative Label) do not match another concept's preferred label.
- Before each release, run automated scripts or manual audits to verify consistency and validation.
- Document any found inconsistencies and remediate them prior to publishing.

Figure 18: Style guide governance snapshot.

## Conclusion

The takeaway is simple. A controlled vocabulary is the smallest effective unit of semantic governance. By making language consistent and computable, it multiplies the value of your content, your analytics, and your AI—without requiring you to remodel reality. Start there, keep it tight, and let every other semantic layer build on that firm ground. A controlled vocabulary prepares terminology for increasingly complex semantic data models, the next step of building in the Ontology Pipeline.

Every organization speaks its own language, but many lack controlled vocabularies. Language within organizations is how we communicate with each other and machines. But often, agreeing upon language is embedded in company culture, a strange and wild landscape cluttered with the creative lingo of marketing and branding, the complex nuances of technical terms, business concepts, acronyms, and domain-specific jargon that evolves organically over time.

Language, and for that matter, vocabulary, are influenced by company culture and are inherently political. When immersed in the daily grind of work, humans often lose sight of how internal, organizational language and vocabularies drift from delivering true semantics, the art of detailing the context and meaning of words and language. That acronym everyone throws around as the piece-de-resistance of a company initiative? It means nothing if it's not well-defined, associated with its actual definition, and spelled out in nomenclature.

Language becomes a source of confusion, inconsistency, and lost productivity when it remains undocumented, unstructured, and ungoverned.

That's where a controlled vocabulary can deliver immense value in context engineering efforts. Controlled vocabularies guided by the SKOS data model and ontology further lend a systematic approach to managing terminology and can transform how your organization communicates, searches, and makes sense of information.

CHAPTER 2

# Metadata Schema

Metadata is the lowest common semantic denominator in most data ecosystems. Metadata, put simply, is data about data. Metadata can manifest in a multitude of ways—as simple text-literal labels, tags applied to resources and documents, and even as database schemas that define rows, columns, and tables in relational databases.

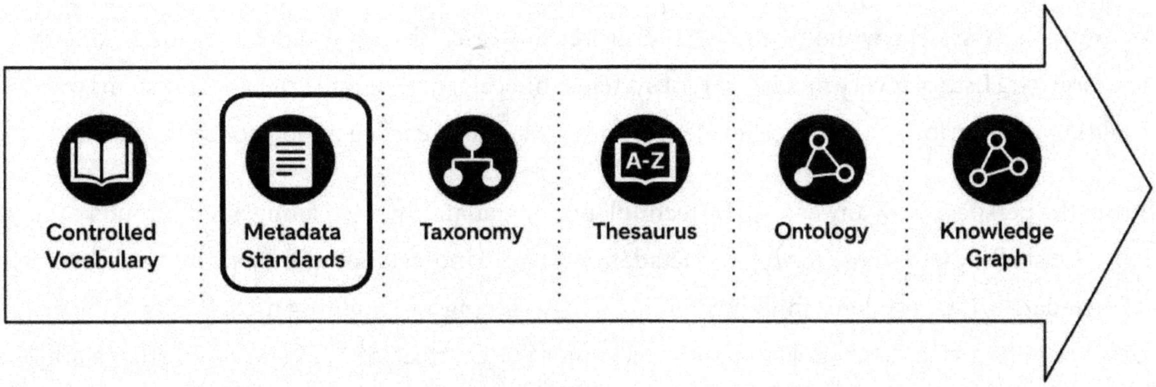


Figure 19: The Ontology Pipeline framework.

But how do we operationalize metadata to derive semantic context and meaning from it? The library and information science domain has been refining, iterating on, and evolving operationalized metadata in digital ecosystems since the advent of computer systems and digital environments. The goal? Improve findability, search, and discovery for humans and machines.

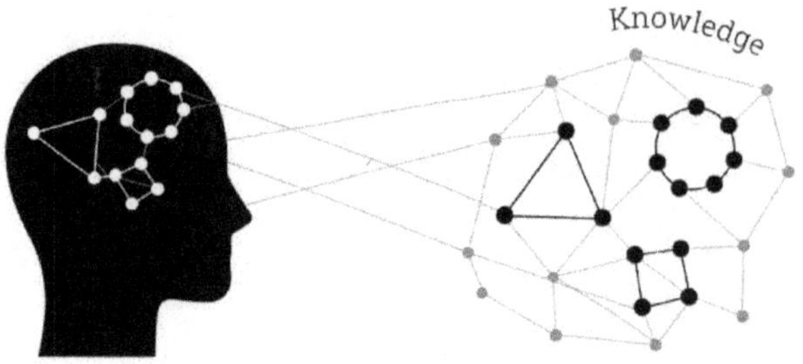


Figure 20: Metadata gets us a step closer to our attempt to fully and richly "express the complexity of interrelations in human knowledge" (https://www.ontotext.com/blog/semantic-metadata/).

## A systems thinking perspective

In the new, AI-infused information technology movement, metadata discussions tend to revolve around data catalogs, lexical and text labels, and API services. I can't imagine designing, modeling, or building a system without understanding the historical background of an idea, concept, or technology. History is very much a part of systems thinking, even if most metadata systems overlook building upon prior art, historical evidence, and work that preceded an idea or technology.

From the perspective of any enterprise technologist, metadata emerged alongside computer systems. This is a shallow lens to use to look at metadata systems. Understanding the centuries-old evolution of metadata brings a systems thinking approach to designing and building metadata systems capable of transmitting rich descriptive semantics. In other words, treat metadata as a holistic data model, capable of interoperability and machine readability.

## The enterprise metadata conversation

Enterprise data conversations and proposed solutions focus on addressing immediate metadata needs, providing hot fixes, and promoting shiny new technologies, all decoupled from the rich history of metadata and the relevant systems. To really understand the evolution and foundations of metadata, as well as to make sense of how to build robust, operationalized metadata systems that scale and extend, we must study the history of metadata, fundamentals of semantics, and principles of organizing. And the very concept of a system is at the heart of understanding semantic, interoperable, extensible metadata. This is why systems thinking is necessary: to unlock the value of metadata.

The NIST CSRC definition of a system is useful to level-set our understanding of a system: "A discrete set of resources organized for the collection, processing, maintenance, use, sharing, dissemination, or disposition of information."[5] By way of this definition, we can better understand the critical importance of a data model for substantiating and proliferating metadata as a first-class data asset.

From their 2015 paper, *A Definition of Systems Thinking: A Systems Approach,* authors Arnold and Wade work through meta definitions of systems thinking, and arrive at three distinct qualifiers:

1. Elements (in this case, characteristics).
2. Interconnections (the way these characteristics relate to and/or feed back into each other).
3. A function or purpose.

Notably, the least obvious part of the system, its function or purpose, is often the most crucial determinant of the system's behavior.[6] Most enterprise systems do not treat metadata as a system of elements, interconnected and designed to serve, with function and purpose.

Metadata in modern business-oriented data ecosystems is often reserved for the semantic layer, data catalogs, and business glossaries, to be managed by master data management programs with general oversight from a data governance entity. Enterprise metadata is often treated as a byproduct or an appendage of a data system, rarely integrated holistically as a logical system and data model. Failing to treat metadata as a holistic system and data model has led to disjointed systems, unable to

---

[5] NIST definition of a system: NIST Computer Security Resource Center (CSRC) glossary, entry "information system" (csrc.nist.gov/glossary).

[6] Arnold, R. D., & Wade, J. P. (2015). "A Definition of Systems Thinking: A Systems Approach." Procedia Computer Science, 44, 669–678.

reconcile disparate metadata elements and incapable of transmitting interoperable semantics that are rich with context and meaning.

If metadata serves as a translation layer and, functionally, translates syntactic structures into a common business language, then why aren't we designing metadata as a system? How do we expect to build for semantics if we are not treating metadata as a holistic system that is both scalable and extensible?

## The library science approach

Library science does not evangelize a single metadata standard or a single schema to rule them all. Quite the contrary. Library science takes a more holistic approach, recognizing that there are foundational, general-purpose data fields or elements that can support robust semantics while also enabling machine readability and interoperability. Essentially, librarians and information scientists operationalize metadata through frameworks, standards, and formats so that lexical labels and descriptions are not uncoupled from digital infrastructure frameworks. This is because all library metadata systems are declared data models woven into the fabric of digital ecosystems and are fundamental to the principles of information retrieval.

Figure 21: Traditional library card catalog (https://mundaneum.org/en/the-mundaneum/history/).

From clay tablets to library card catalogs to the web, metadata has persistently been utilized to support access to information and findability. The Library of Alexandria tied tags to scrolls with titles, authors, and subjects, a practice that foreshadowed modern surrogate records and, later, card catalogs. Libraries have long treated metadata as the scaffolding that makes collections intelligible and findable.

## *Standardizing the record format*

Early inventories and indexes—simple lists of holdings—gave way to card catalogs that let users search by author, title, or subject, and to shared rules that made records consistent across institutions. Released in 1967, the Anglo-American Cataloguing Rules (AACR, later AACR2) standardized what to record and how to phrase it, so "Mark Twain" and "Samuel Clemens" could be collocated and users could get comparable results anywhere. In effect, libraries paired disciplined description with navigable data models to turn shelves of items into searchable knowledge systems.

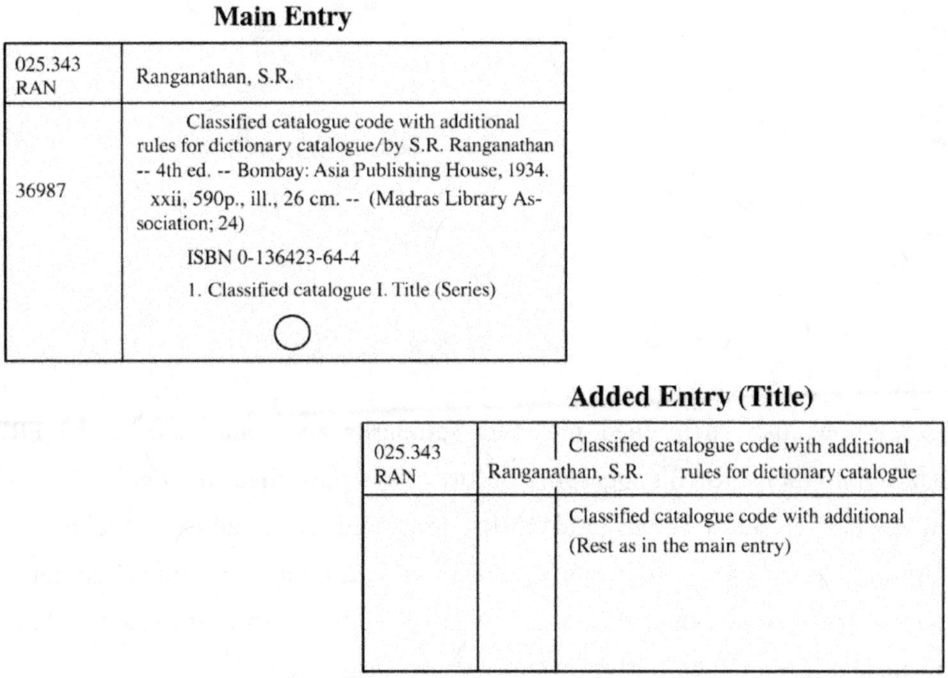


Figure 22: Standardizing records (https://tinyurl.com/AACR-standard).

Digitization pushed analog practices into computer systems and later, onto the web. To address the demands and opportunities posed by new digital systems, Henriette Avram, with support from the Library of Congress, developed the standardized MARC (Machine Readable Catalog) between 1965 and 1968. Catalog records were transformed into machine-readable formats, powering the development of integrated library systems. However, MARC's library-specific structure traveled poorly outside of library catalogs.

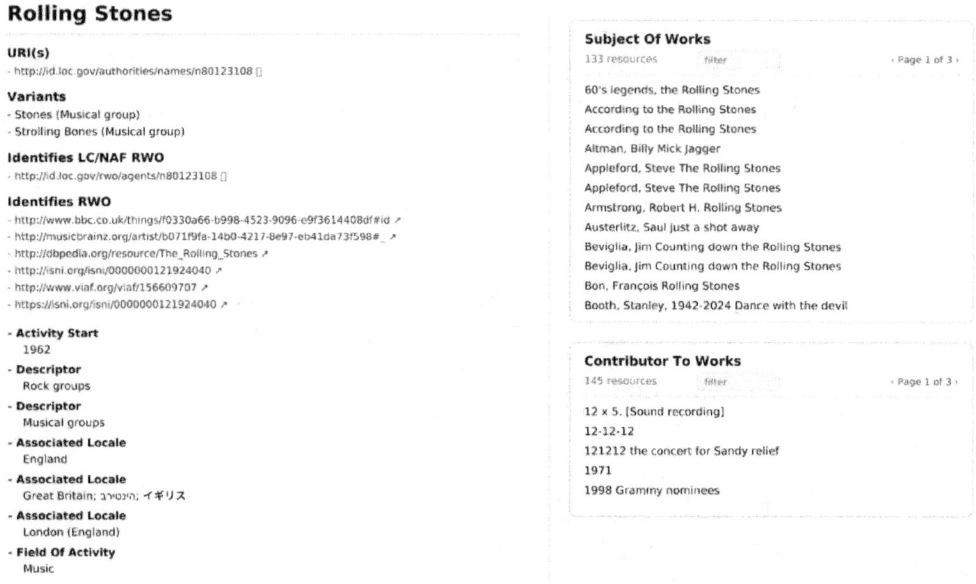


Figure 23: Human readable MARC 21 record (https://id.loc.gov/authorities/names/n80123108.html).

## *FRBR-ize It*

Alongside the previously mentioned metadata standards and data models, the FRBR model (Functional Requirements for Bibliographic Records) was published in 1998 by the International Federation of Library Associations and Institutions (IFLA) to address the management of relationships between resources and resource provenance. A conceptual entity-relationship model, FRBR reframes bibliographic metadata through linked entities, abstracted as Work, Expression, Manifestation, and Item, a departure from single flat records (OCLC).

As a data model, FRBR enables clustering expressions and manifestations under works and serves as the conceptual foundation for RDA (Resource Description and Access, described below) (OCLC).

The FRBR legacy and its evolution continued in the IFLA Library Reference Model (2017), which consolidates FRBR with FRAD and FRSAD, to guide contemporary metadata design (IFLA).

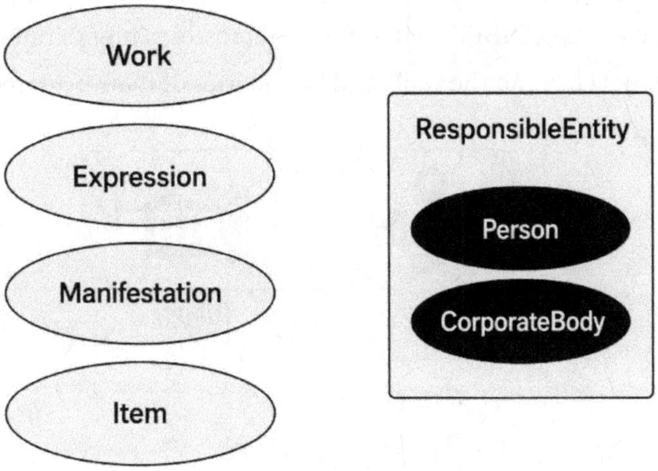


Figure 24: The FRBR model (https://commons.wikimedia.org/wiki/File:FRBR-Group-2-entities-and-relations.svg).

### *Carrier types and linked data*

RDA, the modern descriptive cataloging standard released in June 2010, was developed in 1997 to replace AACR2 and is maintained collectively through international professional library associations and committees. Rooted in FRBR, FRAD, and FRSAD, and aligned with IFLA's Library Reference Model, it provides element sets and instructions designed for user-focused, linked-data applications.

In practice, RDF-based RDA Vocabularies and the RDA Toolkit have enabled wide adoption, enabling interoperable, machine-readable bibliographic metadata across institutions and the web. RDA also provided methods for accurately categorizing ever-expanding carrier types. Note: In metadata, a carrier refers to **the physical or digital medium on which information is stored or transmitted**, such as a book's paper, a CD, a DVD, or an online server.

| Dataset link | Recording method | Scenario | Example |
|---|---|---|---|
| **Name/title of entity** | Unstructured descriptions | Flat file | Printed bibliography |
| **Access point for entity** | Structured descriptions | Bibliographic/Authority | MARC 21 catalog |
| **Identifier for entity** | Identifier | Relational/Object-oriented | MS Access database |
| **IRI of entity** | IRI | Linked open data | RDF graph |

Table 3: Dataset link examples (https://tinyurl.com/RDA-Toolkit).

In 2012, libraries developed BIBFRAME as a web-friendly carrier to further improve openness and interoperability, adopting the Resource Description and Access (RDA) standards and format as an updated content standard. Aligned with RDF and linked data, where people, works, and topics are modeled as interlinked entities, BIBFRAME sought to transform bibliographic catalogs and records to operationalize metadata beyond the walls and boundaries of the Integrated Library System.

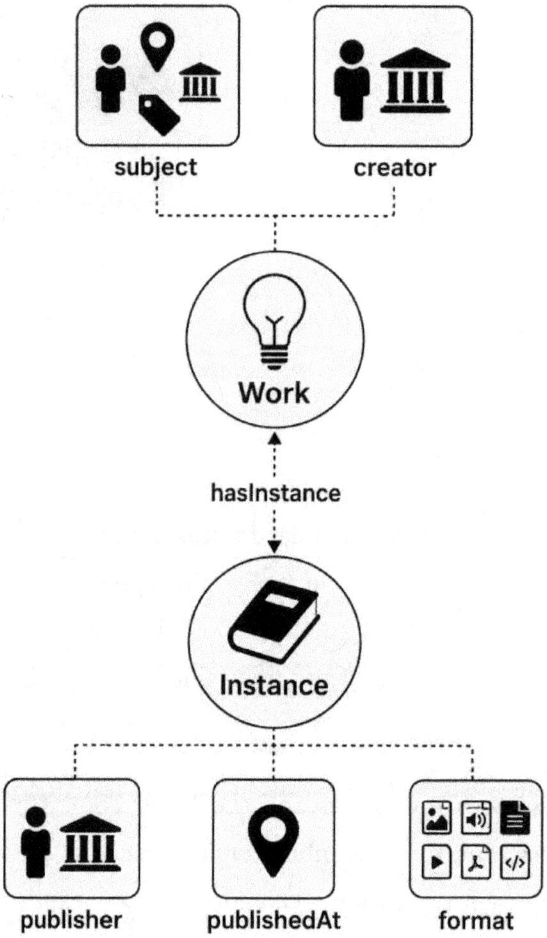


Figure 25: BIBFRAME (https://journals.ala.org/index.php/lrts/article/view/6134/7929).

## *Metadata schemas built for the web*

With this shift from analog to digital systems, librarians also designed domain-appropriate, standardized metadata schemas such as Dublin Core and VRA Core to further support the findability of library and cultural heritage resources in modern digital ecosystems. VRA Core is a community-developed metadata standard from the Visual Resources Association used to describe works of visual culture (art, architecture, and cultural artifacts) and the images that document them.

Dublin Core is a general-purpose metadata standard, originally developed by librarians to capture metadata for publishing documentation on the web. Originally a set of 15 core elements such as Title, Creator, Subject, and Date, Dublin Core was developed by the Dublin Core Metadata Initiative to describe resources of any kind across domains. Like VRA, Core it is community-maintained and interoperable; the difference is scope. Dublin Core aims for broad, cross-domain description, while VRA Core specializes in visual and cultural works.

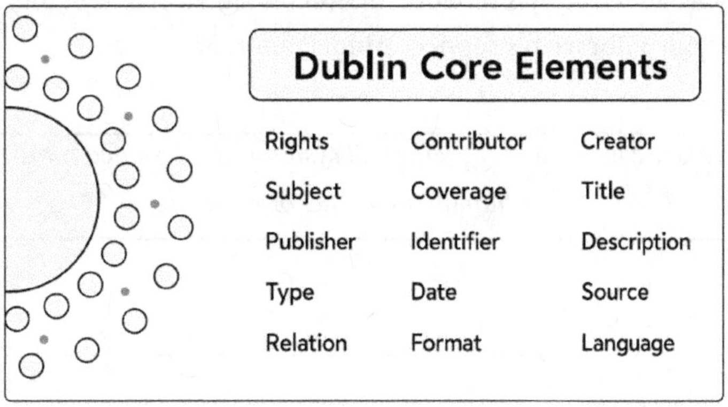


Figure 26: Dublin Core Elements (https://marketplace.heritageinnovation.eu/product/the-dublin-core-metadata-initiative-dcmi/).

## *Historical retrospective*

This high-level historical tour only grazes the compendium of metadata practices and underscores a core truth: library metadata is neither a straight path nor a break from the past. Instead, the field advances by refactoring proven principles into new application profiles, ontologies, and exchange models, carrying forward lessons from card catalogs to MARC, from FRBR to RDA and BIBFRAME, so systems thinking stays anchored in continuity.

## Semantics, metadata, and library science

Librarians continually iterate on schemas, element sets, and governance to meet new retrieval needs, networked architectures, and AI contexts, without discarding the intellectual scaffolding that brought us here. The story is one of heritage fused with invention—methodologies and organizational models that rise with innovation and progress. Never static, always dynamic.

To abandon the historical continuum of metadata is to create disjointed systems, absent of standards and protocols, and void of concrete data models. Metadata schemas, frameworks, standards, repositories, and data models intentionally break down silos while upholding principles of organization, always with a librarian's service-minded approach.

*ALL users are users, and therefore all systems are designed for all users, be it human, machine, or even AI.*

## The metadata difference

Librarian metadata approaches stand in sharp contrast with enterprise metadata approaches. The enterprise metadata management landscape has no shortage of tools and solutions because, let's face it, the business technology world is straight up enterprising!

Businesses are built with high levels of modularity, focused on products, platforms, features, and services. Often, businesses search for metadata solutions as an afterthought, in response to findability challenges and the mismanagement of messy data.

Now that AI demands context and meaning, semantics has placed a more urgent demand for semantic metadata. Data without metadata is bringing organizations to their knees, lacking context and meaning in a sea of syntax-first data ecosystems. AI is not performant with data alone. Metadata is, after all, a way to describe otherwise syntactic data and AI needs this translation layer to make sense of data. Hence, the myopic focus on business intelligence and data analytics functions, such as master data management (MDM) and the semantic layer.

## Where we diverge

### *Mission and time*

Libraries exist to maximize discovery across collections that live for decades, so they invest in durable, conceptual models (FRBR/LRM, RDA, BIBFRAME) that preserve meaning over time. Enterprises optimize for short-term product, analytics, or compliance needs, so metadata is often "just enough" labels tied to current systems, not a domain model.

### *Interoperability incentives*

Libraries *must* share records across institutions (OCLC, union catalogs, authority control), a condition that forces the adoption of common data models. Most enterprises don't exchange rich descriptive metadata beyond a vendor or team boundary, so the incentives to model semantics are weaker.

### *Standards and governance culture*

Library science has a mature stack (content standards, carrier formats, conceptual models, controlled vocabularies) and a distributed governance model. Enterprise metadata is usually owned by individual apps, data warehouses, or catalogs (MDM and BI), where schemas and ownership trump semantics. In fact, enterprises are still grappling with who should even own the semantic layer or standardized semantics. Data engineering? Marketing? Perhaps we should glean some insight from Ole Olesen-Bagneux's 2025 book, *Fundamentals of Metadata Management*, in which he proposes creating a data discovery team to mitigate conflicting metadata interests that traditionally exist within organizations. Recognizing organizational dysfunctions opens the way to new ways of operating.

### *Tooling and skills*

Library toolchains were built around structured descriptions from the start, ontologically rich and centered on machine-readable formats that maximize opportunities for interoperability and imbue semantics. Enterprise stacks evolved around transactions and analytics, so metadata tends to be in the form of columns and rows, JSON, and tags—useful, but rarely a first-class, semantics-first architecture. Enterprise metadata often exists as text-literal, lexical labels, appended to data files, but is barely interoperable and not reliably extensible.

## What the enterprise can learn from library sciences

Some sectors model metadata deeply, such as pharma with the Clinical Data Interchange Standards Consortium (CDISC), finance with the Financial Industry Business Ontology (FIBO), e-commerce with GS1 and schema.org, and manufacturing with the Product Lifecycle Management collection of related standards. In no way am I discounting the work of industry standards, created out of necessity and regulatory affairs. Rather, I am shining a light on what is missing from metadata management in most enterprise organizations: a cohesive semantic data model. Every organization can benefit from a pragmatic bridge, by adopting purpose-built metadata frameworks such as application profiles and a SKOS-like "Knowledge Graph Lite" type of semantic data model. By doing so, a metadata-first data model stabilizes terms as URIs, governs labels and relationships, and lets systems map to the model—bringing the library playbook to enterprises without boiling the ocean.

## A systemic problem

Perhaps the most fundamental flaw in enterprise metadata management approaches is the organizational divide that exists between governance and semantic design. In most enterprise architectures, data governance teams focus on compliance, quality metrics, and business process alignment, while semantic concerns are relegated to technical teams implementing search interfaces or analytics tools. This separation creates what information scientist Marcia Bates calls "semantic fragmentation."

*Semantic fragmentation is where the rules governing data have no meaningful connection to the conceptual models that should give that data meaning.*

Figure 27: Semantic fragmentation.

## The separation of concerns is not helping

Library science demonstrates why this separation is systemically harmful. Governance and semantics are inseparable in library metadata systems. Cataloging rules like RDA don't just specify data quality requirements; they embed rich semantic relationships directly into the descriptive process. When a librarian applies RDA rules to describe a resource, they're simultaneously enforcing data quality standards and building a conceptual model that connects that resource to broader networks of meaning. Every cataloging decision is a semantic decision—there is no such thing as 'neutral' metadata governance. This integration is why library systems achieve genuine interoperability across institutions. When two libraries both follow Dublin Core or RDA, they're not just ensuring consistent data entry; they're building compatible conceptual models that enable meaningful data exchange. Enterprise systems that separate governance from semantics produce what appears to be clean, well-governed data that nonetheless remains semantically opaque and impossible to integrate meaningfully across system boundaries.

## Data models as semantic infrastructure

The absence of true data modeling in enterprise metadata systems is most evident in failed integration projects. Organizations spend millions on data integration platforms, master data management suites, and semantic layers, yet struggle to achieve basic interoperability between business units or external partners. The problem is not technical—it's conceptual. Integration becomes an endless exercise in mapping between incompatible worldviews when organizations lack shared data models that define both entities and their semantic relationships.

And let me reiterate, this does not mean one data model to rule them all.

*Library science's successes with interoperability stem from its commitment to explicit data modeling as the foundation of semantic systems.*

FRBR, for instance, doesn't just define the four entity types of Work, Expression, Manifestation, and Item, it also specifies the semantic relationships between them and provides rules for interpreting and maintaining those relationships. This creates what metadata theorist Michael Gorman calls "semantic scaffolding": a conceptual framework that enables both human catalogers and machine systems to make consistent, meaningful decisions about how to organize and relate information.

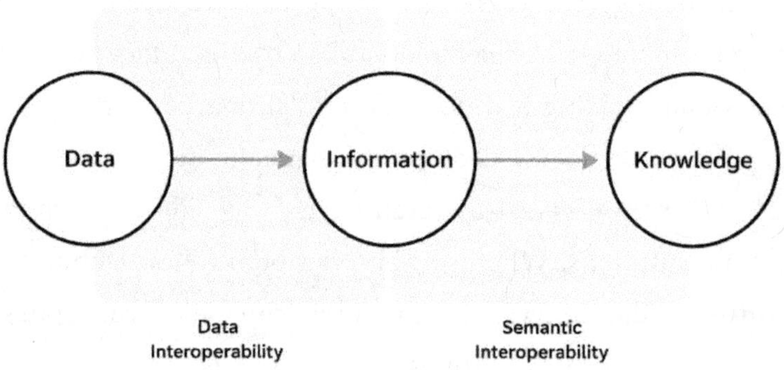


Figure 28: Data interoperability (https://doi.org/10.1016/j.dim.2024.100068).

Enterprise systems that skip this modeling step, treating metadata as labels rather than relationships, inevitably hit semantic walls. A "customer" entity in one system may seem equivalent to a "client" entity in another. Still, integration remains superficial without explicit modeling of what these terms mean, how they relate to other concepts, and what semantic constraints govern their use. The result is what appears to be unified data that represents incompatible conceptual models underneath: impossible to reconcile and thread through a data infrastructure.

## Why semantic layers fall short

Modern enterprise semantic layers, despite their sophisticated interfaces and natural language capabilities, often perpetuate rather than solve these fundamental problems. Tools that promise to "semanticize" enterprise data typically work by applying labels and descriptions to existing data structures without addressing the underlying absence of conceptual modeling. This creates what we will call "semantic theater."

*Semantic theater is a system that appears to provide rich meaning but instead offers better search and visualization of the same semantically impoverished data.*

The difference becomes apparent when these systems encounter the basic challenges that library metadata handles routinely: variant forms of names, changing organizational structures, multilingual descriptions, or temporal relationships. A semantic layer might successfully map "CEO" and "Chief Executive Officer" as equivalent terms. Still, it cannot address the deeper semantic question of how the concept of organizational leadership relates to other business entities, how it changes over time, or how it should be interpreted across different cultural or regulatory contexts.

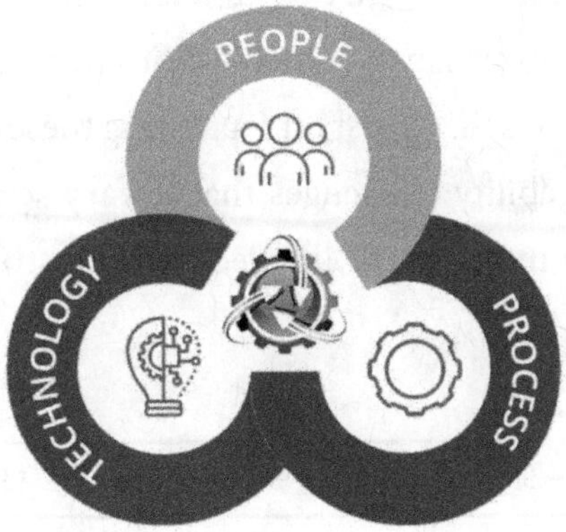


Figure 29: We need all three (https://tinyurl.com/PPT-Framework).

Library metadata systems address these challenges through what the late cataloging expert Sheila Intner calls "semantic architecture": explicit conceptual frameworks that define not only terms but also the logical relationships and constraints that give those terms meaning in specific contexts. This is why library authority control systems can distinguish between "River" as a personal name and "River" as a geographic feature, or why BIBFRAME can represent the complex temporal and administrative relationships involved in serials (items published under the same title, generally as separate issues or annual texts) cataloging.

---

## Semantic-first governance

> *The solution for enterprise metadata systems is not better labeling or more sophisticated search interfaces, but fundamental reorganization around semantic-first governance composites.*

This means designing data governance processes that begin with conceptual modeling, where every business rule and quality metric is grounded in explicit semantic relationships. It means treating controlled vocabularies not as afterthoughts, but as foundational infrastructure, and designing system integrations around shared conceptual models rather than technical protocols.

Most importantly, it means recognizing that sustainable metadata systems require what library science has always understood: governance and semantics must be co-designed and co-evolved as an integrated system. Organizations that insist on separating these concerns will continue to struggle with the fundamental interoperability challenges that library science solved decades ago through patient, principled attention to metadata as intellectual infrastructure rather than as a technical convenience.

> *Ownership and management of metadata are often treated as a hot potato.*

Does the onus of metadata management reside with data engineering, business intelligence (BI), or data analytics? Or is metadata every contributor's and team's responsibility? Where did enterprise systems go wrong with metadata?

In practice, metadata ownership cannot sit with any single function. Data engineering owns the pipelines that move it, business intelligence and analytics own many of the questions it must answer, and domain teams own the meaning of the terms—but none of them alone owns the metadata itself. By treating metadata as a byproduct of individual systems rather than as shared infrastructure, metadata is created inconsistently, documented nowhere, and governed by no one.

The fix is to make metadata a first-class, cross-functional asset with explicit stewardship—which is exactly what a metadata application profile and a semantic layer are built to enforce.

## MDM and the semantic layer

If an organization takes data and records metadata management seriously, there will be a cross-functional team or governance function tasked with building and maintaining master data management (MDM) systems. Their mandate will be to harmonize data, thereby unifying data and metadata in the process. A core function of MDM is to create golden records and canonical definitions, to ultimately create a metadata "single source of truth." In a similar vein, data engineering, data analytics, and business users implement semantic layers to bridge the gap between technical data ecosystems and business users, and to translate complex data representations into common vocabularies and terminologies for end users. MDM and semantic layers can and do work together; however, each is typically unique in its processes and technical components.

While organizations struggle to imbue data systems with rich context and meaning, MDM and semantic layers have fairly drawn the attention of practitioners and vendors alike. It is no secret that AI demands rich semantics, not syntactic data representations, to understand the context and meaning of data within domains and businesses. MDM and semantic layers promise to deliver the holy grail of rich context, mainly through text-literal labels and metadata. However, true structured and semi-structured semantic data representations are not usually threaded through the underlying code to drive contextual understanding efforts for the benefit of AI.

Even though MDM and semantic layers can be effective components of data architecture and data management, both systems tend to fall short in holistically managing metadata. To treat metadata as a data model, machine-readable, interoperable code must accompany metadata models to support a metadata program with teeth. Beyond metadata encoding structures, a metadata model supports AI's contextual understanding while also sustaining crosswalks, transformers, and translation layers, all with the end goal of negotiating organizational metadata alignment. I'm not talking about one model to rule them all. I'm talking about a machine-readable, interoperable manifestation of metadata and its related contexts.

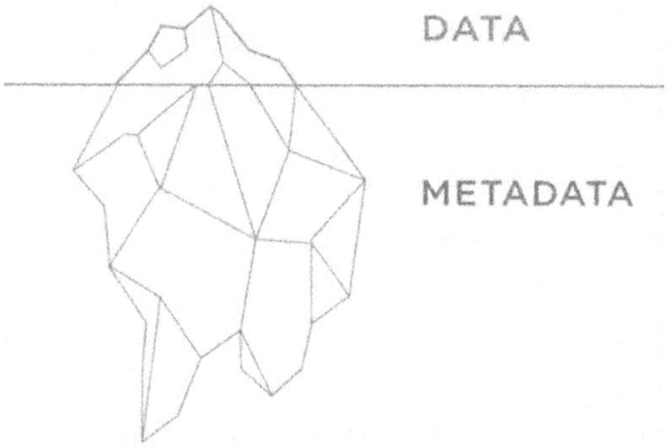


Figure 30: Data is just the tip of the iceberg.

Library science has devised a methodology known as the metadata application profile, or MAP, to address the risks and realities of metadata management. In no way a replacement for MDM or semantic layers, the MAP provides a roadmap of an organization's metadata and methodologies for metadata synchronization and reconciliation. A well-crafted MAP supports teams, organizational data systems, and AI while structuring metadata according to defined metadata and a metadata reconciliation layer. Consider the MAP a form of living, breathing documentation, able to deliver rich context and meaning that are so sorely lacking in most data and business environments.

---

## The semantic crisis

Organizations struggle with metadata and semantic consistency. According to a 2021 Gartner report, 75% of MDM programs fail to meet business objectives. The financial impact reaches astronomical levels when we account for poor data quality, which costs organizations an average of USD $12.9 million to $15 million each year. At the macroeconomic level, IBM discovered that in the U.S. alone, businesses lose $3.1 trillion annually due to poor data quality.

Metadata and semantic inconsistency emerge as primary culprits when we dig into the root causes. According to O'Reilly research, more than 60% of respondents to a survey selected "Too many data sources and inconsistent data" as their top challenge, followed by "Disorganized data stores and lack of metadata," which was selected by just under 50% of respondents. The operational impact? Data teams spend 30–40% of their time addressing data quality issues rather than working on revenue-generating activities.

Organizations have invested millions in MDM platforms that promise to be the "single source of truth" for data. Meanwhile, the BI team has built elaborate semantic models in tools like dbt or Looker that define what a "customer" means for analytics and business user purposes. These two systems speak different languages, use different standards, and typically do not interoperate.

The result? Data engineers spend countless hours writing translation code. Business analysts create spreadsheets to manually map between systems. And executives wonder why their "single source of truth" feels more like multiple sources of confusion.

---

## The metadata application profile

A metadata application profile (MAP) is, at its core, a declaration of the metadata terms an organization uses, how it uses them, and the constraints that apply in specific contexts. As elegantly defined by Dublin Core, an application profile is "an assemblage of metadata elements selected from one or more metadata schemas and combined in a compound schema."

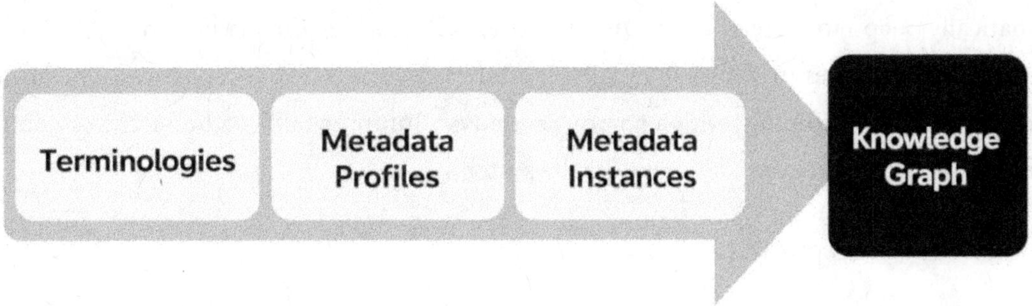


Figure 31: Metadata profiles make terminologies usable in practice and act as templates that bridge the gap between loose terminologies and a consistent knowledge graph.

That compound schema defines fields, encodes semantics, manages relationships, and most crucially, provides crosswalks between different vocabularies. Think of a MAP as a Rosetta Stone for your data ecosystem. It doesn't replace your MDM or your semantic layer; instead, it provides the translation instructions that allow them to communicate fluently. How crosswalks and translations between metadata schemas are operationalized depends upon data architectures, a topic we'll tackle in greater depth later.

---

## The CatChums example

Let me share a really fun example from the library science world that perfectly illustrates how MAPs work in practice. The CatChums metadata application profile was designed for a fictional nonprofit organization creating a searchable database of cat videos. Though whimsical and a little dated, it provides a perfect example of metadata management principles that can be directly applied to enterprise challenges.[7]

The CatChums MAP does several things that are directly applicable to enterprise data management. First, it defines 18 specific metadata elements, from basic fields like "Title" and "Creator," to domain-specific attributes like "CATegories" (including Drama, Comedy, and Musical cat videos) and "Cat Breed," using The International Cat Association's recognized breeds as a controlled vocabulary.

Second, and this is crucial, it provides crosswalks to four different metadata standards: MODS, Dublin Core, VRA 3.0, and VRA 4.0. This means a video tagged with a "Creator" in a local schema automatically maps to "Creator" in Dublin Core, "Creator.Personalname" in VRA 3.0, and to specific agent structures in VRA 4.0. Finally, it establishes controlled vocabularies. The vocabulary includes terms like "Jumping" with a narrower term of "Jumping fail"—a hierarchical relationship that maintains semantic consistency across the system.

---

[7] Alicia Houston, "Program Outcome 3 — Organization of Recorded Knowledge and Information," Alicia Houston, accessed August 19, 2026, http://www.aliciahouston.com/program-outcome-3.html.

Of note, a MAP in the library science domain almost always delivers rich ontological semantics as part of the specifications. Consider the RDF ontology rendering as a hyper machine-readable semantic layer, one that is less focused on SQL syntax and more on supporting interoperability. This means that a MAP supports MDM's objective of unifying and harmonizing data, delivering text-literal labels for business users while supporting AI systems with rich contextual understanding.

## MAPs solve the semantic layer disconnect

The fundamental tension between MDM and semantic layers isn't a technology problem—it's a semantics problem. Master Data Management wants to create a single, authoritative version of truth. Think of it as trying to establish one perfect dictionary that everyone must use. Meanwhile, human-readable text labels derived from semantic layers manifest as glossaries, data catalogs, and human-friendly BI dashboards, all intended to capture the languages of the business.

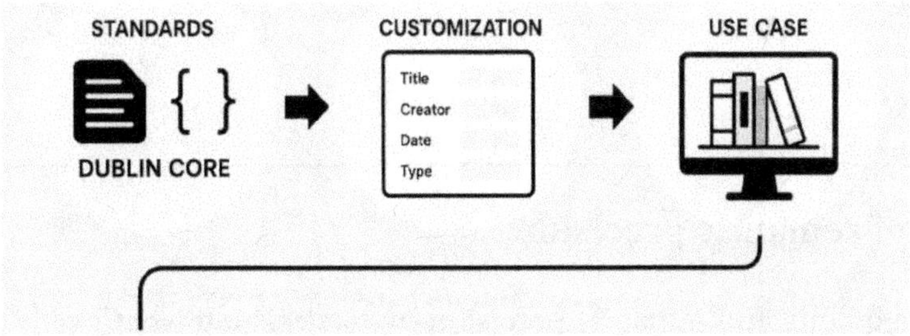


Figure 32: Metadata application profile.

The problem isn't that either approach is wrong—it's that each is solving different parts of the same problem, without a translation mechanism between them. This is where a MAP comes in, acting as a semantic treaty that allows both approaches to coexist productively.

## The three-layer solution

Think of a metadata application profile as having three interconnected layers:

- **The canonical layer**: Establishes your organization's core semantic model, which is what MDM has been trying to create all along. But instead of forcing this model directly onto every system, the MAP documents it as a reference standard. For instance, you define that a "Customer" has certain essential attributes, such as an identifier, legal name, and status. This becomes your semantic North Star, but it's not an operational straitjacket.

- **The implementation layer**: Where MAPs diverge from traditional MDM. Instead of forcing every system to use the canonical model exactly, you document how each system implements these concepts. Your CRM might extend "Customer" with interaction history and lead scores, while your financial system adds credit limits and payment terms. The MAP doesn't fight these differences—it documents them as legitimate variations of the canonical concept.

- **The translation layer**: Provides the semantic crosswalks that maintain meaning across systems. When the CRM's "prospect" becomes the financial system's "credit-pending customer," the MAP contains the rules that preserve semantic meaning during this transformation. While crosswalks support the arduous task of field mapping, a MAP can preserve the meaning of mapped fields through machine-readable formats and encoded definitions.

---

## Data quality and semantic precision

MAPs address data quality and semantic precision by establishing what I call "semantic contracts" at multiple levels. Much like a data contract, a MAP can accommodate semantic variations while supporting agreed-upon terms for data use and production. In fact, a data contract works beautifully with MAPs, operationalizing agreements, conditions, data types, and formats.

For example, at the field level, a MAP specifies whether a date exists, how it should be encoded (e.g., ISO 8601), which time zone assumptions apply, and which business rules govern its validity. When your order management system says an order was placed on "12/01/2024," the MAP ensures every consuming system knows whether that's December 1st or January 12th, whether it's UTC or local time, and whether it includes or excludes the timestamp. This may seem like a no-brainer, but believe me, I recently worked with database systems where there was zero conformance within a single database, and in most tables, I was lucky to even find a date for a record or row. Shudder.

Referring back to the CatChums example, notice in Table 3 how its MAP handles video duration. It's not just stored as a number. It specifies ISO 8601 encoding, distinguishes between display formats (code vs. text), and maintains relationships with related concepts such as file size. This level of semantic precision is exactly what's missing in most enterprise data architectures. If you are working with a system that offers this level of precision and accuracy, consider yourself blessed and way ahead of the curve.

**Length**
**Definition: The duration of the resource**

| | Attributes |
|---|---|
| **Subelement** | **<lengthOfVideo>** |
| **Encoding Scheme** | ISO 8601 |
| **Obligation** | Required |
| **Maximum Occurrence** | 1 |
| **Input Guidelines** | |
| **Example** | <length><br><lengthOfVideo type="code">O3N21S</lengthOfVideo><br><lengthOfVideo type="text">3:21</lengthOfVideo><br></length> |

Table 4: From the CatChums MAP example.

---

## Threading semantics

Crosswalks are perhaps the most under-appreciated component of metadata application profiles. They're essentially mapping tables that show how elements in one metadata schema correspond to elements in another. Crosswalks in a MAP extend beyond field mappings—they preserve semantic relationships across systems by including the RDF, XML, and JSON interpretations of relations. Think of a crosswalk as a framework for metadata transformers that enables direct translations between corresponding or equivalent fields.

In enterprise data, teams and systems are permitted to maintain individual metadata schemes and naming conventions, while the MAP crosswalk enables dynamic reconciliation of metadata. An MDM system might define a customer using one schema, a CRM may use another schema, and your data warehouse yet another. A properly designed MAP with crosswalks ensures that when MDM updates a customer's status from "prospect" to "client," this change propagates with the correct semantic meaning, aligning through the MAP to negotiate meaning with every connected system.

Traditional MDM fails at interoperability because it tries to force semantic uniformity, an unrealistic strategy where the social aspects of naming things typically depart from uniformity. Language is unduly political, but it's also a sign of healthy doses of human agency and autonomy. MAPs succeed because they enable "semantic polymorphism"—the idea that the same concept can have different valid representations in different contexts while maintaining its essential meaning.

---

## Governing semantics with structured metadata

Metadata application profiles also serve as governance frameworks that enforce semantic consistency without stifling innovation. Governance operates through three mechanisms: semantic precision, controlled evolution, and enforcement mechanisms.

### *Semantic precision*

Each element receives an unambiguous definition that eliminates interpretation variance. When the profile defines dc:creator as "the individual or organization with primary responsibility for data accuracy," there's no confusion about whether this means the technical team that built the system or the business owner who validates the data.

### *Controlled evolution*

Changes to semantic definitions follow formal processes. New meanings require new elements rather than overloading existing ones. For example, if using the Dublin Core element relations, there may eventually be a need to capture many different types of relations. We can implement Dublin Core sub-elements and/or qualifiers to support schema expansion and complexity. The logical reasoning model of the underlying metadata ontology and encoding scheme should support schema evolution.

| | | |
|---|---|---|
| Relation | Is Version Of<br>Has Version<br>Is Replaced By<br>Replaces<br>Is Required By<br>Requires<br>Is Part Of<br>Has Part<br>Is Referenced By<br>References<br>Is Format Of<br>Has Format<br>Conforms To | URI |

Figure 33: Dublin Core (https://www.dublincore.org/specifications/dublin-core/usageguide/qualifiers/).

Notice the relationship types detailed in this image, which can add context and clarity to the types of element relations supported.

### *Enforcement mechanisms*

A MAP includes validation rules that prevent semantic drift. These same rules can be specified as hard constraints detailing allowable values, obligation key, and requirement key within database schemas and serialization frameworks.

## Practical implementations

How do we adapt this library science concept to modern data architectures? Let's dive into a practical approach.

### *Start with a core schema*

Define your organization's fundamental data elements—not just their names and types, but their semantic meaning and relationships. Dublin Core has a great starter pack of 15 core elements that can be applied and adapted by almost any organization. Pick and choose what is useful and riff off this spec to derive the most meaningful element set for metadata coverage.

### *Document system-specific profiles*

For each major system (MDM, CRM, data warehouse, BI tools), create a profile that shows how it implements the core schema. Include encoding rules, validation constraints, and transformation logic.

### *Build comprehensive crosswalks*

Create detailed mappings between all profiles. These should handle not just one-to-one field mappings, but also complex transformations (like how a single MDM field might map to multiple BI dimensions). Most organizations have more than one metadata system and metadata can vary wildly from team to team.

I am not suggesting one MAP to rule them all. Perhaps your organization has each system's metadata owner create a MAP that is submitted to a central entity. I worked at one organization where my team managed crosswalks for the entire company, with a requirement to submit a revised MAP quarterly. There are many ways to handle crosswalks. Just keep in mind that crosswalks are extremely valuable for connecting data and semantics across an enterprise.

### *Establish controlled vocabularies*

Define authoritative controlled vocabularies for language, labels, and tags. Like the cat breeds in our MAP example, these ensure consistency while allowing for system-specific extensions. This becomes your input for your value vocabulary. According to a W3C Library Linked Data Incubator Report, a value vocabulary "defines resources (such as instances of topics, art styles, or authors) that are used as values for elements in metadata records.... They are 'building blocks' with which metadata records can be populated.... A value vocabulary thus represents a 'controlled list' of allowed values for an element. Examples include: thesauri, code lists, term lists, classification schemes, subject heading lists, taxonomies, authority files, digital gazetteers, concept schemes, and other types of knowledge organization systems."[8]

---

[8] Antoine Isaac et al., "Library Linked Data Incubator Group: Datasets, Value Vocabularies, and Metadata Element Sets," W3C Incubator Group Report, World Wide Web Consortium (W3C), 25 Oct. 2011, www.w3.org/2005/Incubator/lld/XGR-lld-vocabdataset-20111025/.

### *Enable extensibility through semantic evolution*

MAPs enable what I think of as "guided evolution." When a new system needs to extend the canonical model, such as adding social media handles to customer records, the MAP provides a framework to logically capture the newly added data type and format. The new attributes are documented as extensions to the canonical model, with clear relationships to existing MAP schema elements. With clearly detailed definitions of all elements and capture of semantic relationships between elements, new data types and formats are incorporated into the MAP, thereby making the newly added metadata available and interoperable.

### *Version and govern*

Treat your MAP as living documentation. Track changes, maintain lineage, version the MAP, and establish governance processes for updates.

---

## Real-world implementation patterns

Organizations successfully implementing metadata application profiles follow consistent patterns. Do not try to boil the ocean. Each organization has unique needs and nuanced data architectures.

My experience yields the following advice:

- **Start small:** Begin with a critical business entity (products, customers, or content) and prove value before expanding.
- **Build incrementally:** Add elements and relationships gradually, rather than attempting comprehensive coverage immediately.
- **Federate ownership**: Let domain experts own their metadata while maintaining central coordination of standards.
- **Automate validation**: Implement automated checks to ensure profile compliance and maintain consistency at scale.

- **Visualize relationships**: Create intuitive displays of metadata networks to help users understand connections. A visualization dashboard also provides observability when implemented well.

- **Measure impact**: Track metrics like search effectiveness, integration success rates, and data quality scores.

MAPs offer organizations a proven methodology for creating unified data ecosystems. By adopting library science principles—formal element definitions, controlled vocabularies, systematic crosswalks, and structured governance—enterprises can transform fragmented data landscapes into coherent knowledge networks. The MAP serves simultaneously as **technical specifications** that systems can execute, **governance frameworks** that enforce policies, **quality standards** that ensure consistency, **living documentation** that evolves with needs, and **semantic roadmaps** that guide integrations.

## Conclusion

When MDM systems and semantic layers unite through properly constructed metadata application profiles, the result is not just better data management, but a fundamental transformation in how organizations understand and leverage their information assets. The path forward requires recognizing that metadata management is not merely a technical challenge but a semantic discipline that requires rigor and a systematic approach.

The disconnect between MDM and semantic layers isn't just a technology problem— it's a semantics problem. We've been trying to solve it with more ETL pipelines and more integration tools, but what we really need is a semantic bridge.

Metadata application profiles provide that bridge. They're not new technologies to purchase or platforms to implement. They're a methodology—borrowed from librarians who've been managing complex, distributed metadata for decades—that can transform how we think about semantic consistency in modern data architectures.

CHAPTER 3

# Taxonomy

Taxonomies occupy a peculiar position in the landscape of knowledge organization. Everyone acknowledges their importance—for search, for navigation, for AI training, for enterprise knowledge management—yet writing about them coherently has proven stubbornly difficult. The challenge is not with the concepts themselves, which library science has refined over decades. The challenge is that every domain suggests different cuts through the material, every use case demands different emphases, and the gap between theory and implementation can feel impossibly wide.

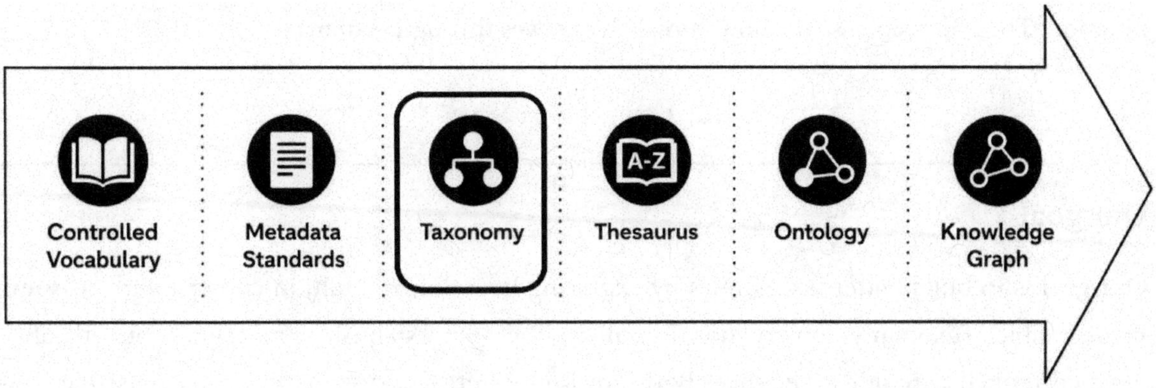


Figure 34: The Ontology Pipeline framework..

## A different approach

My approach is different. I'm not interested in presenting yet another abstract framework. Instead, I'm offering actual taxonomies, woven into narratives that examine how and why they take their shapes. We'll visit taxonomies across different domains and use cases, moving from foundational principles through construction methods to deployment considerations.

Our community technology taxonomy will be one such structure. I hope that by experiencing taxonomies in their working forms, you will gain an understanding of these classification and categorization artifacts, which encode real decisions about scope, granularity, hierarchy, and relationships.

*Drawing from years of building controlled vocabularies across organizations and enterprises, I've learned that taxonomy work lives in the details.*

The difference between a taxonomy that serves its purpose and one that becomes shelfware often comes down to choices made during construction: how you handle polyhierarchy, where you draw boundaries between concepts, when to use associative relationships, and how to structure your notation. These decisions shape how knowledge moves through systems.

## Our goal

Our goal is to build better taxonomies by exploring how they're built, in context, with reasoning made visible. Taxonomy construction is a discipline with established principles, but it's also a practice refined through experience. Both are important: the systematic approaches that make taxonomies coherent and sustainable, and the practitioner's knowledge of what works when abstraction meets application.

Whether you're starting your first taxonomy project or refining your approach after years of work, my schema aims to make sense of a practice that's essential to knowledge infrastructure yet often treated as a mysterious craft.

Let's demystify methodologies through understanding.

A taxonomy is a low-fidelity semantic structure with high returns on investment. Through hierarchical relationships alone, taxonomies support definitions, establish context, create meaning, and enable inference, without the complexity or the overhead of full ontological modeling. Taxonomy is the third stage in the Ontology Pipeline framework, yet it's often the first semantic structure organizations attempt to build. It's also the structure many enterprises rush to automate, absent of a controlled vocabulary.

This creates problems.

Taxonomies become unwieldy, inconsistent, and difficult to maintain without controlled vocabularies and metadata standards in place. But when built correctly, as part of a rigorous, iterative process, taxonomies deliver measurable value for both human navigation and machine reasoning.

This is why taxonomies do not have to be static or fail to capture new concepts and definitions. If built correctly with defined processes and workflows, a taxonomy becomes more robust and resilient over time. Just as a library system constantly updates its classification schemes and controlled vocabularies to account for new resources, materials, and formats, so should an organization attend to the care and feeding of its own classification schemes and controlled vocabularies.

And yes—a taxonomy *is* a classification scheme.

This chapter focuses on taxonomy construction. We'll examine what taxonomies are, how they function within the larger semantic ecosystem, when to build them with and without AI assistance, and how to implement them systematically. The examples come from real-world taxonomies: non-governmental organizations, government, education, marketing and advertising, software products, and comprehensive knowledge management systems spanning multiple domains.

Here, we're focused on prep work—the essential phase that helps you design and plan for taxonomy construction. The prep work becomes the scope for the work and the framework for the taxonomy build itself. Taxonomy construction is more difficult and far less predictable without planning and a solid design framework, often failing to meet organizational needs or lacking sufficient coverage.

While the prep work may seem arduous, it's well worth the effort because the resulting taxonomy will deliver accurate, data-driven coverage for domain concepts.

And who doesn't love processes and informed decision-making?

---

## What a taxonomy is (and is not)

*A taxonomy is a hierarchical classification system that structures controlled vocabulary terms from broad to specific, establishing parent-child relationships between concepts.*

The hierarchy creates navigable paths through knowledge domains, enabling both discovery and context. Let's examine this three-level taxon (sub-hierarchy) from one of my projects, the Bee Taxonomy, part of the Shock knowledge graph.

```
–» Community empowerment
   └── Caregiving
       └── Eldercare
           └── Home repair
           └── Grocery shopping
```

Figure 35: The Bee Taxonomy, part of the Shock knowledge graph.

This four-level hierarchy tells us that 'Grocery shopping' is a subcategory of 'Eldercare,' which is a type of 'Caregiving,' which is a type of 'Community empowerment' (This is set theory). Each level in the hierarchy narrows the scope, defining a thing in terms of its parts. The structure provides content and event classification, user navigation, reasoning paths for algorithms, and rich sensemaking for AI systems.

A taxonomy is not:

- A flat list of terms (That's a list and maybe a controlled vocabulary).

- A network of associative relationships (That's a thesaurus which we'll go into detail in the next chapter).
- An ontological system consisting of complex relations governed by rules and constraints.

Taxonomy construction is when we take our controlled vocabulary—a flat list or index of defined, disambiguated terms—and introduce a hierarchical structure. Nothing more, nothing less. Also, important to note: a taxonomy is a type of controlled vocabulary, structured as a hierarchy, to support categorization and inference.

---

## Classification, navigation, and reasoning

*Taxonomies serve three essential functions in knowledge management systems: classification, navigation, and reasoning.*

### *Classification*

We are building a classification scheme when we create categories. If we classify "Book clubs" under "Literary events," which sits under "Library activities," which belongs to "Cultural activities," we're asserting that book clubs share properties with other literary events, and that literary events share properties with library activities. The hierarchy becomes a classification engine.

```
—» Cultural activities
   └── Library activities
       └── Literary events
           └── Book clubs
```

Figure 36: Classification scheme example.

### *Navigation*

Users can browse from general to specific, discovering related concepts along each path. A taxonomy provides multiple entry points into content and for website navigation trees. By searching broadly for "Cultural activities," a user can narrow results and navigate down through "Library activities" to "Literary events" to find "Book clubs." The structure guides discovery while also supporting the accurate tagging of assets.

### *Reasoning*

AI systems can traverse the hierarchy to infer relationships. If the system knows that clinical trials require participant consent, and "Human Drug Trials" are a type of "clinical trial," it can infer that human drug trials also require participant consent. The taxonomy enables semantic reasoning without explicit rules for every concept.

```
–» Health & Medical
   └── Clinical Research
       └── Clinical Trials
           └── Human Drug Trials
               └── Investigational New Drug
               └── Clinical Trial Registration
               └── Clinical Trial Eligibility
```

Figure 37: Semantic reasoning example.

---

*These three functions of classification, navigation, and reasoning make taxonomies essential infrastructure for search systems, content management platforms, recommendation engines, and AI applications.*

---

## Before we get started

While I would love folks to jump into taxonomy construction without pause, taxonomy construction requires planning and thoughtful research. Why? Because you are building an artifact for digital systems, and you intend it to be used for specific reasons and use cases. Just as we shape software features and products with user requirements, use cases, and product requirement documents (PRDs) in mind, a taxonomy has its own processes to justify its construction and guide architecture decisions.

Prerequisites for designing and building a taxonomy include:

- Metadata schema(s) and Metadata Application Profile (MAP).
- A controlled vocabulary (see Chapter 1: Controlled Vocabularies).

We guide taxonomy construction with the following activities, requirements, and processes:

- ANSI Z39.19 Guidelines for Construction of Monolingual Vocabularies and Thesauri (reference for guidance).
- Use cases.
- Domain research—internal and external.
- Coverage model.
- Taxonomy requirements document.

We can build our taxonomy with very simple tooling:

- OpenRefine or Excel for data cleaning and manipulation.
- Taxonomy editors such as:
  - Enterprise-grade Graphwise Taxonomy Builder or TopQuadrant.
  - Low price to no cost TopBraid or VocBench.
  - Excel or Google Sheets.

Let's walk through the steps and prepare for taxonomy construction. But first, we need to start with the Ontology Pipeline framework.

---

## Ontology pipeline

I created the Ontology Pipeline as a framework for building semantic knowledge infrastructures to guide builders and thinkers through the logical steps that lead to reliable, logical knowledge systems. Each stage of the Ontology Pipeline prepares us for the next stage of building and provides a repeatable and measurable process for organizing information and knowledge.

We start with controlled vocabularies because we need clean, disambiguated concepts to model coherent, machine-readable and human-readable knowledge. Poor term quality can lead to circular logic, resulting in self-referential data.

Another common error in taxonomy building is the failure to reconcile and represent synonyms and acronyms as part of concepts and their preferred terms. In other words: a lack of vocabulary control. A machine (and some people) will treat these unresolved entities as duplicates or get confused by multiple first-class terms sharing the same definitions and meanings.

A controlled vocabulary is the first step in building a semantic knowledge ecosystem, as detailed by the Ontology Pipeline framework. That's why it was the subject of the first chapter of this book. For many organizations, simply establishing operationalized controlled vocabularies delivers immense benefit, with or without artificial intelligence entering the equation.

After we've created a controlled vocabulary, we move on to metadata schemas. Metadata schemas inform our knowledge architectures as to how data is represented using metadata. They also tell us how data is transported through systems, successfully or unsuccessfully. Metadata provides greater insight, clarifying ownership of data assets and metadata, and exposing gaps within metadata systems and data catalogs. Metadata schemas inform our building, while also illuminating gaps in machine and human understanding.

The third stage of the Ontology Pipeline is taxonomy, and yes—here we are.

We have our controlled vocabulary, our analysis of metadata schemas, and hopefully, a metadata application profile (MAP) to account for the metadata highways and byways within an organization. We use our controlled vocabulary as a foundation for structuring a hierarchy when designing and constructing a taxonomy.

Metadata schemas serve as architectural blueprints for the taxonomy, while controlled vocabularies provide the material from which we construct it. Together, the first two stages of the Ontology Pipeline prepare builders for taxonomy construction, leading to more reliable taxonomy-building processes that account for how language and metadata are leveraged within existing systems.

With our controlled vocabulary, metadata schemas, and MAP at the ready, we can now create a coverage model to ensure we build a taxonomy that is fit for purpose. A coverage model includes the controlled vocabulary as part of the input, so we can assess coverage gaps, which amount to opportunities for category expansion in our taxonomy-building phase.

The first step in assembling a coverage model is to gather use cases and define taxonomy requirements.

## Use cases and requirements

There are likely one or more reasons for needing a taxonomy. What are the use cases? For most organizations, the reasons for a taxonomy are simple, such as improving search and retrieval for a machine learning project that seeks to detect overpayments or improving the accuracy of LLM output for a customer-facing product.

Gather all current and potential taxonomy use cases. Don't be afraid to collect existing use cases from information and knowledge management workspaces such as SharePoint and Confluence. Use cases are about identifying problems and opportunities.

Create a spreadsheet where you can organize each use case, identify the problem(s) to be solved, and articulate how taxonomy can solve the stated problems. An example appears in Table 5.

| Use Case | Problem Statement | How Taxonomy Can Solve the Stated Problems | Priority Level | Stakeholder Owner | Status (TRUE=Complete FALSE=In Progress) |
|---|---|---|---|---|---|
| **Streamline Content Discovery** | Users cannot quickly find relevant documents or resources; inconsistent keyword tagging across systems. | Provides standardized vocabulary for consistent tagging and hierarchical structure for efficient browsing and search filtering. | High | Marketing/Sales | ☑ |
| **Improve Data Governance & Compliance** | Duplicate data entries and conflicting definitions lead to audit failures and reporting inaccuracy. | Establishes a single source of truth for key terms, definitions, and relationships, simplifying data validation and compliance checks. | High | Legal/Compliance | ☑ |
| **Enhance Personalization Engine** | Recommendation engine provides irrelevant suggestions due to poor categorization of user behavior and product attributes. | Standardizes product and content attributes, allowing the recommendation algorithm to accurately map user interests to relevant items. | Medium | Product Development | ☐ |

| Use Case | Problem Statement | How Taxonomy Can Solve the Stated Problems | Priority Level | Stakeholder Owner | Status (TRUE=Complete FALSE=In Progress) |
|---|---|---|---|---|---|
| **Optimize Digital Asset Management (DAM)** | Teams cannot reliably find or reuse existing assets because files are tagged inconsistently or not at all, leading to duplicated work and off-brand content. | Creates a controlled vocabulary for metadata tagging (e.g., subject, format, usage rights), making asset retrieval precise and scalable. | High | Creative Services | ☑ |
| **Standardize API Documentation** | Developers struggle to integrate services due to inconsistent terminology and lack of defined relationships between service components. | Defines a common language for service components, operations, and data models, improving interoperability and reducing integration time. | Medium | IT Operations | ☐ |
| **Facilitate Cross-Departmental Reporting** | Reports from different departments (e.g., Finance, HR) use different terms for the same concept, making reconciliation impossible. | Maps disparate business terms to a unified enterprise vocabulary, ensuring consistent meaning and reliable aggregate reporting. | High | Executive Leadership | ☑ |

Table 5: Taxonomy use cases.

Your requirements document will guide you in determining the starting point for your taxonomy build, as well as the appropriate level of granularity required to represent concepts. If we keep our scope constrained and start with the first listed item, 'Streamlining Content Discovery,' we have enough input to start the coverage model research, discovery, and reconciliation processes.

Pick one and, if possible, multiple use cases, choosing according to priority, scope, and feasibility of taxonomy implementation and integration within systems. This means there will be a fair amount of diplomacy required to reach agreements with teams and organizations to coordinate with workflows and product management. You will likely have to engage in formal product and project discussions, with proposals and presentations. In some organizations, proposing a taxonomy project as a pilot or proof-of-concept (POC) can fast-track it, bypassing organizational formal processes.

And with that, we are off to the races.

## Coverage model

Let's talk coverage and coverage models—the planning phases of taxonomy construction. A coverage model is a structured assessment of what your taxonomy must cover to serve its intended purpose. It maps your domain boundaries, identifies required concept areas, and establishes completeness criteria before you begin hierarchical construction. Without a coverage model, you're building blind—you don't know if you've captured 40% or 90% of your domain, whether critical gaps exist, or if you're over-investing in areas that don't matter to users. The coverage model answers four essential questions:

1. What topics do we need to include?
2. How deep should each branch go?
3. What level of granularity do users and digital systems need?
4. What are competitors or comparable organizations covering that we need to match or exceed?

Answering these questions requires domain research to surface sufficient input to guide the coverage model.

The coverage model itself will include a spreadsheet workbook, documents, and assets, organized in a dedicated file folder or server file where you will collocate your research. This will become your collection of information and knowledge assets. A coverage model also serves as a foundational research framework, ensuring your taxonomy reflects the actual language, concepts, and organizational needs of your domain. Rather than designing a taxonomy based on assumptions or a single stakeholder's perspective, the coverage model systematically captures terminology from the full breadth of sources that your taxonomy will eventually serve. This approach grounds your controlled vocabulary in evidence, revealing both the explicit terms people use and the implicit conceptual structures that organize their thinking. Because a coverage model relies upon domain research as input, let's be specific about what we are looking for in our research tasks. Have your controlled vocabulary at the ready before you embark on your quest for more input. Our controlled vocabulary tells us what is already accounted for and represented.

We are looking to identify gaps in coverage and where the business departs from how the rest of the world defines concepts and practices. Aligning on definitions and how things are represented on the web and in the real world is critical, especially when an AI system will be an end user. Mismatches between internal and real-world definitions often result in AI system failures, as a model's training data comes from the open internet, whose sense of reality is shaped by crowdsourced understandings of what things are and what they mean.

This misalignment—between the real world and internal vocabularies—should be captured and lightly documented, to flag concepts whose definitions contradict more widely accepted definitions. For example, if your organization defines "Journey" as a product feature used to construct a customer journey for marketing campaigns, a taxonomy should support the unique concept definition of Journey through definitions and parent-child relationships. This is what we mean when we say "context" in relation to the value proposition of taxonomies. In Figure 38, the Journey Taxonomy for Acme Products defines the concept, Journey, through its parent and child relations.

```
—» Acme Products
   └── Acme Analytics
       └── Journey (Feature)
           └── Manage journeys
           └── Market segmentation
           └── Send time optimization
           └── Timezone management
```

Figure 38: The Journey Taxonomy for Acme Products.

The Journey Taxonomy by Claude Opus 4.5 is not wrong; it's just not how Acme defines Journey as a feature in a product.

```
—» Journey
   └── Transformation
       └── Phase
           └── Departure
           └── Trial
           └── Passage
           └── Return
```

Figure 39: 'Journey' can assume different meanings.

As you can see, the concept 'Journey' can assume different meanings through a hierarchy, where parent-child relations add context and meaning to each category in the classification scheme.

"Journey" could also mean the stadium rock band, but we will save that taxonomy for another day.

## Gathering from diverse formats and file types

Effective coverage modeling begins by casting a wide net across your organization's documentary landscape. Sample documents should include unstructured content such as reports, policy documents, marketing materials, and internal communications in formats ranging from Word documents and PDFs to presentation decks.

Structured sources prove equally valuable. Spreadsheets containing product catalogs, customer data fields, or inventory classifications often reveal hidden taxonomic logic embedded in column headers and categorical values. Legacy databases, CRM systems, and enterprise applications contain metadata schemas that represent previous attempts to organize information. Even email subject lines and help desk ticket categories offer insight into how people naturally categorize their work. The goal is not an exhaustive collection, but rather a representative sampling–enough variety to surface terminology patterns.

## Sourcing across organizational boundaries

Internal coverage should extend across departmental silos, since different teams often develop their own vocabularies for overlapping concepts. Marketing may describe products using customer-facing language, while Engineering uses technical specifications, Legal employs regulatory terminology, and Sales focuses on competitive positioning.

Gathering term lists from each stakeholder group reveals these dialectical variations and highlights where synonymy, homonymy, and conceptual gaps exist. Interview subject matter experts, review departmental documentation, and examine taxonomies already embedded in team wikis,

SharePoint sites, and project management tools. This cross-functional approach ensures your taxonomy can serve as a bridging vocabulary rather than privileging one department's worldview.

Figure 40: Stakeholder term lists.

## Leveraging external and industry taxonomies

Beyond internal sources, publicly available taxonomies and classification schemes provide invaluable benchmarks for coverage and structure. These external resources offer tested conceptual frameworks and reveal industry-standard terminology that your stakeholders may expect. See the "Resources" section at the end of this book for useful assets related to open, available taxonomies. Competitor analysis also belongs in external coverage work. Examine how similar organizations structure their navigation, tag their content, and categorize their offerings. This competitive intelligence reveals both opportunities for differentiation and baseline expectations within your industry.

## The capture, collection, and reconciliation process

With sources identified, the practical work of term harvesting begins. Capture involves extracting candidate terms through manual review, automated text analysis, corpus analysis, or a combination of these. Natural language processing tools can surface frequently occurring noun phrases and named entities, while human review catches contextual nuances that algorithms miss. Maintain provenance throughout—record which terms came from which sources, preserving the connection between vocabulary and origin.

Let's focus on corpus analysis, as I find it to be the most reliable and easiest way to gather high-quality vocabulary terms.

### *Corpus analysis*

Corpus analysis involves the TF (Term Frequency) and TF-IDF (Term Frequency-Inverse Document Frequency) algorithms. TF measures how often a word appears in a document, focusing locally on a document's word count. A variety of corpus analysis methods and tools can be found in the "Resources" section at the end of this book.

Another option is to partner with an engineer to assist in corpus analysis. The most important part of corpus analysis is to keep all assets together for each source. This is to maintain the provenance and source for extracted terms.

To reconcile the corpus results, populate the extracted terms and term collection in a spreadsheet workbook, with a dedicated tab for each corpus source. For example, the terms extracted from a collection of documents and resources from marketing will populate a workbook tab you will name 'marketing'. This is one of the core grind tasks in vocabulary harmonization.

### *Reconciling harvested terms*

The mechanics of worksheet reconciliation deserve their own treatment—it's a methodical process with decision points and edge cases that benefit from detailed consideration.

For now, here's the high-level approach. Your reconciliation workbook needs to account for three conditions: term provenance (which source each term came from), term frequency (how often it appeared in that source), and mapping status (how the term relates to your existing controlled vocabulary). Work through the harvested terms in three passes:

- **First pass, exact matches**: Resolve exact matches between harvested terms and your existing controlled vocabulary. These are terms you already have—the corpus analysis simply confirms they're in active use. Note the match, capture the frequency data, and move on. High frequency across multiple sources validates your vocabulary choices. Exact matches that appear rarely might signal that your vocabulary uses terminology that doesn't reflect actual usage, which is worth flagging for review.

- **Second pass, cluster like terms**: For terms that are not exact matches, use clustering to group similar terms. These are synonyms, spelling variants, acronyms, and related expressions that orbit the same concept. Map these clusters to existing categories in your controlled vocabulary. The clustered terms become candidates for alternative labels—different ways of expressing concepts you already have. The clustered terms can also be candidates for subcategories in your taxonomy—narrower terms that help round out the description of a category. Term frequency within clusters helps you see which variants are common enough to merit inclusion.

- **Third pass, new candidate terms**: Terms that aren't an exact match and can't thematically cluster with existing concepts are your new candidates. These represent potential gaps in your vocabulary—concepts the domain uses that you haven't yet captured. Note each new candidate term along with its source, marking it as a candidate for expansion. Don't add these to your vocabulary yet; flag them for evaluation during the structuring phase.

### *What you now have*

At the end of reconciliation, you have your working material: your original controlled vocabulary (validated and annotated with frequency data), clustered terms ready to become alternative labels, and a list of new candidate terms, with all terms noting their provenance.

---

## Mapping to industry standard vocabularies

Map your existing controlled vocabulary to publicly available industry-standard vocabularies and taxonomies to expand your vocabulary. This is an additional or alternative way to capture more terms to be considered.

Standard vocabularies represent the accumulated work of domain experts and standards bodies. Mapping to them reveals terminology your organization hasn't adopted, concepts you haven't named, and relationships you haven't articulated.

Many of these vocabularies are published in SKOS format and available as linked data, enabling automated mapping using SKOS mapping properties such as exactMatch, closeMatch, broadMatch, and narrowMatch. Alignment with industry-standardized vocabularies is a powerful mechanism for staying relevant within a domain and the industry as a whole, especially in AI.

While an organization may have its own marketing and branding terminology, that same terminology may not make sense outside its walls. This may look like adopting industry standard terminology as alternative labels, ultimately enabling more robust category definitions and improved entity reconciliation.

---

## Why domain coverage is important

If I'm covering a domain—any domain—I want coverage for the domain, not just my company. This matters because, for LLMs, we need to cover not just what we know but also what we don't. This allows us to discover new opportunities in the marketplace and maintain a handle on the competitive landscape.

A taxonomy that includes terminology uncommon in company-speak is valuable for creating a tech radar of the domain or industry. This supports signal detection for upcoming trends, forecasting, and competitive analysis. It also helps describe domains more fully and contextualize concepts by grounding them in facts beyond internal assumptions.

This aspect of taxonomy building always catches folks off guard: Why cover concepts that aren't within the things an organization cares about right now?

I once worked at a company where the subject matter experts (SMEs) took it upon themselves to remove half of the concepts from a vocabulary because it was not relevant to the domain or the company. The SMEs viewed the extra concepts as noise, but in reality, they were a competitive advantage.

As a librarian, I understand that distribution and fair coverage of subject areas, topics, and domains are critical to understanding. Comprehensive coverage mitigates bias.

*A vocabulary built only from internal sources reflects internal blind spots.*

A vocabulary built from domain-wide corpus analysis and mapped to industry standards reveals the full landscape—including the parts your organization hasn't noticed yet, the terminology competitors use that you don't, and the emerging concepts that haven't made it into your operational language.

This is how taxonomies become strategic assets.

---

## Coverage model as a framework

After assembling the research and doing the prep work, the next step is to assemble the actual coverage model, which will serve as your design framework for taxonomy construction.

The coverage model, once complete, includes:

- The existing controlled vocabulary.
- Metadata schemas.
- Metadata application profile.
- Use cases.
- Taxonomy requirement document.
- Collections of documents and resources used for corpus analysis.
- The workbook with harvested terms, one tab per source.
- The reconciliation work (exact match, clusters, and candidate terms).

The framework itself will be a requirements document that serves as your taxonomy blueprint, informing hierarchy depth decisions (how many levels are needed), preventing scope creep, and providing stakeholders with concrete metrics for completeness. You'll know when you are done when you've achieved the coverage targets you defined upfront.

The coverage model documentation becomes your framework for informed taxonomy design decisions. You can identify emergent themes by tracking which sources contributed which terms. Perhaps customer service documentation emphasizes problem categories that product documentation ignores, or recent materials introduce terminology absent from legacy content. These patterns inform scope decisions about what your taxonomy must cover comprehensively and what it should cover peripherally.

Concept frequency analysis reveals depth requirements. Domains where many fine-grained distinctions appear in source materials warrant deeper hierarchical development, while areas with sparse or generic terminology may need only shallow coverage. Trend analysis across document dates can show evolving vocabulary, helping you anticipate where your taxonomy will need flexibility for emerging concepts.

Finally, source documentation supports governance. The coverage model provides evidence-based justification when stakeholders question why certain terms were included or excluded, or why particular hierarchical relationships were established. This transparency builds trust in the taxonomy as a representation of organizational reality rather than an arbitrary imposition, and it establishes the baseline against which future taxonomy evolution can be measured.

---

*People don't care about concepts, naming conventions, and taxonomies until THEIR concepts and naming are challenged.*

---

Retaining term sources will come in handy when there is a word war. It's best to come prepared with citations.

The coverage model is the necessary prep work that drives key structural decisions. It helps determine how many levels your hierarchy needs—where depth serves precision and where it creates unnecessary complexity. It identifies where alternative labels are essential to capture the varying ways people describe the same concepts, ensuring your vocabulary meets users where they are, rather than forcing them to guess your preferred terminology. And it highlights areas requiring attention: gaps in domain coverage, ambiguities where a single term carries multiple meanings that need disambiguation, and overlaps where concepts blur and require clearer boundaries.

---

## Transforming flat vocabulary into a structured hierarchy

Now that we've established the groundwork for taxonomy construction, which includes gathering use cases, conducting domain research, building a coverage model that maps your controlled vocabulary against organizational needs, and reconciling terms organized into clusters, exact matches, and new candidates, it's time to transform that flat vocabulary into a structured hierarchy.

Our focus turns to building taxonomies using simple, portable structures that work in any tool or format. We will use parent-child relationships, definitions, and alternative labels to capture synonyms and acronyms. No specialized vocabulary standard is required.

Why start *without* SKOS (Simple Knowledge Organization System)? Because the fundamental logic of taxonomy construction exists independently of any encoding standard. Understanding how to structure hierarchies, write definitions, and manage alternative labels prepares you for any implementation, whether that's a spreadsheet, a content management system, a taxonomy editor, or eventually a SKOS-compliant RDF data model that can be leveraged as part of a knowledge graph. The principles transfer; the format is secondary. We'll get to SKOS at the end of this chapter, introducing this concept to readers who are ready to formalize their taxonomies using linked data principles.

---

## What we're building

A taxonomy without SKOS consists of four essential components:

- **Preferred labels:** The authoritative term for each concept, the name that appears in navigation, search facets, and tagging interfaces.

- **Hierarchical relationships:** Parent-child connections that organize concepts from broad to narrow, establishing the is-a or is-a-type-of relationships that create taxonomy structure.

- **Definitions:** Clear, concise descriptions that disambiguate each concept, explaining what belongs in a category and what does not.

- **Alternative labels:** Synonyms, acronyms, and variant terms that users might search for, mapped to their corresponding preferred labels.

That's it. Four components. Everything else, including associative relationships, scope notes, editorial notes, and mapping properties, belongs to SKOS taxonomies and thesauri, which we'll address in the next chapter. This non-SKOS taxonomy, built simply in a spreadsheet, stays simple. This constraint is also a feature, for its elegant simplicity.

---

## From coverage model to hierarchy

Your coverage model produced three categories of terms:

- **Exact matches:** Terms already in your controlled vocabulary.
- **Clustered terms:** Synonyms and variants grouped around existing concepts.
- **New candidate terms:** Concepts your vocabulary doesn't yet capture.

Each category requires different handling as we move into hierarchy construction.

---

## Starting with top-level categories

Begin by identifying your top-level categories, the broadest groupings that will anchor your hierarchy. These typically emerge from your use cases and domain research. Top-level categories might include Products, Industries, Solutions, and Resources for a content taxonomy supporting a marketing organization. You might see Programs, Services, Populations, and Outcomes for a taxonomy.

Top-level categories should be mutually exclusive and collectively exhaustive within your defined scope. Mutual exclusivity means a concept belongs to one branch, not multiple branches. Collective exhaustiveness means every concept in your domain fits somewhere in the structure.

The mutually exclusive, collectively exhaustive paradigm is rooted in the work of librarian S. R. Ranganathan.

Ranganathan published "Prolegomena to Library Classification" in 1939, presenting a set of classification principles to guide library cataloging activities. Ranganathan was brilliant, presenting his principles as canons. My method for building taxonomies draws heavily on Ranganathan's book. After all, a taxonomy can be a classification scheme that also serves to organize resources and provide rich semantics.

Ranganathan defines exhaustiveness and exclusiveness as:

- **The Canon of Exhaustiveness:** The classes in any array of classes should be totally exhaustive of their common immediate universe.
- **The Canon of Exclusiveness**: The classes in an array should be mutually exclusive.

If you find concepts that don't fit any top-level category, you either need a new category or you need to revisit your scope.

Let me illustrate with an example from the Bee Taxonomy, part of the Shock knowledge graph, an NGO focused on community empowerment. The top-level categories reflect the organization's core domains:

| Top-Level Category | Scope |
|---|---|
| **Community empowerment** | Activities and services that build community capacity |
| **Economic development** | Programs supporting financial stability and growth |
| **Health and wellness** | Services addressing physical and mental health |
| **Education and training** | Learning opportunities and skill development |

Table 6: Bee Taxonomy example.

These four categories create distinct branches. A concept like Eldercare fits clearly under Community empowerment. Job training fits under education and training. The boundaries are clean.

## The Is-a test

Every parent-child relationship in a taxonomy must pass the Is-a test. The child concept must be a type of the parent concept. This sounds simple, but the test catches many taxonomy errors.

Consider this list of terms and let's try to step through the logic of a possible hierarchy:

**Community empowerment**
**→ Caregiving**
**→ Eldercare**
**→ Grocery shopping**

Figure 41: Community empowerment.

**Apply the Is-a test at each level:**

**Is Caregiving a type of Community empowerment?** Yes. Caregiving is an activity that builds community capacity by supporting vulnerable members.

**Is Eldercare a type of Caregiving?** Yes. Eldercare is a form of caregiving focused on older adults.

**Is Grocery shopping a type of Eldercare?** Yes, in this context. Grocery shopping as an eldercare service is a specific eldercare activity.

Now, consider an example of an invalid hierarchy:

**Vehicles**
**→ Cars**
**→ Wheels**

Figure 42: Invalid hierarchy.

Are Wheels a type of Car? No. Wheels are a component of cars, not a type of car. This is a part-of relationship (meronymy), not an is-a relationship. Part-of relationships belong in thesauri or ontologies, not taxonomies.

## Taxonomy levels

Taxonomy depth should reflect actual complexity in your domain, not arbitrary decisions. Most operational taxonomies function well at three to four levels. Deeper than that, and you risk over-specification. Shallower, and you lose precision.

The Is-a test keeps your taxonomy logically coherent. Every time you add a term to a branch, ask: Is X a type of Y? If the answer is no, you need a different parent or a different structure. The coverage model guides depth decisions. If your corpus analysis reveals many fine-grained distinctions in a domain area, that branch needs more depth. If an area has sparse or generic terminology, keep it shallow. Consistent depth across all branches is ideal but not always achievable.

*What matters is that depth serves purpose, not aesthetics.*

Consider two approaches to the same concept:

**Shallow (two levels)**

```
-» Cultural activities
   └── Book clubs
```

**Deeper (four levels)**

```
-» Cultural activities
   └── Library activities
       └── Literary events
           └── Book clubs
```

Figure 43: Two approaches to the same concept.

Which is correct? It depends on your use case. The deeper structure serves you if you need to distinguish between library-based literary events and non-library literary events, or between literary events and other library activities, such as computer classes. The shallow structure is sufficient and easier to maintain if those distinctions don't matter for your classification or navigation needs.

## Writing definitions

*Definitions do the heavy lifting in taxonomy disambiguation.*

A well-written definition tells users what belongs in a category and, equally important, what doesn't. Without definitions, hierarchical position provides some context, but ambiguity creeps in at scale.

### *The genus-differentia pattern*

The most reliable pattern for taxonomic definitions is the genus-differentia pattern, borrowed from classical logic. A definition identifies the broader category (genus) and the distinguishing characteristics (differentia) that set this concept apart from siblings.

Pattern: [Preferred Label] is a [genus/parent concept] that [differentia or distinguishing characteristics].

**Examples**

- Eldercare is a form of caregiving that focuses on supporting older adults with daily living activities, health management, and social engagement.
- Clinical trials are research studies that test medical interventions in human participants to evaluate safety and efficacy.
- Book clubs are literary events where participants gather to discuss a shared reading, typically meeting on a regular schedule.

Notice how each definition references the parent concept (genus) and specifies what makes this concept different from its siblings (differentia). The definition for Clinical trials identifies the genus—research studies—and the differentia—testing medical interventions in human participants, evaluating safety and efficacy. You can navigate the SNOMED medical taxonomy (See "Resources" at the end of this book) to explore how these concepts are organized.

## What makes a good definition

Good taxonomy definitions share several characteristics:

- **Concise:** One to two sentences. If you need more, you're probably overloading the definition with scope notes or usage guidance that belongs elsewhere.
- **Non-circular:** The definition should not use the term being defined. "Eldercare is care for elders" tells us nothing.
- **Consistent:** Use the same grammatical structure across definitions. If you start with "A type of..." for one term, use that pattern throughout.
- **Boundary-setting:** The definition should help users understand edge cases. The definition hasn't done its job if it's not clear whether something belongs.
- **Neutral:** Avoid promotional language, value judgments, or organizational jargon unless that jargon is specifically being defined.

---

## Managing alternative labels

Alternative labels capture the various ways users express the same concept. They enable search systems to match user queries to preferred labels, improve content discovery, and acknowledge that language varies across users, departments, and contexts.

### *What becomes an alternative label?*

Your coverage model produced clusters of related terms. Within each cluster, you selected one term as the preferred label. The remaining terms in the cluster become alternative labels. These typically include:

- **Synonyms:** Different words with the same meaning. "Elder care" and "Senior care" might be alternatives to "Eldercare."
- **Acronyms and abbreviations:** Always use the spelled-out form as the preferred label and the acronym as an alternative label. "Artificial intelligence" is preferred; "AI" is an alternative. This ensures clarity for users unfamiliar with acronyms.
- **Spelling variants:** British versus American spellings, hyphenated versus unhyphenated forms. "Organisation" as an alternative to "Organization."

- **Legacy terminology:** Older terms that users might still search for. "Handicapped parking" as an alternative to "Accessible parking."
- **Common misspellings:** Only when frequent enough to warrant inclusion. This is more common in search systems than in classification taxonomies, but I often include them deliberately, as a small courtesy to users who mistype a term—a quiet safety net that still returns the right result.

---

## The acronym rule

Almost every organization I've worked with had an 'Acronym Glossary,' usually poorly maintained and often containing duplicate acronyms. Imagine the acronym silage that exists at a mega-organization like Amazon. There may be five distinct meanings for the acronym SSS, each represented as a unique entity. You will be doing essential, unglamorous work to reconcile and semantically represent the tangle of acronyms in a logical, consistent, and accurate way.

With that in mind, capturing acronyms is critical to reconciling vocabulary terms in an organization. Always default to spelled-out versions for preferred labels. Acronyms become alternative labels. This rule has few exceptions.

| Preferred Label | Alternative Label |
|---|---|
| Artificial intelligence | AI |
| Natural language processing | NLP |
| Customer relationship management | CRM |
| Non-governmental organization | NGO |

Table 7: Preferred labels.

The rare exception is when an acronym has become the dominant term and the spelled-out form is rarely used. "Scuba" is preferred over "Self-contained underwater breathing apparatus." "ISBN" is preferred over "International Standard Book Number." Use frequency data from your corpus analysis to make this determination.

## Structuring your taxonomy in a spreadsheet

While taxonomy editors offer specialized features, many practitioners build and maintain taxonomies in spreadsheets. A well-structured spreadsheet can capture all the essential components and export to various formats, including SKOS-ready structures when you're ready for that transition.

The spreadsheet format I recommend uses hierarchical concept columns that visually represent the taxonomy structure, making parent-child relationships apparent immediately. This format is both human-readable and machine-parseable, and it sets you up for a smooth transition to SKOS.

### *The column structure*

The spreadsheet has two areas: a fixed area containing mandatory columns, and an optional area for additional properties.

We will include these fields:

- **Scheme:** The name of your taxonomy or concept scheme. This identifies which taxonomy a concept belongs to, which is essential when managing multiple vocabularies.
- **Concept L1, concept L2, concept L3:** Hierarchical concept columns representing each level of depth. Top concepts appear in concept L1, their children in concept L2, and so on. This visual nesting makes the hierarchy immediately readable.
- **Definition:** The genus-differentia definition for the concept.
- **altLabel:** Synonyms, acronyms, and spelling variants. Use semicolons to separate multiple values.

Optional fields:

- **Notation:** A code or identifier for the concept, useful for system integration.
- **Custom attributes:** Any domain-specific properties like source, status, or owner.

Important! All column headers should be lowercase. This convention ensures compatibility with tools that parse the spreadsheet into structured formats. We will remove the L1, L2, and L3 type header labels when we move our work to the SKOS format.

*Example spreadsheet structure*

Here's how a taxonomy branch appears in this format:

| scheme | concept L1 | concept L2 | concept L3 | definition | altLabel |
|---|---|---|---|---|---|
| **Bee Taxonomy** | | | | | |
| | Community empowerment | | | Activities that build community capacity | |
| | | Caregiving | | Support services for vulnerable populations. | Care work |
| | | | Eldercare | A form of caregiving focused on older adults. | Senior care; Elder care |
| | Education and training | | | Learning opportunities and skill development. | |
| | | Financial literacy | | Educational programs for money management. | Money management; Personal finance |
| | | | Budgeting | Skill focused on income allocation | Budgeting skills; Budget planning |

Table 8: Taxonomy branch example.

Notice how the hierarchical concept columns, such as concept L1, concept L2, and concept L3, create a visual tree structure. Each row represents one concept. The concept appears in the column corresponding to its depth, with parent columns left empty. This makes the parent-child relationships immediately visible—Caregiving is a child of Community empowerment because it appears in concept L2, following a concept L1 entry.

---

## Reading the hierarchy

The hierarchy is determined by concept position and row order:

- A concept in concept L2 is a child of the most recent concept L1 entry above it.
- A concept in concept L3 is a child of the most recent concept L2 entry above it.
- Top concepts (concept L1) have no parent—they sit directly under the scheme.

This format scales cleanly. Add concept L4, concept L5, and so on as your taxonomy requires deeper levels. The visual structure remains intuitive.

---

## How AI systems utilize taxonomies

A taxonomy maintained in a spreadsheet is not a lesser artifact—it's a portable, system-agnostic knowledge structure that AI systems can readily consume. Understanding how AI leverages taxonomies helps you design structures that maximize value for both human users and machine processes.

### *Hierarchical inference*

When you export your spreadsheet as CSV or JSON, you've created a machine-readable file that large language models, search systems, recommendation engines, and classification pipelines can ingest. Parent-child relationships enable AI systems to understand that content tagged with "Budgeting" also belongs to "Financial literacy" and "Education and training," thereby supporting query expansion and semantic inference without complex ontological reasoning.

Consider a user searching for "money management courses." Without a taxonomy, the search system only returns exact matches. With a taxonomy, the system recognizes that "money management" is an alternative label for "Financial literacy," which is a type of "Education and training." The search can now expand to include content tagged at any level of this branch, dramatically improving recall while maintaining precision.

### *Definitions as training signals*

The definitions you've written become training signals, helping AI systems understand not just what a concept is called, but what it means and where its boundaries lie. When a language model encounters ambiguous content, the definition provides disambiguation logic. Is this article about "financial planning" in the retirement sense or the corporate strategy sense? The genus-differentia definition answers that question.

Definitions improve chunk retrieval by providing semantic context in retrieval-augmented generation (RAG) systems. When the system retrieves content to inform a response, it can use definitions to assess relevance beyond keyword matching. A well-defined taxonomy turns RAG from a keyword search into a genuine semantic search.

### *Alternative labels and synonym resolution*

Alternative labels prove particularly valuable for AI applications. When a language model encounters "money management" in user input, the alternative label mapping tells the system to treat this as equivalent to "Financial literacy"—enabling accurate classification even when users don't apply your preferred terminology. This synonym resolution happens at the data layer, not through prompt engineering or model fine-tuning. The spreadsheet taxonomy becomes a lightweight knowledge base that grounds AI behavior in your organizational understanding of concepts, reducing hallucination and ensuring that AI-generated content aligns with how your domain organizes knowledge.

### *Classification and tagging*

AI systems can use your taxonomy to automatically classify incoming content. Given a document, the system matches text against preferred labels, alternative labels, and definitions to assign appropriate categories. The hierarchical structure enables multi-level classification—the system can tag content with both the specific concept, "Budgeting," and its ancestors, "Financial literacy" and "Education and training" without redundant processing. This automated classification at scale is where taxonomies deliver measurable ROI. What once required human taggers to review every piece of content can now be automated, with the taxonomy ensuring consistency that human taggers often struggle to maintain across thousands of items.

### *Grounding LLM output*

Large language models benefit from taxonomy grounding in two ways. First, the taxonomy provides a controlled vocabulary for output. The model selects from your defined concepts instead of generating arbitrary category names. Second, the hierarchy constrains logical relationships, preventing the model from asserting anything that contradicts your domain structure.

When you provide your taxonomy to an LLM as context, you're giving it a map of your domain's conceptual territory. The model can navigate that map rather than invent its own geography. This is particularly valuable for enterprise applications where consistency with existing systems and terminology is non-negotiable.

---

## Building a branch example

Let's walk through building a single branch from reconciled terms to a completed taxonomy structure.

### *Starting Material*

From your coverage model, you have a cluster of terms related to financial literacy:

**Cluster:** Financial literacy, Money management, Personal finance, Budgeting, Budgeting skills, Financial education, Financial planning basics, Budget planning.

Your corpus analysis also identified these as high-frequency terms in your domain. Your existing controlled vocabulary doesn't include these concepts.

### *Step 1: Select the preferred label*

Choose the term that best represents the concept for your users. "Financial literacy" is the broadest and most used term in educational contexts. It becomes the preferred label.

### *Step 2: Determine placement*

Where does Financial literacy fit in your hierarchy? Review your top-level categories. In our NGO taxonomy, it belongs under Education and training as a type of educational program.

|Education and training

→ Financial literacy

**Apply the Is-a test:** Is Financial literacy a type of Education and training? Yes. The hierarchy is valid.

*Step 3: Identify subcategories*

Look at the remaining terms in the cluster. Do any represent narrower concepts that warrant their own categories?

"Budgeting," "Budget planning," and "Budgeting skills" represent the same narrower concept. "Budgeting" becomes a subcategory.

"Financial planning basics" represents another narrower concept distinct from budgeting. It becomes a sibling subcategory.

*Step 4: Assign alternative labels*

The remaining terms become alternative labels for their corresponding preferred labels:

- **Financial literacy:** Money management; Personal finance; Financial education.
- **Budgeting:** Budgeting skills; Budget planning.

*Step 5: Write definitions*

Apply the genus-differentia pattern:

- **Financial literacy:** Educational programs that develop understanding of money management concepts, including budgeting, saving, investing, and debt management.
- **Budgeting:** A financial literacy skill focused on planning income allocation and tracking expenses to meet financial goals.
- **Financial planning basics:** Introductory financial literacy content covering goal-setting, savings strategies, and long-term financial decision-making.

### *Step 6: Document in Spreadsheet Format*

The completed branch in the hierarchical spreadsheet format looks like this:

| scheme | concept L1 | concept L2 | concept L3 | definition | altLabel |
|---|---|---|---|---|---|
| Bee Taxonomy | | | | | |
| | Education and training | | | Learning opportunities and skill development. | |
| | | Financial literacy | | Educational programs for money management. | Money management, Personal finance |
| | | | Budgeting | Skill focused on income allocation. | Budgeting skills; Budget planning |
| | | | Financial planning basics | Introductory content on goal-setting. | |

Table 9: Completed branch in the hierarchical spreadsheet format.

Both Budgeting and Financial planning basics appear in concept L3, following Financial literacy in concept L2, making them siblings—both are children of Financial literacy.

---

## Common pitfalls and how to avoid them

### *Mixed granularity*

Users struggle to navigate consistently when one branch has five levels of depth and another has two levels of depth. Aim for balanced depth across branches. If one area genuinely requires more granularity, document why.

### *Orphan terms*

Terms that don't fit anywhere often signal gaps in your top-level structure or scope creep. Every term should have a logical home. Revisit your category architecture if you end up with orphans.

### *Circular definitions*

"Caregiving is the act of providing care" tells users nothing. Always define the concept using different words than the term itself. The genus-differentia pattern prevents this by requiring reference to a broader category.

### *Overlapping categories*

Your categories aren't mutually exclusive if content could legitimately belong to multiple categories. Either refine the definitions to clarify boundaries or restructure to eliminate overlap. Polyhierarchy, where one concept has multiple parents, exists in some taxonomies, but it adds complexity and should be used judiciously, not as a workaround for unclear boundaries.

### *Institutional jargon as preferred labels*

Internal acronyms and project names rarely make good preferred labels. Your taxonomy should be understandable to new employees, external partners, and AI systems that don't share your organizational context. Use plain language for preferred labels; capture jargon as alternative labels.

---

## Quality checklist

Before finalizing a taxonomy branch, verify:

- Every parent-child relationship passes the Is-a test.
- Every concept has a definition using the genus-differentia pattern.
- Definitions are precise, not circular.
- Acronyms are alternative labels, not preferred labels.
- Sibling categories are mutually exclusive.
- Depth is consistent within and across branches.
- All terms from the coverage model are accounted for as preferred labels, alternative labels, or documented exclusions.
- Column headers are lowercase.
- The scheme column identifies the taxonomy consistently.

## Why SKOS?

The taxonomy structure we've built, with preferred labels, parent-child hierarchies, definitions, and alternative labels, is complete and functional. It can be implemented in spreadsheets, content management systems, or taxonomy editors. The spreadsheet format we've used is *almost* SKOS-ready. The column names—scheme, concept, definition, altLabel—align with the SKOS vocabulary framework. So why formalize with SKOS?

SKOS provides a standard vocabulary and RDF data model for expressing the exact structures we've discussed. Machines can understand and process it without custom parsing when your taxonomy uses SKOS. You can link your concepts to external vocabularies like Wikidata, DBpedia, and the Library of Congress. You can publish your taxonomy as linked data. And you gain access to a rich ecosystem of tools built to work with SKOS.

Now, we will translate everything we've built here into full SKOS notation, showing how the spreadsheet columns map to SKOS properties, how to add URIs for concept identification, and what tools to leverage for visualization and publishing. The concepts don't change, but the encoding becomes standardized, machine-readable, interoperable, and knowledge graph ready.

Building a taxonomy without SKOS strips the work down to its essentials: preferred labels that name concepts clearly, hierarchical relationships that pass the Is-a test, definitions that set boundaries using genus-differentia patterns, and alternative labels that capture the many ways users express the same ideas.

This is the essence of taxonomy construction. It's the classification logic that underlies every taxonomy, regardless of encoding format or tooling choice. Master this, and you can build taxonomies in any environment. The spreadsheet format I've provided here provides a SKOS-ready structure that can be exported, transformed, and immediately integrated with AI systems.

The coverage model you built earlier gives you the raw material, the clay with which you will model. The principles I've outlined here give you the construction methods.

*The work is iterative, building branch-by-branch, concept-by-concept, definition-by-definition, until your flat vocabulary becomes a structured hierarchy ready to support classification, navigation, and reasoning—for both human users and the AI systems that increasingly depend on well-organized knowledge.*

Next, we'll formalize these structures using SKOS, preparing your taxonomy for the linked data ecosystem and enabling interoperability with external vocabularies. The logic stays the same. The encoding becomes standardized, interoperable, and machine readable.

As a reminder, SKOS (Simple Knowledge Organization System) is the W3C standard and recommendation for representing taxonomies, thesauri, and classification schemes. SKOS gives your taxonomy a grammar that machines can parse, that systems can exchange, and that the broader Semantic Web can discover and integrate.

You do not incorporate SKOS in your process until the construction logic is solid. Validating hierarchies, writing definitions, and reconciling synonyms exist independently of any encoding standard. You must understand *what* you're building before learning *how* to encode it.

Practitioners who leap straight to SKOS tooling without grasping these structures produce technically valid RDF that is semantically hollow. The encoding is correct, but the knowledge organization is not.

There is a second reason SKOS matters now. The rise of large language models, retrieval-augmented generation architectures, and agentic AI systems has made structured knowledge *more* valuable, not less. SKOS taxonomies can serve as a grounding layer that constrains output, resolves ambiguity, and enables reasoning, serving as a critical component of a knowledge infrastructure. SKOS is the format that makes your taxonomy consumable by these systems, at scale.

## What SKOS adds to your spreadsheet taxonomy

Let's be clear about what SKOS gives you that a spreadsheet does not before we dive into syntax. What becomes *possible* when your taxonomy speaks RDF? The topics and material are dense, but I will do my best to break down the SKOS standard while also teaching you how to structure a taxonomy with SKOS.

First things first: you will need to reference the SKOS W3C standard to follow along. Also, we will be using the Bee Taxonomy, part of the Shock knowledge graph, the same demo taxonomy I referenced earlier.

### *Concept identity through URIs*

The concept Community empowerment is a text string. Two organizations can both use the term "Community empowerment" and mean entirely different things. In SKOS, every concept is identified by a URI—a globally unique identifier that distinguishes your concept from every other concept on the web. The preferred label is *attached to* the concept; it does not *constitute* the concept. This means that taxonomy concepts are no longer a list of words. The concepts become a collection of identifiable, referenceable items.

How do large language models handle concept URIs? When a language model encounters the string "Financial literacy," it must infer meaning from context. When it encounters a URI that resolves to a SKOS concept with a definition, a hierarchy, alternative labels, and links to external vocabularies, it has structured knowledge to reason against. The concept becomes a node in a knowledge graph rather than an ambiguous token.

The difference is worth noting for classification pipelines. Without SKOS, assigning the string "Budgeting" means the concept could match different concepts across different taxonomies, on a wing and a prayer. In SKOS, we assign shock:Budgeting, which is globally unambiguous and uniquely encoded, bolstered by a URI that makes the concept unique and specific.

### *Formal concept schemes*

Recall the scheme column from earlier? SKOS formalizes it as skos:ConceptScheme—a named container for your taxonomy. A concept scheme declares scope: these concepts belong together, were curated together, and should be interpreted together. The skos:hasTopConcept property identifies the entry points to your hierarchy, and skos:inScheme asserts membership. When you publish a concept scheme, you are making a claim about the coherence and completeness of a knowledge organization effort.

### *Documentation properties*

The work of creating constraints by way of definitions is work we have completed in the spreadsheet taxonomy build. That was intentional—you needed to see that definitions alone could carry a taxonomy before adding complexity. SKOS provides a much richer toolkit. Beyond skos:definition, you gain:

- **skos:scopeNote**: Clarifies what falls inside and outside a concept's boundaries.
- **skos:editorialNote**: Maintenance annotations visible to taxonomy managers, not end users.
- **skos:historyNote**: Documents how a concept has evolved over time.
- **skos:changeNote**: Records specific modifications to a concept.
- **skos:example**: Illustrates usage with concrete instances.

These properties transform your taxonomy from a static classification structure into a documented, maintainable knowledge asset. For AI implementations specifically, documentation properties serve as context engineering material—structured natural language that can be injected into prompts, used as retrieval signals, or parsed into classification rules. I'll unpack each one shortly.

### *Hidden labels*

Think of skos:hiddenLabel as an integrated allow and deny list. skos:hiddenLabel captures lexical strings that should be accessible to search and indexing but should *not* be displayed to users in navigation or browsing interfaces. If users search for "finanance literacy" when they mean "Financial literacy," a hidden label catches that query without exposing the misspelling in your faceted navigation.

Hidden labels are also useful for deprecated terms that should still resolve in search. When a concept's preferred label changes—say, "Handicapped parking" becomes "Accessible parking"—the old term moves to a hidden label, ensuring search continuity without sanctioning outdated language. For AI systems ingesting user queries, hidden labels dramatically improve recall without requiring the model to infer synonymy from context.

### *Mapping properties*

Perhaps the most consequential addition SKOS provides is its family of mapping properties for linking concepts *across* different concept schemes. The properties skos:exactMatch, skos:closeMatch, skos:broadMatch, skos:narrowMatch, and skos:relatedMatch allow you to declare how your concepts correspond to concepts in other vocabularies—how your "Financial literacy" can be formally linked to an equivalent concept in an industry standard vocabulary, to a Wikidata entity, or to a partner organization's taxonomy. For AI systems, these links become traversal paths—ways to expand a knowledge base without retraining a model.

---

## Anatomy of a SKOS taxonomy

We will use the Turtle serialization format for all RDF examples. Turtle is the most human-readable RDF syntax and the one encountered most commonly in SKOS work. If you can read a spreadsheet, you can read Turtle. The structures are the same; the punctuation is different.

### *Namespace declarations*

Every SKOS file begins with namespace prefix declarations—shorthand references to the vocabularies your taxonomy uses.

```
@prefix skos:  <http://www.w3.org/2004/02/skos/core#> .
@prefix rdf:   <http://www.w3.org/1999/02/22-rdf-syntax-ns#> .
@prefix dct:   <http://purl.org/dc/terms/> .
@prefix xsd:   <http://www.w3.org/2001/XMLSchema#> .
@prefix shock: <https://shock.org/taxonomy/> .
```

Figure 44: SKOS structure.

skos: is the SKOS vocabulary itself. dct:gives you Dublin Core metadata terms for describing the scheme. shock: is the taxonomy demo namespace—the base URI under which the Bee Taxonomy concepts will live. In production, this would be a URI you control.

### *The concept scheme*

The concept scheme declares your taxonomy as a coherent whole.

```
shock:BeeTaxonomy a skos:ConceptScheme ;
    dct:title       "Bee Taxonomy"@en ;
    dct:creator     "Shock Knowledge Team" ;
    dct:created     "2026-02-01"^^xsd:date ;
    dct:description "A three-level taxonomy for classifying
        community empowerment programs, education and training
        initiatives, workforce development activities, and
        health and wellness services."@en ;
    skos:hasTopConcept shock:CommunityEmpowerment ,
        shock:EducationAndTraining ,
        shock:WorkforceDevelopment ,
        shock:HealthAndWellness .
```

Figure 45: Concept scheme.

The skos:hasTopConcept declarations identify the entry points to the hierarchy. Every concept in the Bee Taxonomy traces its lineage back to one of these four top concepts through skos:broader relationships. Ranganathan's Canon of Exhaustiveness applies here: these four top concepts should be collectively exhaustive of the taxonomy's domain.

### *Concepts and labels*

Each row in the taxonomy spreadsheet that represents a concept becomes a skos:Concept. Let's take the Financial Literacy branch and render it in SKOS.

The definitions, the alternative labels, the hierarchy—all of it transfers directly from the spreadsheet. What's new is the concept identity. shock:FinancialLiteracy is a globally unique URI, not a text string.

The misspellings that might land in a search box are now skos:hiddenLabel values—accessible to indexing, but invisible to users. And the Is-a test still applies Budgeting *is a type of* Financial literacy. The validation logic does not change because the encoding has changed.

```
shock:EducationAndTraining a skos:Concept ;
    skos:inScheme      shock:BeeTaxonomy ;
    skos:topConceptOf shock:BeeTaxonomy ;
    skos:prefLabel     "Education and training"@en ;
    skos:definition    "Programs and initiatives focused on
        developing knowledge, skills, and capabilities across
        community members of all ages."@en ;
    skos:narrower      shock:FinancialLiteracy .


shock:FinancialLiteracy a skos:Concept ;
    skos:inScheme     shock:BeeTaxonomy ;
    skos:prefLabel    "Financial literacy"@en ;
    skos:altLabel     "Money management"@en ;
    skos:altLabel     "Personal finance"@en ;
    skos:altLabel     "Financial education"@en ;
    skos:hiddenLabel "finacial literacy"@en ;
    skos:hiddenLabel "financal literacy"@en ;
    skos:definition  "Educational programs that develop
        understanding of money management concepts, including
        budgeting, saving, investing, and debt management."@en ;
    skos:broader      shock:EducationAndTraining ;
    skos:narrower     shock:Budgeting ,
        shock:FinancialPlanningBasics .


shock:Budgeting a skos:Concept ;
    skos:inScheme    shock:BeeTaxonomy ;
    skos:prefLabel  "Budgeting"@en ;
    skos:altLabel     "Budgeting skills"@en ;
    skos:altLabel     "Budget planning"@en ;
    skos:definition "A financial literacy skill focused on
        planning income allocation and tracking expenses to
        meet financial goals."@en ;
    skos:broader     shock:FinancialLiteracy .
```

Figure 46: The Financial Literacy branch.

## *Hierarchical relationships*

Parent-child relationships map to skos:broader (child → parent) and skos:narrower (parent → child). These are inverses. You need to assert in one direction only. A SKOS-aware system can infer the other. In practice, I recommend asserting both explicitly. It makes the Turtle file self-documenting and eliminates reliance on inference for basic navigation.

The Is-a test catches invalid hierarchies in SKOS exactly as it does in a spreadsheet. Wheels are a *component of* cars, not a type of car. That meronymic relationship belongs in a thesaurus or ontology. SKOS won't stop you from asserting invalid hierarchies—it will faithfully encode your mistake. The Is-a test is your validation layer, not the syntax. And the Is-a test is what prevents the introduction of faulty logic and problems you'll need to fix.

## From spreadsheet to SKOS: A column-by-column translation

Our spreadsheet format used lowercase column headers: scheme, concept L1, concept L2, concept L3, definition, and altLabel. The L1, L2, and L3 suffixes were visual scaffolding for the spreadsheet; in SKOS, hierarchy is expressed through skos:broader and skos:narrower relationships rather than column position.

Here is how each column maps:

| Spreadsheet Column | SKOS Property | Notes |
|---|---|---|
| **scheme** | skos:ConceptScheme | The scheme name becomes a ConceptScheme resource with Dublin Core metadata. |
| **concept L1** | skos:Concept + skos:topConceptOf | Level 1 concepts are top concepts of the scheme. |
| **concept L2** | skos:Concept + skos:broader → L1 | The most recent L1 entry above determines the broader concept. |
| **concept L3** | skos:Concept + skos:broader → L2 | The most recent L2 entry above determines the broader concept. |
| **definition** | skos:definition | Same genus-differentia text; add language tag (@en). |
| **altLabel** | skos:altLabel (one triple per term) | Semicolon-separated values become individual altLabel triples. |

Table 10: Column mapping.

This is a mechanical translation. Every row becomes a skos:Concept. The column position determines the skos:broader relationship. What SKOS adds—URIs, hidden labels, documentation properties, and mapping—are net-new enrichments layered on top of the existing structure.

## Documentation properties in practice

Earlier, we used definitions alone to document concepts. Now, we open the full SKOS documentation toolkit. Here is how to use each property effectively, illustrated with examples from the Bee Taxonomy.

### *skos:definition*

The genus-differentia pattern still applies: State the broader category (genus) and the distinguishing characteristics (differentia). In SKOS, the definition becomes a formal triple with a language tag. Nothing changes about how you write them; the encoding simply makes them machine-readable.

Definitions function as semantic grounding in AI systems—they tell a language model not just what a concept is called, but what it *means* and where its boundaries lie. When a model encounters ambiguous content, the definition provides disambiguation logic. Is this article about "financial planning" in the retirement sense or the corporate strategy sense? The genus-differentia definition answers that question without requiring the model to guess from context.

### *skos:scopeNote*

A definition tells you what a concept *is*. A scope note tells you what it *includes* and what it does not. Scope notes are operational documentation—they tell taggers, classifiers, and automated systems where the boundaries are.

```
shock:Caregiving a skos:Concept ;
    skos:prefLabel  "Caregiving"@en ;
    skos:definition "Activities that build community capacity
        by supporting vulnerable members through direct
        assistance and personal care."@en ;
    skos:scopeNote  "Use for direct care activities provided
        to individuals. For community-level program planning
        and coordination, use Community empowerment. For
        health-specific interventions, use Health and
        wellness."@en .
```

Figure 47: skos:scopeNote.

Notice how the scope note references sibling and adjacent concepts by name. This is deliberate. Scope notes help users navigate *between* concepts, not just understand a concept in isolation. They keep taggers honest and search results precise. Scope notes are essentially classification instructions written in natural language for an AI classification system. When you include a scope note in a prompt alongside a document to be classified, you are giving the model explicit disambiguation rules: "If the content is about X, use this concept; if it is about Y, use that concept instead." This is context engineering at the data layer—embedding classification logic directly into the knowledge structure rather than relying solely on prompt engineering.

### *skos:editorialNote*

Editorial notes are for taxonomy managers, not end users. They capture maintenance decisions, open questions, and governance context. Think of them as comments in code—invisible to the consumer, but essential for the maintainer.

```
shock:GroceryShopping a skos:Concept ;
    skos:prefLabel    "Grocery shopping"@en ;
    skos:definition   "An eldercare service involving the
        purchase and delivery of food and household supplies
        for older adults."@en ;
    skos:editorialNote "Placed as narrower (Eldercare) based
        on the is-a test: Grocery shopping as an eldercare
        service IS a type of Eldercare. Review after six
        months of tagging data to confirm this placement
        reflects actual usage."@en .
```

Figure 48: skos:editorialNote.

Remember the Is-a test discussion about whether Grocery shopping is a type of Eldercare? That placement decision and the reasoning behind it now live inside the taxonomy itself, not in a separate meeting note or Slack thread where it will be lost within a month.

### *skos:historyNote and skos:changeNote*

```
shock:FinancialLiteracy a skos:Concept ;
    skos:prefLabel   "Financial literacy"@en ;
    skos:historyNote "Originally a candidate term from
        coverage model. Promoted to concept L2 under Education
        and training after corpus analysis confirmed high
        frequency in the domain."@en ;
    skos:changeNote  "v1.0 (2026-02): Initial release. Three
        cluster terms reconciled as altLabels: Money
        management, Personal finance, Financial
        education."@en .
```

Figure 49: skos:historyNote and skos:changeNote.

### *skos:example*

Examples ground abstract concepts in concrete instances. They are particularly valuable when the boundary is difficult to articulate in definitional language alone.

```
shock:Budgeting a skos:Concept ;
    skos:prefLabel "Budgeting"@en ;
    skos:example   "Monthly income and expense worksheets;
        envelope budgeting workshops; youth savings
        challenges; family budget planning sessions."@en .
```

Figure 50: skos:example.

Examples do double duty for AI implementations: they ground human understanding and provide few-shot learning material, a handful of labeled examples that guide a model's behavior, for language models. When a classification system encounters borderline content, the examples offer concrete reference points that a definition alone may not capture. Include them in any concept where the boundary between this concept and its siblings is genuinely difficult to navigate.

---

## How much documentation is enough?

Not every concept needs every document property. Use skos:definition on every concept, no exceptions. Use scope notes on concepts with real ambiguous boundaries. Use editorial notes when a placement decision needs institutional memory. Use history and change notes when you need an audit trail. A well-placed scope note on a confusing concept is worth more than scope notes on every concept in the taxonomy. Over-documentation creates maintenance burdens and dilutes the signal value of notes that matter.

---

## Connecting through mapping properties

Mapping properties are how your taxonomy joins the linked data ecosystem. They declare how your concepts align with external vocabularies, transforming an isolated internal asset into a participant in the Semantic Web.

| Property | When to Use |
|---|---|
| **skos:exactMatch** | The concepts are interchangeable across a wide range of applications. Use sparingly—true exact matches are rare across independently developed vocabularies. |
| **skos:closeMatch** | The concepts are similar enough to be interchangeable in some applications. This is the most common mapping relationship. |
| **skos:broadMatch** | Your concept is narrower than the target concept. Your "Budgeting" maps broadly to an external vocabulary's "Personal Finance." |
| **skos:narrowMatch** | Your concept is broader than the target concept. Your "Education and training" maps narrowly to an external vocabulary's "Financial Literacy Programs." |
| **skos:relatedMatch** | The concepts are associated but neither is broader nor narrower. A meaningful connection that is not hierarchical. |

Table 11: The mapping properties.

```
shock:FinancialLiteracy a skos:Concept ;
    skos:prefLabel  "Financial literacy"@en ;
    skos:closeMatch <http://www.wikidata.org/entity/Q2979> ;
    skos:broadMatch <http://id.loc.gov/authorities/subjects/
        sh85048256> .    # LCSH "Finance, Personal"
```

Figure 51: skos:closeMatch.

The skos:closeMatch to Wikidata says: Our concept and Wikidata's concept for financial literacy are close enough to be interchangeable in many contexts. The skos:broadMatch to Library of Congress Subject Headings says: Our Financial literacy concept is narrower than LCSH's broader "Finance, Personal" subject heading. Both assertions are useful. The Wikidata match enables discovery and disambiguation. The LCSH match enables interoperability with library and information science standards.

Mapping properties are traversal paths into external knowledge for AI systems. An agentic system that understands your internal taxonomy can follow skos:exactMatch and skos:closeMatch links to discover relevant information in Wikidata, DBpedia, or partner vocabularies—effectively expanding its knowledge base without retraining. A RAG system can use mappings to retrieve content tagged against different taxonomies, dramatically improving recall across organizational boundaries. Your SKOS taxonomy becomes a bridge between organizational knowledge and the world's structured data.

The ability to align internal taxonomies with external standards, such as IPTC NewsCodes, Library of Congress Subject Headings, the Getty Art & Architecture Thesaurus, or GeoNames, becomes a strategic capability rather than a one-off integration project as organizations mature their semantic infrastructure. Build mapping review into your taxonomy governance cycle.

---

## The complete financial literacy branch

Earlier, we built the Financial literacy branch step-by-step—from raw cluster terms through preferred label selection, hierarchy placement, alternative label assignment, definition writing, and spreadsheet documentation. Let's see that same branch in its final SKOS form, with the full documentation toolkit applied. For reference:, see Table 12.

| scheme | concept L1 | concept L2 | concept L3 | definition | altLabel |
|---|---|---|---|---|---|
| Bee Taxonomy | | | | | |
| | **Education and training** | | | Programs and initiatives focused on developing knowledge, skills, and capabilities... | |
| | | **Financial literacy** | | Educational programs that develop understanding of money management concepts... | Money management; Personal finance; Financial education |
| | | | Budgeting | A financial literacy skill focused on planning income allocation... | Budgeting skills; Budget planning |
| | | | Financial planning basics | Introductory financial literacy content covering goal-setting... | |

Table 12: Spreadsheet fragment.

Every preferred label, every definition, and every alternative label from the spreadsheet is present. What's new is the URI, the annotation properties, the documentation properties, and the mapping properties. The taxonomy is the same. Semantic encoding makes it concise, interoperable, and machine-readable.

```
# --- Level 3: Budgeting ----------------------------------------
# URI: https://shock.org/taxonomy/Budgeting
# prefLabel: "Budgeting"

shock:Budgeting a skos:Concept ;
    skos:inScheme    shock:BeeTaxonomy ;
    skos:prefLabel  "Budgeting"@en ;
    skos:altLabel   "Budgeting skills"@en ;
    skos:altLabel   "Budget planning"@en ;
    skos:definition "A financial literacy skill focused on planning
        income allocation and tracking expenses to meet financial
        goals."@en ;
    skos:scopeNote  "Use for workshops and curricula centered on
        creating and maintaining budgets. For broader introductory
        content, use Financial planning basics."@en ;
    skos:example    "Monthly income and expense worksheets; envelope
        budgeting workshops; youth savings challenges; family
        budget planning sessions."@en ;
    skos:broader    shock:FinancialLiteracy ;
    skos:closeMatch
        <http://www.wikidata.org/entity/Q179330> ;
    skos:relatedMatch
        <http://dbpedia.org/resource/Budget> .

# --- Level 3: Financial Planning Basics ----------------------
# URI: https://shock.org/taxonomy/FinancialPlanningBasics
# prefLabel: "Financial planning basics"

shock:FinancialPlanningBasics a skos:Concept ;
    skos:inScheme    shock:BeeTaxonomy ;
    skos:prefLabel  "Financial planning basics"@en ;
    skos:altLabel   "Intro to financial planning"@en ;
    skos:definition "Introductory financial literacy content
        covering goal-setting, savings strategies, and long-term
        financial decision-making."@en ;
    skos:scopeNote  "Use for foundational planning content aimed
        at beginners. For detailed budgeting instruction, use
        Budgeting."@en ;
    skos:broader    shock:FinancialLiteracy ;
    skos:closeMatch
        <http://www.wikidata.org/entity/Q613301> ;
    skos:broadMatch
        <http://id.loc.gov/authorities/subjects/sh85048256> ;
    skos:relatedMatch
        <http://dbpedia.org/resource/Financial_planning_(personal)> .
```

Figure 52: full documentation toolkit.

## SKOS taxonomies as AI infrastructure

We have explored how AI systems use taxonomies for hierarchical inference, synonym resolution, automated classification, and LLM grounding. SKOS amplifies every one of these capabilities. But the relationship between SKOS and AI goes deeper than amplification. A SKOS taxonomy becomes a critical component of AI and knowledge infrastructure, shaping how AI systems reason, retrieve, classify, and communicate. Let's walk through the specific mechanisms.

### *Context engineering at the data layer*

The most valuable AI systems are not the ones with the largest models. They are the ones with the best context. Context engineering—the practice of structuring the information surrounding a language model's tasks—is increasingly recognized as the differentiator between AI systems that hallucinate and those that perform. A SKOS taxonomy expressed in RDF is a context engineering artifact.

Let's examine the context a SKOS concept delivers. A preferred label names the concept in organizational language; alternative labels capture the various ways users refer to the concept. The definition establishes meaning through embedded natural language; a scope note can provide classification rules, and examples offer concrete instances.

Mapping properties connect the concept to the broader world of structured knowledge, including external knowledge infrastructures such as Wikidata, DBpedia, the Getty, and VIAF. Each of these properties serves a distinct function when injected into a prompt or used as a retrieval context. The definition grounds. The scope note disambiguates. The examples calibrate. The alternative labels expand recall. The mapping links cross boundaries and align with ontology-rich data sources.

Mapping properties should not be confused with prompt engineering. Prompt engineering is an interaction-level practice—you craft prompts for a specific task. Implementing a SKOS model is context engineering and operates at the infrastructure level. The SKOS taxonomy encodes organizational knowledge in a form that any prompt, any pipeline, any agent can leverage. Every AI system in the organization benefits.

### *Retrieval-Augmented Generation (RAG)*

RAG architectures retrieve relevant documents to ground a language model's response in factual content. The quality of a RAG system depends almost entirely on the quality of its retrieval. This is where SKOS taxonomies create a measurable advantage. Let's take the case of a user asking about "money management courses." A naive RAG system embeds this query as a vector and retrieves documents with similar embeddings.

A taxonomy-enhanced RAG system drives with precision. It resolves "money management" to the concept shock:FinancialLiteracy via the skos:altLabel mapping, then retrieves documents tagged with that concept or any of its narrower concepts. It uses the skos:scopeNote to determine whether the user means budgeting workshops or investment courses. It can traverse skos:broader to include documents tagged at the Education and training level. It can follow skos:closeMatch to discover relevant content in external knowledge bases tagged against different vocabularies. The SKOS taxonomy is the compass.

The result is a retrieval that is both more precise and more comprehensive than vector similarity alone. The taxonomy acts as a semantic index that understands what the user means, not just what the user typed. This is the difference between keyword search with better math and genuine semantic search grounded in domain knowledge.

### *Automated classification and tagging*

Automated classification is where taxonomies deliver measurable ROI. SKOS makes classification pipelines more robust in several specific ways.

Concept URIs eliminate ambiguity. The system assigns shock:Budgeting, not the string "Budgeting"—which could match different concepts across different taxonomies or even different branches of the same taxonomy. URI-based classification is the only approach that scales without collisions in multi-taxonomy environments.

The value of the full label set is immense. Each concept URI and prefLabel can carry multiple alternative and hidden labels. The label set provides a rich surface for text matching. A classification model does not need to learn that "budgeting skills" and "budget planning" map to the same concept; the taxonomy encodes this equivalence declaratively. The model's job simplifies from semantic inference to label resolution.

Scope notes are often overlooked or ignored but can function as classification instructions if you choose. When a classifier encounters content that could reasonably fall under Caregiving or Health and wellness, the scope note "Use for direct care activities provided to individuals; for health-specific interventions, use Health and wellness" provides the disambiguation rule. This is structured guidance that can be included in a classification prompt or codified as a rule in a deterministic pipeline.

Inference is baked into the SKOS structure. The hierarchy enables multi-level classification without redundant processing. Because skos:broader relations are formally encoded, tagging content with shock:Budgeting automatically implies shock:FinancialLiteracy and shock:EducationAndTraining. The system traverses the graph rather than running multiple classification passes. The SKOS concept scheme taxonomy becomes a stable, manageable pipeline that can reliably handle heavy workloads.

Large language models generate fluent, confident text. The challenge is ensuring the text is accurate and consistent with the organization's knowledge. SKOS taxonomies provide grounding in two complementary ways.

First, the taxonomy provides a controlled vocabulary for output. Instead of generating arbitrary category names—which a model will happily do, with slight variations each time—the model selects from your defined concepts. This consistency is non-negotiable in enterprise applications where taxonomy terms appear in reports, dashboards, and downstream systems. If your taxonomy says "Financial literacy" is the preferred label, the model should never output "Financial Literacy," "financial literacy education," or "money management" as a category name. The SKOS structure provides the constraints.

Second, the hierarchy constrains logical relationships. If a model is generating a classification hierarchy on the fly, it might assert that Budgeting is a type of Workforce development, which would fail the Is-a test. When the model operates within a SKOS taxonomy, it inherits the validated hierarchical structure rather than inventing its own. The model navigates your domain map rather than drawing its own geography.

### *Agentic AI and knowledge navigation*

AI agents—systems that autonomously plan and execute multi-step tasks—need structured knowledge to reason against. An agent tasked with "find all training programs relevant to community financial wellness" must decompose the query, identify relevant concepts, determine what counts as relevant, retrieve appropriate content, and synthesize results.

*Without a taxonomy, every step depends on the agent's pretrained knowledge and probabilistic inference. With a SKOS taxonomy, the agent has a map.*

The agent resolves "financial wellness" to shock:FinancialLiteracy via label matching. It traverses skos:narrower to discover Budgeting and Financial planning basics as subtopics. It reads the skos:scopeNote to understand boundaries. It follows skos:closeMatch to Wikidata to discover related entities. It uses skos:broader to check whether the parent Education and training has other relevant children. Each step is a deterministic graph traversal, not a probabilistic generation. The agent's reasoning is auditable, reproducible, and grounded in organizational knowledge rather than model weights.

### *Cross-domain knowledge integration*

The mapping properties deserve particular attention for AI applications. In practice, organizations rarely operate with a single taxonomy. A marketing team uses one vocabulary, a product team another, a compliance team a third. AI systems that need to reason across these domains face a vocabulary alignment problem that no amount of model training can solve because the problem is not about language understanding, but about organizational knowledge that exists nowhere except in the heads of people who work across teams.

SKOS mapping properties externalize this knowledge. When your taxonomy declares skos:closeMatch between your "Financial literacy" and a partner organization's "Financial education programs," an AI system can traverse that link to retrieve, classify, or reason across organizational boundaries. When it declares skos:broadMatch to a Library of Congress subject heading, the system gains access to a century of bibliographic classification. These are not theoretical capabilities. They are the operational advantages that differentiate an AI implementation that works within a single silo from one that works across the enterprise.

### *The taxonomy as a shared contract*

Think of a SKOS taxonomy as a shared contract between humans and machines. For humans, it provides a consistent vocabulary for communication. For AI systems, it provides structured context and a vehicle for definitions and disambiguation. For the organization, it provides a single source of truth about how concepts are named, defined, related, and bounded. Every AI implementation that touches the same taxonomy inherits the same understanding. This is how you achieve consistency across chatbots, search systems, classification pipelines, and analytics dashboards without building and maintaining parallel knowledge structures for each.

---

## Governance and lifecycle

A SKOS taxonomy is a living artifact. The documentation properties we discussed—editorial notes, change notes, history notes—are governance tools. But they need to be situated within a broader framework.

### *Version control*

SKOS taxonomies serialized as Turtle files are plain text. This means they can and should be managed in version control systems like Git. You get change tracking, branching for proposed modifications, pull request workflows for review, and full audit trails. Treat your taxonomy with the same rigor you would apply to production code, because for AI systems, it *is* production code. A breaking change to your taxonomy—renaming a concept, restructuring a branch, deprecating a term—can propagate through every AI system that depends on it. Version control ensures those changes are deliberate, reviewed, and reversible.

### *Validation*

Validation in SKOS goes beyond the Is-a test. SKOS defines a set of integrity conditions that tools can check:

- A concept may have at most one skos:prefLabel per language tag.

- skos:prefLabel, skos:altLabel, and skos:hiddenLabel are pairwise disjoint—the same string cannot serve as both preferred and alternative label for the same concept.
- Hierarchical cycles (A broader than B, B broader than C, C broader than A) are invalid.
- Top concepts should not have broader concepts within the same scheme.

Tools like Skosify, SKOS Play !, and qSKOS automate these checks. qSKOS is particularly useful for quality assessment, detecting disconnected concepts, label conflicts, cyclic hierarchical relations, and other structural issues. All are open-source and can be integrated into CI/CD pipelines—run validation on every commit, just as you would run tests on production code.

---

## Lifecycle management

Concepts are born, evolve, and occasionally die. SKOS does not prescribe a lifecycle model, but a mature taxonomy operation needs one. Consider a simple lifecycle:

proposed → approved → active → deprecated → retired

Editorial notes capture lifecycle state. Change notes document transitions. History notes explain why. When a concept is deprecated, its preferred label may become a hidden label on its replacement concept, ensuring search continuity while redirecting users to the current preferred term.

Lifecycle management is no different and no less important for AI implementations. A deprecated concept that is not properly handled will lead to classification drift—AI systems will continue assigning content to a concept that no longer reflects the current organizational understanding. Hidden labels on the replacement concept ensure that existing content tagged with the old term remains discoverable, while new classification routes lead to the current concept.

---

## Tooling

You do not need specialized software to create SKOS taxonomies. A text editor and the Turtle syntax are sufficient. That said, tooling can accelerate the work.

### *Taxonomy editors*

Dedicated taxonomy management tools Graphwise, Metaphacts, Stardog, and TopQuadrant include taxonomy management tools as part of their offerings that provide graphical interfaces for building and managing SKOS vocabularies, with built-in validation, collaboration features, and integration capabilities. These are enterprise tools appropriate for large-scale taxonomy programs.

VocBench offers an open-source alternative with strong SKOS support and collaborative editing for smaller projects. TemaTres is also a great open-source tool for building SKOS taxonomies and thesauri. Check out SKOS Play ! for SKOS spreadsheet conversion and SKOS validation.

### *Visualization*

All the tools listed above provide some forms of SKOS taxonomy visualization. Visualization helps identify structural problems, such as orphaned concepts, unbalanced hierarchies, and missing relationships, that are difficult to spot in raw Turtle files. Consistent depth across branches, for instance, becomes immediately obvious in a tree diagram.

### *Programmatic access*

SKOS taxonomies can be loaded into triple stores and queried with SPARQL for integration with content management systems, search platforms, and AI pipelines. Libraries like rdflib (Python) and rdf-ext (JavaScript) provide programmatic access for custom integrations. This is where the investment in formal encoding pays its highest dividends—your taxonomy becomes queryable infrastructure rather than a static reference document. An AI pipeline can issue a SPARQL query to retrieve all narrower concepts of a classification result, all alternative labels for synonym expansion, or all scope notes for disambiguation context—at runtime, programmatically, with no custom parsing required.

## Quality checklist for SKOS taxonomies

Everything from the quality checklist introduced earlier still applies: Is-a test validation, genus-differentia definitions, no circular definitions, acronyms as alternative labels, mutual exclusivity among siblings, and consistent depth. SKOS adds:

- Every concept has a URI within your namespace.
- Every concept declares skos:inScheme.
- Top concepts use both skos:topConceptOf and skos:hasTopConcept.
- Every concept has exactly one skos:prefLabel per language.
- Acronyms are skos:altLabel values, not preferred labels.
- Common misspellings are skos:hiddenLabel values.
- No label can be both skos:prefLabel and skos:altLabel, on the same concept.
- Every concept has a skos:definition.
- Ambiguous concepts have skos:scopeNote values.
- Mapping properties link to *external* concept schemes, not internal hierarchy.
- No hierarchical cycles exist.
- Validation passes in Skosify or qSKOS.

SKOS Play ! has a nice, web-accessible tool that can help you understand the full depth of the SKOS validation matrix.

## The thesaurus horizon

SKOS supports more than taxonomies. The skos:related property enables associative relationships between concepts that are neither broader nor narrower, but are meaningfully connected—the hallmark of a thesaurus. Associative relationships belong to SKOS taxonomies and thesauri, not to simple spreadsheet structures. Now that we're in SKOS, the door is open.

When you find yourself wanting to say that Financial literacy and Workforce development are related but neither subsumes the other, you are ready to extend your SKOS taxonomy into a SKOS thesaurus. This is the natural progression of the Ontology Pipeline framework: controlled vocabulary to taxonomy, to thesaurus to ontology, each stage adding semantic richness while building on the rigor established in previous stages.

The thesaurus extension adds lateral reasoning for AI implementations. A taxonomy gives AI systems vertical understanding—Budgeting is a type of Financial literacy, which is a type of Education and training. A thesaurus gives AI systems a horizontal understanding—Financial literacy is related to Workforce development, suggesting that someone researching financial literacy programs might also benefit from workforce training content. This lateral reasoning is precisely the kind of serendipitous semantic discovery that makes AI systems hum.

The transition from taxonomy to thesaurus within SKOS is an extension. You add skos:related triples to your existing model. Everything else stays. And beyond thesauri, SKOS serves as ontology training wheels—a way to model shared understanding through a simplified domain model. The discipline of modeling concepts, defining relationships, maintaining consistency, and thinking in triples prepares practitioners for the more complex ontological modeling that OWL enables.

So far, we've moved deliberately from foundation to formalization. We started by preparing the ground, reviewing use cases, conducting domain research, reconciling concepts, and developing coverage models. Then, we built the structure: validated hierarchies, genus-differentia definitions, and alternative labels, all in a portable spreadsheet format. This was followed by giving the structure a formal identity in the linked data ecosystem through SKOS.

---

*The constant thread through all three phases is that encoding is secondary to understanding.*

---

A SKOS taxonomy requires care and precision, built on rigorous concept reconciliation and clear definitions to shape validated hierarchies. The standards and syntax are important because they encode carefully-made decisions. And as we learned from our discussion of the coverage model, we have a solid foundation of domain knowledge, stakeholder input, and a clear understanding of how *both humans and machines* will use the taxonomy.

That last phrase, "both humans and machines", deserves emphasis. Practitioners reading this book will build taxonomies that support human navigation, search, and understanding. But increasingly, the most consequential consumers of these taxonomies are AI systems: classification pipelines that tag thousands of documents per hour, RAG architectures that retrieve context for language model responses, agents that navigate knowledge graphs to answer complex questions, and grounding layers that keep generated output consistent with organizational reality. SKOS is the format that makes your taxonomy legible to all stakeholders, whether they're human or machine.

*Taxonomies are infrastructure. Like all infrastructure, they are invisible when they work well and are painfully visible when they do not.*

The investment in doing this work properly—progressing through the Ontology Pipeline stages rather than skipping to encoding—builds an elegant semantic system and organizational asset. SKOS makes a good taxonomy interoperable, discoverable, and machine-readable. It gives your careful work the reach it deserves.

## Conclusion

Taxonomy building is patient work. It requires listening to how people actually talk about their domains, respecting the accumulated wisdom of industry standards, and holding space for what your organization doesn't yet know it needs to name. The payoff is a vocabulary that doesn't just organize what exists—it illuminates what's emerging, reveals blind spots, and positions your organization to see the full landscape of its domain.

A well-built taxonomy is quiet infrastructure with a loud impact. It enables searches, makes AI systems smarter, and makes knowledge findable. Start with coverage. The structure will follow.

CHAPTER 4

# Thesaurus

At the close of the last chapter, we reached the thesaurus horizon. We had a working SKOS taxonomy for the Financial literacy branch of a taxonomy, with preferred labels, a broader/narrower hierarchy, definitions, and alternative labels, all of it built and validated. Then we added the single associative link: Financial literacy is related to Workforce development; two concepts that are meaningfully connected even though neither one sits above the other. That one triple is the doorway into this chapter.

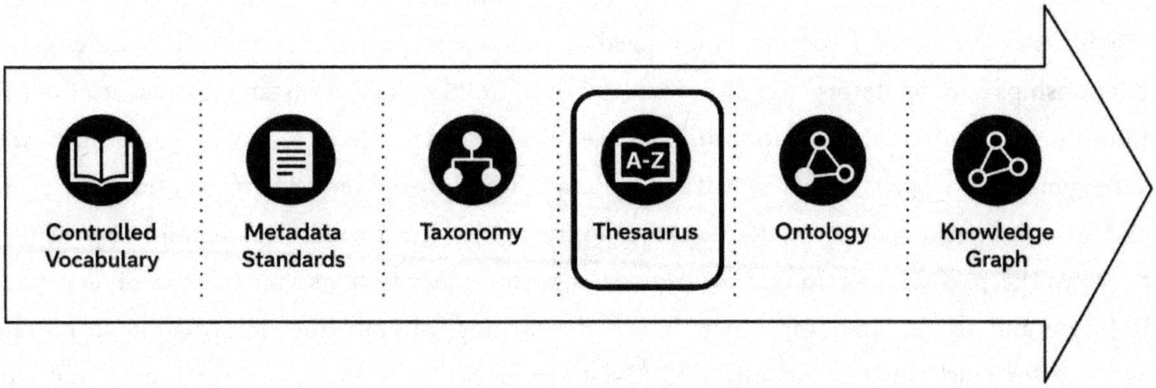


Figure 53: The Ontology Pipeline framework.

A thesaurus is a taxonomy that has grown up. It keeps everything the taxonomy gave us and, as the Ontology Pipeline promises, everything from the taxonomy remains. We do not start over. Instead, we extend. The taxonomy you've already built becomes the backbone of a richer structure. This chapter is about what that richer structure adds, what it means for AI, and where its edges are. Most of all, it is about how to mature a taxonomy, the SKOS you wrote in Chapter 3, to include the equivalence and associative relationships that turn it into a thesaurus.

---

## A thesaurus outside of machines

The word thesaurus comes from the Latin and Greek for "treasury" or "storehouse." In ordinary use, a thesaurus is the sense in a dictionary or word processor and was made famous by Roget's Thesaurus (1852). A thesaurus is a reference work that groups words by meaning: it clusters synonyms, and often antonyms, so a writer can find an alternative word that captures a particular shade of an idea. Its job is to help you find the right word, vary your vocabulary, and avoid repetition. It is a writer's tool, organized around words and their near-equivalents.

---

## A thesaurus as defined by ANSI/NISO Z39.19

In information science, the term means something more specific. Z39.19-2005 (R2010) defines a thesaurus as "a controlled vocabulary arranged in a known order and structured so that the various relationships among terms are displayed clearly and identified by standardized relationship indicators."[9] There are three relationship types: equivalence (a preferred term with its non-preferred synonyms, shown as altLabel / hiddenLabel), hierarchical (broader term / narrower term, BT / NT), and associative (related term, RT). A taxonomy carries the hierarchical relationship while a thesaurus keeps that hierarchy and adds equivalence and association. Its stated purpose is consistent indexing and reliable retrieval rather than better writing, to embolden information search and retrieval for machines and humans. ISO 25964 carries the same model internationally and adds interoperability between vocabularies.[10]

---

9 National Information Standards Organization. ANSI/NISO Z39.19 (R2010): Guidelines for the Construction, Format, and Management of Monolingual Controlled Vocabularies. NISO, 2005.

10 International Organization for Standardization. ISO 25964-1:2011, Information and Documentation—Thesauri and Interoperability with Other Vocabularies—Part 1: Thesauri for Information Retrieval; and ISO 25964-2:2013, Part 2: Interoperability with Other Vocabularies. ISO, 2011–2013.

The two definitions for a thesaurus diverge in what they organize. The information science thesaurus is a structured system of concepts, joined by all three relationship types—equivalence, hierarchy, and association—and built for retrieval; the everyday thesaurus used for writing, gathers synonyms and antonyms for a writer choosing words. We are building the information science flavor of a thesaurus, intended to disambiguate the labels and meanings of concepts.

## A thesaurus as represented by SKOS

SKOS (Simple Knowledge Organization System, a W3C standard) does not define "thesaurus" in prose; it supplies the data model for expressing one on the web and in digital environments.[11] It represents the structure and content of concept schemes such as thesauri, taxonomies, classification schemes, and subject heading lists in Resource Description Format (RDF), which build triple statements.

In SKOS terms, a thesaurus is a skos:ConceptScheme made of skos:Concept resources, each identified by a Uniform Resource Identifier (URI) or an International Resource Identifier (IRI). Each concept has a skos:prefLabel, can have one or many of skos:altLabel, and skos:hiddenLabel. The concept hierarchy is structured using skos:broader and skos:narrower. Beyond the taxonomic structure, a thesaurus adds skos:related (associative), and joins across concept schemes through the mapping properties, skos:exactMatch, skos:closeMatch, skos:broadMatch, skos:narrowMatch, and skos:relatedMatch. SKOS is the machine-readable encoding of the Z39.19 / ISO 25964 model, how the standards' thesaurus is ported to the web and digital environments so machines can read it. The mapping properties are more powerful than they appear, as this makes it possible to network multiple concept schemes, which is handy for the messy realities that exist in most organizations, allowing for a distributed, semantic architecture.

A thesaurus is a workhorse, beneficial for information retrieval and discovery systems, and exponentially endurant when it comes to symbolic AI. Symbolic AI, also known as Good Old-Fashioned AI (GOFAI), is one of the earliest paradigms in artificial intelligence. Current commercial

---

[11] W3C. SKOS Simple Knowledge Organization System Reference. Edited by Alistair Miles and Sean Bechhofer, W3C Recommendation, 18 Aug. 2009, www.w3.org/TR/skos-reference/.

AI systems, such as OpenAI's ChatGPT, are deep-learning, generative AI systems—specifically, autoregressive large language models built on the transformer architecture. In contrast with symbolic AI, ChatGPT does not rely on handcrafted rules or explicit knowledge bases. Instead, it harnesses statistical patterns in data to produce human-like text, making it highly flexible but also less inherently transparent than a rule-based system.

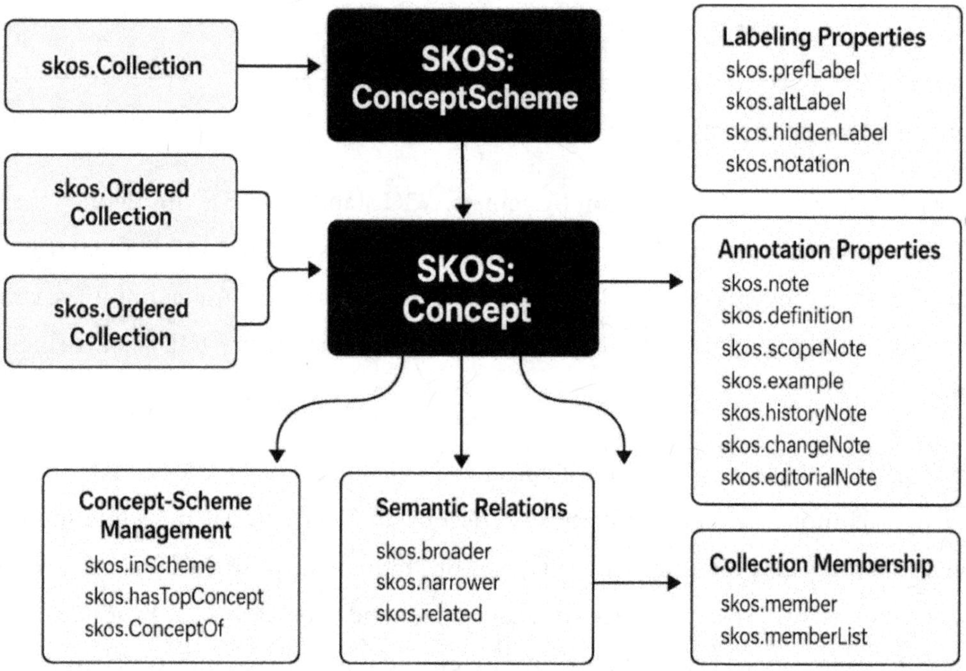


Figure 54: The full SKOS data model.

The through line: Z39.19 and ISO 25964 serve as guidelines, defining what a thesaurus is and how to build one; SKOS details how to encode a taxonomy or thesaurus for machines. And with a SKOS thesaurus, we build a concept graph that represents the relationships between concepts, expressed through a triple store. That is different from an ontology or knowledge graph, which connects real-world entities and the facts about them. The ontology and knowledge graph come later, in Chapters 5 and 6. For this chapter, we model the concept graph.

We will not rebuild the vocabulary or the taxonomy here; that work is done. Instead, we pick up where we left off, with the Financial literacy example, and add the elements necessary to build a thesaurus: associative relations, mapping relations that connect across vocabularies, the SKOS extension called SKOS-XL, and collections.

To pick up where we left off, there was a doorway triple with the close of the taxonomy chapter, that is our lead-in to the thesaurus, where we modeled an associative relationship within the taxonomy. The moment we connected Financial literacy to Workforce development, we crossed from taxonomy into thesaurus, by connecting one taxonomy to another. However, we built the Financial literacy taxonomy, without full visibility into the Workforce development controlled vocabulary structure. We will build the thesaurus from the Workforce development concept to fully realize the shape of a thesaurus and how a SKOS-based networked architecture is enabled.

## The Thesaurus and Generative AI

As AI systems move from narrow, task-specific assistants, such as chatbots, to general-purpose partners for all things digital, the quality and precision of the "context" they're given have become the single biggest determinant of whether they perform reliably or hallucinate spectacularly. Context is the relational structure that holds meaning in place: the web of relationships, definitions, and distinctions that lets a system read a fact correctly and connect it to the facts around it.

An LLM meets context through its context window, the finite span of tokens it can attend to at once when a user submits a request, query, or instruction set. The window is only a delivery mechanism, sized by token economics; context itself is larger than any window, and it exists wherever meaning is made explicit, in the prompt, retrieval store, or in a curated vocabulary. The act of building a thesaurus or any other part of the Ontology Pipeline is to build a robust context engineering practice, which means treating context as an intentional arrangement of domain-specific information and knowledge, enabling AI to synthesize responses reliably.

Knowledge organization is how we make that context explicit and reusable. Controlled vocabularies, taxonomies, thesauri, ontologies, and knowledge graphs each structure context as encoded relationships and meaning, turning loose text into disambiguated facts that surface the right information at the right moment. They structure context rather than invent it, so that LLM responses are vetted, connected, and unambiguous.

Structured, machine-readable knowledge provides context and clarity for machines, and a thesaurus is one of the most direct ways to supply it. Built with SKOS, a thesaurus structures concepts through hierarchical (broader and narrower), associative (related), and equivalence (preferred and non-preferred label) relationships. This structured simplicity reduces complexity, making data easier for both humans to curate and machines to interpret.

---

## The Thesaurus and Symbolic AI

A thesaurus is a workhorse, beneficial for information retrieval and discovery systems, and remarkably durable when it comes to symbolic AI. Symbolic AI, also known as Good Old-Fashioned AI (GOFAI), is one of the earliest paradigms in artificial intelligence. Classic examples of symbolic AI include rule based expert systems such as MYCIN (medical diagnosis) and DENDRAL (chemical analysis), the Cyc common sense knowledge base, logical programming, and decision-tree systems, all which reason over explicit, human authored rules and facts rather than learned statistical weights.

Current commercial AI systems, such as OpenAI's ChatGPT and Anthropic's Claude, are deep learning, generative AI systems, specifically autoregressive large language models built on the transformer architecture. In contrast with symbolic AI, the commercially available frontier AI models do not rely on handcrafted rules or explicit knowledge bases. Instead, they harness statistical patterns in data to produce human-like text, making them highly flexible but also less inherently transparent than rule-based systems.

| Symbolic | Sub-symbolic |
|---|---|
| Symbols | Numbers |
| Logical | Associative |
| Serial | Parallel |
| Reasoning | Learning |
| von Neumann machines | Dynamic Systems |
| Localised | Distributed |
| Rigid and static | Flexible and adaptive |
| Concept composition and expansion | Concept creation, and generalization |
| Model abstraction | Fitting to data |
| Small data | Big data |
| Literal/precise input | Noisy/incomplete input |

Figure 55: Statistical patterns in data (https://ceur-ws.org/Vol-2699/paper06.pdf).

Emerging AI research is discovering that symbolic AI is needed to deliver accurate, reliable results and, even more critically, to bolster AI's natural language conversational capabilities. The thing is, a thesaurus structured with SKOS is technically a form of symbolic AI and a fundamental, machine-readable representation of knowledge. As illuminated by Gary Marcus in his paper, "The Next Decade in AI: Four Steps Towards Robust Artificial Intelligence": "To build a robust, knowledge-driven approach to AI we must have the machinery of symbol-manipulation in our toolkit. Too much of useful knowledge is abstract to make do without tools that represent and manipulate abstraction, and to date, the only machinery that we know of that can manipulate such abstract knowledge reliably is the apparatus of symbol-manipulation."[12]

## Explicit concept hierarchies and relations

A thesaurus modeled using the SKOS ontology makes taxonomic relations, such as skos:broader and skos:narrower, first-class citizens in a machine-readable format. By modeling concepts as URIs and linking concepts with properties, a reasoner can traverse the hierarchy, infer implicit broader/narrower links (e.g., transitive closures), and classify new instances under the correct concepts. This explicit structure is essential for symbolic AI systems that rely on rule-based classification and inheritance of properties.

## Lightweight inference support

Although a SKOS thesaurus is less expressive than an ontology modeled using Web Ontology Language or OWL, SKOS defines a core subset of semantics that many RDF and OWL reasoners can process out-of-the-box. For example, a SKOS-aware reasoner can automatically infer that if Concept A is a skos:broader of Concept B, and Concept B is a skos:broader of Concept C, then Concept A is also a broader concept of Concept C. This kind of lightweight inferencing accelerates symbolic rule engines, enabling efficient query answering and classification over a large thesaurus.

[12] Marcus, Gary. "The Next Decade in AI: Four Steps towards Robust Artificial Intelligence." arXiv, 2020, arxiv.org/abs/2002.06177.

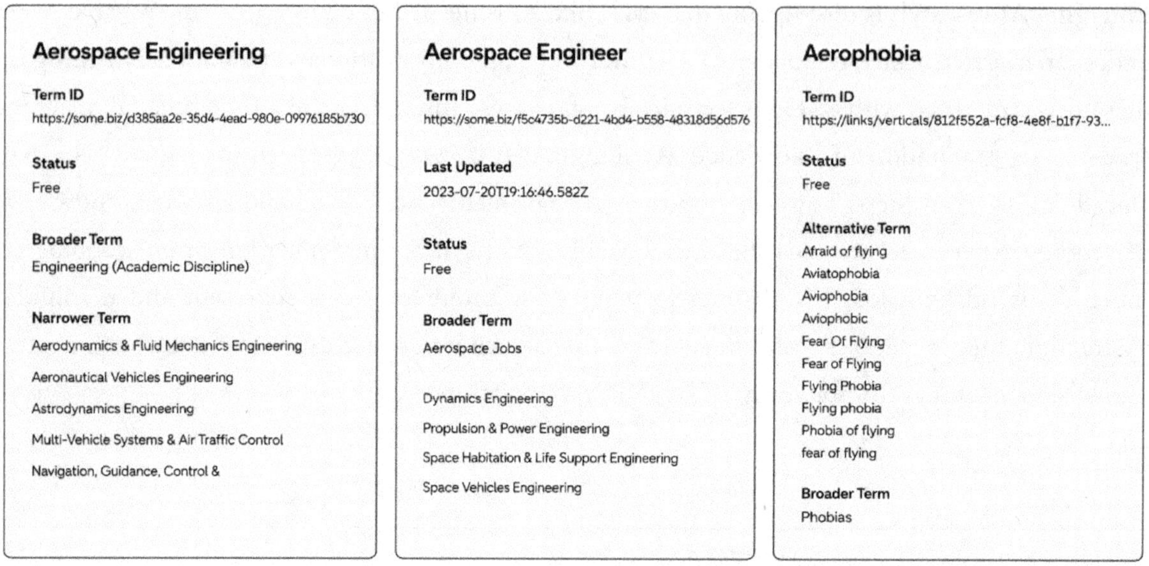


Figure 56 Thesaurus example.

## Synonym and mapping handling

SKOS provides dedicated properties for labels and mappings: skos:prefLabel, skos:altLabel, skos:hiddenLabel, as well as mapping relations like skos:exactMatch and skos:closeMatch. Symbolic AI systems leverage these to normalize synonyms, resolve co-references, and map across different vocabularies, which is crucial for tasks such as semantic search, question answering, and rule-based natural language processing (NLP) pipelines. AI engines can reason about lexical variants and crosswalk disparate datasets without ambiguity by interpreting these label relations symbolically.

## Interoperability and neurosymbolic AI

A SKOS thesaurus serves as a backbone for the symbolic layer in neurosymbolic AI, where symbolic reasoning is combined with neural networks. It anchors learned embeddings to well-defined concepts, enabling hybrid systems to both learn from data and apply logical rules consistently.

A concept graph built with SKOS as a foundational framework provides symbolic modules and elements. The SKOS thesaurus enforces domain constraints, performs logical deduction, and generates explanations, thereby enhancing both interpretability and robustness of AI reasoning. In other words, a SKOS thesaurus can shine some light into the black box that is AI.

SKOS's data model is a thesaurus structure that provides the scaffolding for symbolic knowledge representation, inference, and interoperability—core capabilities that power logical reasoning for AI systems.

---

## Curation of concepts

SKOS supports the thoughtful curation of concepts and the structuring of primary relations between them. This high-level modeling is done by defining what we call candidate concepts. Candidate concepts account for each concept to be considered for promotion, whether a preferred, alternative, or hidden label. The chosen concepts are first modeled as a controlled vocabulary or flat(ter) list.

The curation stage and the refined, resulting concepts are then structured as a taxonomy or hierarchy. Some practitioners choose to model a taxonomy and a thesaurus simultaneously when working with SKOS. As with any other practice, there are benefits and pitfalls to varying the order of operations. My recommendation is to model each stage individually, as SKOS modeling is iterative. You will continue to revise and refine your SKOS model throughout the lifecycle of the thesaurus, so get used to it.

Most candidate concepts can be acquired by collecting all concepts within a system, such as those derived from a system scrape or from lists of metadata terms, data catalogs, disparate taxonomies, or a conglomeration of several source vocabularies. The idea is to collect as many vocabularies and terms in use to establish a collection of terms that will represent a shared understanding of a system, domain, or specific subjects.

Not all candidate concepts become classes or official members of a SKOS concept collection. The idea is to collapse and refine candidate concepts to arrive at a reconciled, disambiguated SKOS vocabulary in which all concepts are defined and unique.

The work of refining a vocabulary requires rigor and discipline, as it's easy to disregard ambiguous terms or to succumb to stakeholder pressure when colleagues insist on certain concepts, such as "Other implementations." The key here is to resist peer pressure and work against ambiguity, for the sake of knowledge.

---

## A shared vocabulary

The process of modeling system concepts using SKOS ultimately focuses on establishing a shared vocabulary, bolstered by SKOS's logical data model. A SKOS vocabulary reduces ambiguity by guiding the modeler through thoughtful curation of concepts and establishing natural workflows to support the reconciliation of duplicate or near-duplicate concepts.

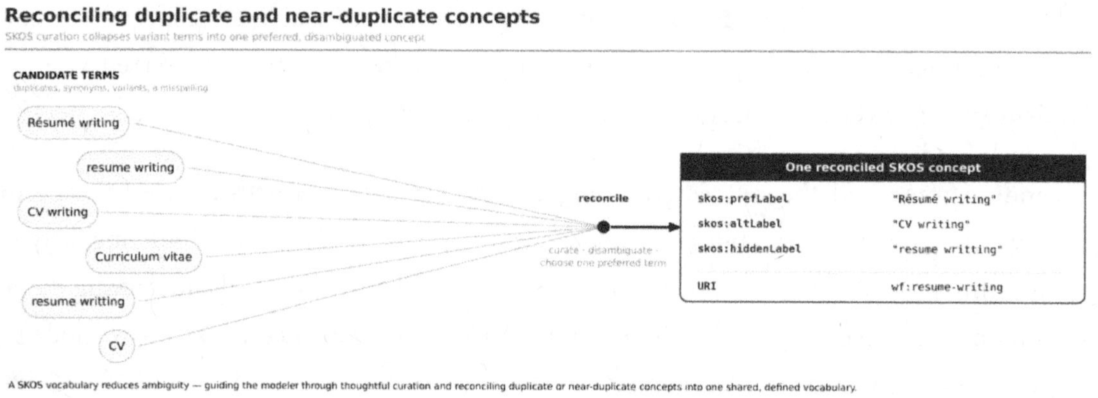


Figure 57: Reconciling duplicate concepts.

For example, when I was working at an educational technology company, I was handed a flat list of over 10,000 terms, the result of GitHub and Stack Overflow web scraping. SKOS provided the framework to reconcile synonyms and acronyms, while shaping the long list into a three-level SKOS taxonomy. 10,000 terms were swiftly reduced to 2,500 well-defined concepts, each with parent-child relations, alternative labels, hidden labels, and related concepts. SKOS modeling is a critical foundation for developing more complex ontologies, as it is impossible to model messy, undefined, or unrefined data. A shared vocabulary establishes baseline definitions, agreed-upon vocabularies, and, in turn, a shared understanding of what is to be further molded and modeled.

## Support iterative development

A thesaurus built with SKOS is agile: it can be quickly prototyped, tested, and adapted as understanding evolves. This scaffolding approach helps teams learn together, maturing their vocabulary as understanding deepens. Because its logic is deliberately small, SKOS is approachable, a place to build a shared, well-defined vocabulary and to develop the discipline of structuring taxonomies and thesauri.

```
Cloud Communications
        Term ID
                https://linksets1/S1unified/5c33bff7-e49c-4111-832e-68a9e3e6c444
        Last Updated
                2023-06-06T20:54:37.626Z
        Status
                Free
        Broader Term
                Cloud Computing
        Narrower Term
                Call Tracking Software
                Cloud Communication Platforms
                VoIP Services
        Related Term
                File Sharing Software

Cloud Computing
        Term ID
                https://linksets1/S1unified/744701ef-7710-47a5-9ce1-c410d00807b4
        Last Updated
                2023-06-07T21:02:20.644Z
        Status
                Free
        Broader Term
                Technology
        Narrower Term
                Cloud Communications
                Cloud Computing Architecture
                Cloud Computing Providers
                Cloud Management
        Related Term
                Cloud Applications
                Cloud Robotics
```

Figure 58: Example of structuring taxonomies and thesauri.

Just as machines appreciate the logical discipline introduced by relationship constraints and definitions, human modelers benefit from the focus that SKOS's small, fixed set of relationship types imposes. It is a way to model a shared understanding through a deliberately simplified vocabulary, with the discipline of one preferred term, defined and disambiguated, for each concept.

A glossary, data catalog, taxonomy, and thesaurus are all excellent candidates for SKOS modeling. Constrain the use cases, start with what exists within any given system, model it with SKOS, and iterate until your data asset can stand on its own as a rich, disambiguated SKOS thesaurus.

Experiment with your SKOS model, use it for Retrieval Augmented Generation (RAG), train your AI model on SKOS, and measure to see how AI output improves. Operationalize SKOS early and often to provide a feedback loop for iterative modeling, until the shared vocabulary model provides enough context and meaning to deliver rich results.

A thesaurus is approachable in a way heavier semantic modeling is not. SKOS is an ideal entry-level semantic data model, well positioned to support stakeholder engagement and collaboration.

Domain experts and non-technical stakeholders alike can more easily participate in SKOS-based modeling, as the primary tasks involve defining concepts and modeling them as parent-child relations. SKOS's simplified logic lowers the barriers for collaboration and validation, ensuring the resulting vocabulary reflects real-world knowledge and needs. And the best feature of SKOS is its simplicity (it's in the name, after all).

---

## When SKOS is enough

SKOS provides a framework specifically designed to represent controlled vocabularies, classification schemes, and thesauri. At its core, SKOS simplifies complex concepts into meaningful yet easily manageable components. It enables basic semantic relations such as hierarchical (broader/narrower), associative (related), and equivalence (synonyms). For many organizations, these fundamental relationships capture all the contextual information needed to power effective AI solutions.

Take, for instance, a business implementing a recommendation engine, with or without AI. Initially, it may seem essential to construct a deeply expressive ontology. However, as explored in the metadata phase, precise metadata is often the simplest and most direct way to impart the meaning and context of data. A SKOS thesaurus model efficiently meets this need by clearly defining concepts, categorizing entities, and articulating basic relations. A SKOS model can act as a sophisticated decision tree. Because a SKOS model is a tree structure expressed as a semantic data model, it is machine-readable and interoperable. It can eliminate ambiguity, provide synonym control, allow testing and validation, and establish relationships among terms.

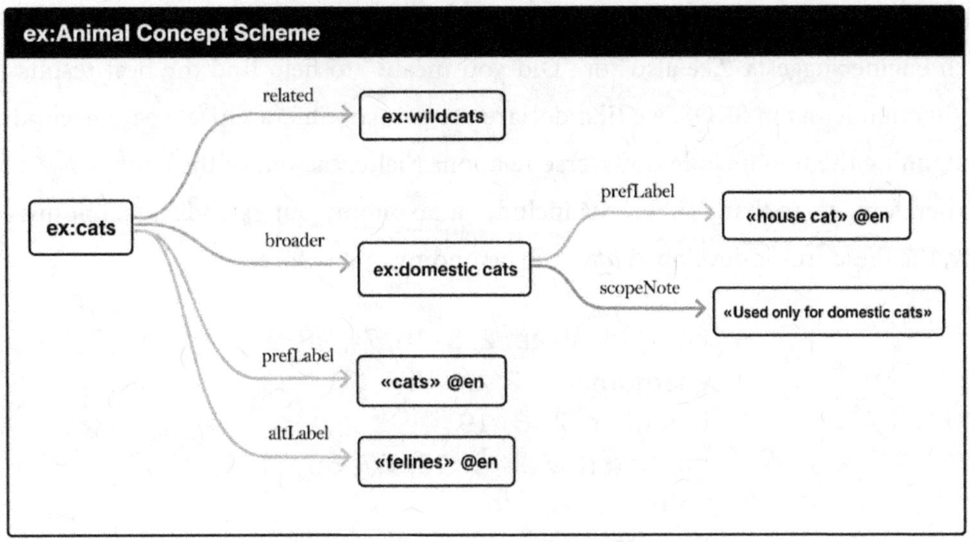


Figure 59: Animal concept scheme (hanami.app/2023/09/21/understanding-skos-and-the-importance-of-data-quality/).

The same SKOS model used for a recommendation engine can, in turn, be used for concept discovery, with the help of a matching framework. This is where a vector database comes in handy. For new concepts entering a system, vectors can be calibrated to discard concepts that match existing SKOS concepts and to map new terms only to corresponding SKOS categories. While this is a seemingly simple implementation, SKOS grounds vector databases with a curated and defined domain model to establish "rules" for concept groupings and attribution. SKOS is a version of human-in-the-loop for vector processing.

## The mighty thesaurus

While SKOS supports controlled vocabularies and taxonomies, a SKOS thesaurus serves as a strong foundational layer for richer structures. A thesaurus organizes concepts, relationships, and metadata in an approachable and extendable format. It is often argued that a thesaurus comes before a taxonomy, and many of these arguments are valid. A thesaurus can serve as an index, providing references to indexed concepts and the information they contain.

Much like a book index, we experience this indexing phenomenon when searching on Google, where the search engine suggests "See also" or "Did you mean?" to help find the best results for a user query. When modeling in SKOS, we first declare the primary, hierarchical (parent-child) relations before extending them to include transverse relations that break out of the confines of a taxonomy model. Therefore, given that a thesaurus includes a taxonomy but extends a taxonomy beyond its hierarchy, the thesaurus is developed *after* the taxonomy, not before.

herbs for sleep, 2, 5, 16, 74, 98-99
chamomile, 12, 36, 58-60
lavender, 2, 6, 19
passion flower, 5, 18, 62-65
valerian, 12, 74
**See also** teas

Figure 60: A recipe book index, with a see also reference relationship.

The "related" element in SKOS can be experienced in a book index where "See also" is enabled by the simple skos:related property. In this example, herbs for sleep are related to teas, working outside of and extending beyond the logical taxonomic parent-child relation. A thesaurus extends the semantic richness of a taxonomy, preparing the ontology for more complex ontologies and relationship types, when ready.

What if the related "thing" is not in the same SKOS vocabulary? There's a SKOS solution for that scenario. The property skos: relatedMatch is one of SKOS's mapping properties, intended to link two SKOS concepts that live in different concept schemes via an associative (non-hierarchical) relationship.

By definition, skos:relatedMatch is a sub-property of both skos:related and skos:mappingRelation, so any triple using skos:relatedMatch also asserts a general skos:related link, plus that it's a mapping relation between schemes.

That's right: You can build and maintain multiple domain SKOS thesauri and extend relations to support a more complex, networked SKOS model. In practice, you use skos:relatedMatch when you want to make clear that two concepts—say one in your in-house taxonomy and one in an external vocabulary—are related, without implying a broader/narrower hierarchy. If you just need an associative link within a single scheme, you'd use skos:related; if you need to show a cross-scheme mapping that happens to be associative, you use skos:relatedMatch.

Because SKOS places no hard integrity constraints on mapping properties, you can even use skos:relatedMatch between concepts in the same scheme (it will still imply mappingRelation), but the convention is to reserve it for inter-scheme links for clarity. I advise that you determine when mapping relations should be used for conformance and consistency.

SKOS offers an elegant entry point into the world of semantic modeling, providing just the right balance of structure and simplicity to build a shared vocabulary that both humans and machines can understand. By iterating through candidate concepts, taxonomies, and thesauri, you cultivate a disciplined approach to disambiguation and definition that compounds in value as your domain knowledge evolves. Its lightweight logic empowers stakeholders, from subject matter experts to semantic engineers, to collaborate on meaningful hierarchies and thesauri without the risks associated with getting lost in the complexity of lower ontologies.

When it's time to graduate to richer ontologies, your SKOS foundation ensures that you're building atop a rigorously curated, interoperable framework. Embrace SKOS early, experiment often, and let its "training wheels" guide you toward truly powerful, dynamic, and scalable knowledge models.

---

## Next steps

We've covered the why and the what. Now it's time to learn how to model a complete SKOS thesaurus for the Workforce development domain.

We'll journey from a controlled vocabulary through a taxonomy to a rich thesaurus, in order, utilizing every SKOS class, property, and relation along the way. We will explore how URIs (Uniform Resource Identifiers) transform our knowledge model from a simple vocabulary into a globally interoperable concept graph that supports entity reconciliation, category discovery, and seamless integration with broader semantic systems. Consider this your practical workshop for building an RDF concept graph that can power RAG systems, improve training data, and bring semantic clarity to AI implementations.

## From controlled vocabulary to thesaurus

We now model the Workforce development domain, the branch we opened at the close of Chapter 3. We move step by step, from a flat controlled vocabulary, through a taxonomy, to a thesaurus, using every SKOS class, property, and relation as we go. Each stage builds on the last.

Before we build, it is worth stating why. The structure we are about to model does three jobs: it grounds a retrieval or RAG system in vetted, disambiguated concepts so it returns the right service; it supplies clean, well-defined concepts for classification tasks; and it gives both people and machines a shared, queryable semantic understanding of workforce-development services. Every modeling choice below serves one of those three ends.

### *A word about URIs*

Before we model, a word about what SKOS brings: every concept gets a unique, dereferenceable URI. This is the foundation that makes a vocabulary interoperable. When I assign https://contextually.com/workforce#job-readiness as the URI for our Job readiness concept, I am creating a globally addressable resource that any system can reference, link to, and reason about.

A URI carries a controlled vocabulary into the wider linked data web and helps manage the problem of entity ambiguity. When a retrieval system meets "PD" in a document, does it mean professional development, public domain, or a police department? The concept wf:Job readiness stands apart from any string it happens to share. One URI holds all facets of a single concept, and that concept can grow into a richer structure later.

### *Now, let's model*

We begin by constructing the Workforce development thesaurus from scratch. Carrying over the taxonomy-building guidelines, we first organize and structure our corpus of terms as a hierarchy in a spreadsheet, accounting for alternative labels, hidden labels, and associative relations. See Table 13.

**Concept scheme: Workforce Development**

| concept L1 | concept L2 | concept L3 | altLabel | hiddenLabel | related |
|---|---|---|---|---|---|
| Workforce development | | | | | |
| | Job readiness | | Employment readiness | | Credit management |
| | | Résumé writing | CV writing | resume writting | Skill assessment |
| | | Interview preparation | Interview coaching | | |
| | Financial capability | | Financial literacy; Financial wellness | | |
| | | Budgeting basics | | | Career planning |
| | | Credit management | | | Job readiness |
| | Career planning | | Career development | | Budgeting basics |
| | | Goal setting | | | |
| | | Skill assessment | | | Résumé writing |

Table 13: The Workforce development branch as a thesaurus spreadsheet, showing preferred terms, alternate and hidden labels, and the related link.

## *The Spreadsheet Elements in SKOS RDF*

Rendered in SKOS, that spreadsheet becomes a small concept scheme, which, when written as a SKOS RDF data model, becomes the Workforce Development skos:ConceptScheme that every concept points to with skos:inScheme. Every concept within the hierarchy lives within the skos: ConceptScheme, and is represented as a skos:Concept, the hierarchical relations expressed using skos:broader and skos:narrower relationship properties. The synonyms and acronyms in the altLabel and hiddenLabel columns are encoded as skos:altLabel and skos:hiddenLabel, while the related column becomes skos:related.

Before introducing our concept scheme, we first declare our prefixes and namespaces, which also form the foundation for URI patterns throughout our SKOS model. The prefixes are shorthand for the namespaces, saving time and space throughout our turtle concept scheme. The declaration of our namespaces and prefixes tells a machine and human what to expect and what to prepare for, as to what we are using to describe the concept scheme.

We declare that we are using the RDF data model and RDFS scheme to express triples; we are using the SKOS data model to declare our thesaurus; and we are using our workforce concept scheme to assert the concepts, their labels, documentation properties, and relationship types. We call the declaration of namespaces and prefixes the preamble.

```
@prefix rdf:    <http://www.w3.org/1999/02/22-rdf-syntax-ns#> .
@prefix rdfs:   <http://www.w3.org/2000/01/rdf-schema#> .
@prefix skos:   <http://www.w3.org/2004/02/skos/core#> .
@prefix wf:     <https://contextually.com/workforce#> .

# wf: is the workforce-development thesaurus we build in this chapter.
# Two more prefixes arrive later: skosxl: at the thesaurus stage (SKOS-XL
# labels), and shock: at the mapping stage – that is Chapter 3's Bee
# Taxonomy, the vocabulary we map back to. See those sections.
```

Figure 61 The preamble.

Two unique namespaces appear in this chapter, each representing a SKOS structure. The first, wf: (https://contextually.com/workforce#), is our own—it represents the Workforce development thesaurus we are building: every concept, label, relationship, and collection. The second, shock: (https://shock.org/taxonomy/), we do not have to build; it is the Bee Taxonomy from Chapter 3, the taxonomy this chapter grew out of. We declare shock: only at the mapping stage, because that is where the two vocabularies meet. Keeping them in separate namespaces is what makes the mapping meaningful: skos:closeMatch, skos:exactMatch, and skos:relatedMatch are cross-scheme relations, so there must be two schemes for them to join. Our wf: thesaurus maps out to Chapter 3's shock: taxonomy, and that link is the carryover between the two chapters, evident in the code.

With the preamble declared, we render the spreadsheet as SKOS in three stages—a controlled vocabulary, then a taxonomy, then a thesaurus—each one building on the last. The staged code follows; the preamble above remains for all three stages.

### *Stage 1: controlled vocabulary—the foundation*

Our controlled vocabulary establishes the core concepts of the Workforce development domain and creates our first concept scheme. Each concept belongs to the scheme and carries a preferred label, alternative labels for synonyms, and a definition. See Figure 62.

Here we see SKOS in its simplest form. Every skos:Concept sits in our skos:ConceptScheme with a preferred label (skos:prefLabel), alternative labels (skos:altLabel) for synonyms, a definition, and, where useful, a scope note. The alternative label "Employment readiness" resolves to the same concept as "Job readiness," so a search for either lands in one place.

```
@prefix rdf:    <http://www.w3.org/1999/02/22-rdf-syntax-ns#> .
@prefix rdfs:   <http://www.w3.org/2000/01/rdf-schema#> .
@prefix skos:   <http://www.w3.org/2004/02/skos/core#> .
@prefix wf:     <https://contextually.com/workforce#> .

wf:workforce-development-scheme rdf:type skos:ConceptScheme ;
    skos:prefLabel  "Workforce Development Concept Scheme"@en ;
    skos:definition "A controlled vocabulary for workforce-development concepts and services"@en ;
    skos:creator    "Contextually" ;
    skos:created    "2025-01-01" .
wf:job-readiness rdf:type skos:Concept ;
    skos:inScheme  wf:workforce-development-scheme ;
    skos:prefLabel "Job readiness"@en ;
    skos:altLabel  "Employment readiness"@en ;
    skos:definition "The competencies and preparation that make a person ready to apply for and succeed in a job"@en ;
    skos:scopeNote "Includes résumé writing and interview preparation"@en .
wf:financial-capability rdf:type skos:Concept ;
    skos:inScheme  wf:workforce-development-scheme ;
    skos:prefLabel "Financial capability"@en ;
    skos:altLabel  "Financial wellness"@en ;
    skos:definition "The knowledge and confidence to manage personal finances"@en .
wf:career-planning rdf:type skos:Concept ;
    skos:inScheme  wf:workforce-development-scheme ;
    skos:prefLabel "Career planning"@en ;
    skos:altLabel  "Career development"@en ;
    skos:definition "Setting career goals and mapping the steps to get there"@en .
```

Figure 62: SKOS controlled vocabulary.

## *Stage 2: taxonomy—building hierarchy*

Now we add hierarchy with skos:broader and skos:narrower, creating a three-level taxonomy. Workforce development sits at the top; Job readiness, Financial capability, and Career planning sit beneath it; and each of those has its own narrower concepts.

We mark the top of the tree with skos:topConceptOf, and skos:broader and skos:narrower build the levels beneath. The skos:example property carries a concrete case, which helps a retrieval system understand context, and when a concept applies.

```
@prefix rdf:    <http://www.w3.org/1999/02/22-rdf-syntax-ns#> .
@prefix rdfs:   <http://www.w3.org/2000/01/rdf-schema#> .
@prefix skos:   <http://www.w3.org/2004/02/skos/core#> .
@prefix wf:     <https://contextually.com/workforce#> .

# Level 1 – top concept
wf:workforce-development rdf:type skos:Concept ;
    skos:inScheme     wf:workforce-development-scheme ;
    skos:topConceptOf wf:workforce-development-scheme ;
    skos:prefLabel    "Workforce development"@en ;
    skos:definition   "Programs and services that help people gain skills, credentials, and readiness for employment"@en .

# Level 2 – major branches
wf:job-readiness rdf:type skos:Concept ;
    skos:inScheme wf:workforce-development-scheme ;
    skos:broader  wf:workforce-development ;
    skos:narrower wf:resume-writing, wf:interview-preparation .

wf:financial-capability rdf:type skos:Concept ;
    skos:inScheme wf:workforce-development-scheme ;
    skos:broader  wf:workforce-development ;
    skos:narrower wf:budgeting-basics, wf:credit-management .

wf:career-planning rdf:type skos:Concept ;
    skos:inScheme wf:workforce-development-scheme ;
    skos:broader  wf:workforce-development ;
    skos:narrower wf:goal-setting, wf:skill-assessment .

@prefix rdf:    <http://www.w3.org/1999/02/22-rdf-syntax-ns#> .
@prefix rdfs:   <http://www.w3.org/2000/01/rdf-schema#> .
@prefix skos:   <http://www.w3.org/2004/02/skos/core#> .
@prefix wf:     <https://contextually.com/workforce#> .

# Level 3 – specific services
wf:resume-writing rdf:type skos:Concept ;
    skos:inScheme   wf:workforce-development-scheme ;
    skos:prefLabel  "Résumé writing"@en ;
    skos:definition "Preparing a résumé that summarizes a candidate's experience and skills"@en ;
    skos:broader    wf:job-readiness ;
    skos:example    "Tailoring a résumé to a job posting"@en .

wf:interview-preparation rdf:type skos:Concept ;
    skos:inScheme   wf:workforce-development-scheme ;
    skos:prefLabel  "Interview preparation"@en ;
    skos:definition "Practice and coaching for job interviews"@en ;
    skos:broader    wf:job-readiness ;
    skos:example    "Mock interviews and common questions"@en .

wf:budgeting-basics rdf:type skos:Concept ;
    skos:inScheme  wf:workforce-development-scheme ;
    skos:prefLabel "Budgeting basics"@en ;
    skos:broader   wf:financial-capability .

wf:credit-management rdf:type skos:Concept ;
    skos:inScheme  wf:workforce-development-scheme ;
    skos:prefLabel "Credit management"@en ;
    skos:broader   wf:financial-capability .

wf:goal-setting rdf:type skos:Concept ;
    skos:inScheme  wf:workforce-development-scheme ;
    skos:prefLabel "Goal setting"@en ;
    skos:broader   wf:career-planning .

wf:skill-assessment rdf:type skos:Concept ;
    skos:inScheme  wf:workforce-development-scheme ;
    skos:prefLabel "Skill assessment"@en ;
    skos:broader   wf:career-planning .
```

Figure 63: SKOS taxonomy branches.

## *Stage 3: thesaurus—adding semantic richness*

Now we cross from taxonomy into thesaurus by adding the associative relationship, skos:related. These relations join concepts that belong together, beyond the parent-child relation expressed in a hierarchy.

```
@prefix rdf:    <http://www.w3.org/1999/02/22-rdf-syntax-ns#> .
@prefix rdfs:   <http://www.w3.org/2000/01/rdf-schema#> .
@prefix skos:   <http://www.w3.org/2004/02/skos/core#> .
@prefix wf:     <https://contextually.com/workforce#> .

# Associative links cross branches, and each is stated both ways
# (skos:related is symmetric). Financial capability's services connect
# out into the career and job branches.

wf:budgeting-basics  skos:related wf:career-planning .
wf:career-planning   skos:related wf:budgeting-basics .

wf:credit-management skos:related wf:job-readiness .
wf:job-readiness     skos:related wf:credit-management .

wf:resume-writing    skos:related wf:skill-assessment .
wf:skill-assessment  skos:related wf:resume-writing .
```

Figure 64: SKOS thesaurus with related.

These relations cross branches. Budgeting basics, under Financial capability, joins career planning; credit management joins job readiness; résumé writing joins skill assessment. Each is stated and the relationship is valid in both directions, because skos:related is symmetric. They deliberately skip siblings: two concepts under the same parent are already related via their shared parent, so relating them directly adds nothing, and a validator flags such a link as valueless.

The related link cannot be expressed by a taxonomy and is the responsibility of the thesaurus. When someone asks about credit management, the system knows to offer job readiness alongside it. This associative tie is also what carries financial capability across into the working life of the vocabulary—the same doorway triple from the close of Chapter 3, when we related Financial literacy to Workforce development.

## *SKOS-XL: when labels need labels*

Now we add a new namespace and prefix. Stages 1 and 2 included only rdf, rdfs, skos, and wf, because plain skos:prefLabel and skos:altLabel were all a controlled vocabulary or taxonomy needed.

SKOS-XL lives in a separate namespace, http://www.w3.org/2008/05/skos-xl#, so the skosxl prefix is declared here, at the thesaurus stage. If you only need to name a concept, skos:prefLabel is enough; when you need to say something about the label itself, you switch that label to skosxl:Label and declare the prefix.

Figure 65: SKOS-XL, turning a label into a resource.

SKOS-XL is deliberately small: one class and five properties. The class is skosxl:Label, a label treated as a resource. Three properties, skosxl:prefLabel, skosxl:altLabel, and skosxl:hiddenLabel, attach a label to a concept, mirroring the plain skos:prefLabel, skos:altLabel, and skos:hiddenLabel. A fourth, skosxl:literalForm, is for the label's text. And the fifth, skosxl:labelRelation, establishes a relationship between one label and another. At its simplest, a concept points to label resources in place of plain strings.

```
@prefix rdf:    <http://www.w3.org/1999/02/22-rdf-syntax-ns#> .
@prefix rdfs:   <http://www.w3.org/2000/01/rdf-schema#> .
@prefix skos:   <http://www.w3.org/2004/02/skos/core#> .
@prefix skosxl: <http://www.w3.org/2008/05/skos-xl#> .
@prefix wf:     <https://contextually.com/workforce#> .

wf:resume-writing-label rdf:type skosxl:Label ;
    skosxl:literalForm   "Résumé writing"@en ;
    skosxl:labelRelation wf:cv-writing-label .
wf:cv-writing-label rdf:type skosxl:Label ;
    skosxl:literalForm "CV writing"@en .
wf:resume-writing skosxl:prefLabel wf:resume-writing-label ;
    skosxl:altLabel wf:cv-writing-label .
```

Figure 66: SKOS-XL labels.

Because a label is now a resource, it can do two things a plain string cannot. First, it can record its own history—when the term changed and what it replaced—so a concept carries the provenance of its terminology with it. Second, one label can be tied to another: an acronym like "CV" points to its full form, "Curriculum vitae," so both surface forms resolve to the same concept.

```
@prefix rdf:    <http://www.w3.org/1999/02/22-rdf-syntax-ns#> .
@prefix rdfs:   <http://www.w3.org/2000/01/rdf-schema#> .
@prefix skos:   <http://www.w3.org/2004/02/skos/core#> .
@prefix skosxl: <http://www.w3.org/2008/05/skos-xl#> .
@prefix wf:     <https://contextually.com/workforce#> .

wf:wd-label rdf:type skosxl:Label ;
    skosxl:literalForm "Workforce development"@en ;
    skos:changeNote  "Preferred term as of 2025, replacing 'Manpower development'"@en ;
    skos:historyNote "In wide use since the 1998 Workforce Investment Act"@en .
wf:workforce-development skosxl:prefLabel wf:wd-label .
wf:cv-label rdf:type skosxl:Label ; skosxl:literalForm "CV"@en .
wf:curriculum-vitae-label rdf:type skosxl:Label ; skosxl:literalForm "Curriculum vitae"@en .
wf:cv-label skosxl:labelRelation wf:curriculum-vitae-label .
```

Figure 67: SKOS-XL history and change note.

The Workforce development label carries a change note and a history note on the label itself, so the term's lineage travels with it. And the acronym "CV" is joined to "Curriculum vitae" through skosxl:labelRelation, so both surface forms resolve to one concept.

## Adding SKOS collections

SKOS collections group concepts for display or navigation, without implying hierarchy. A skos:Collection is an unordered grouping; a skos:OrderedCollection is one where the order of members is declared, using an rdf:List structure.

```
@prefix rdf:    <http://www.w3.org/1999/02/22-rdf-syntax-ns#> .
@prefix rdfs:   <http://www.w3.org/2000/01/rdf-schema#> .
@prefix skos:   <http://www.w3.org/2004/02/skos/core#> .
@prefix skosxl: <http://www.w3.org/2008/05/skos-xl#> .
@prefix wf:     <https://contextually.com/workforce#> .

wf:job-search-skills rdf:type skos:Collection ;
    skos:prefLabel "Job search skills"@en ;
    skos:member    wf:resume-writing, wf:interview-preparation .
wf:career-planning-steps rdf:type skos:OrderedCollection ;
    skos:prefLabel  "Career planning steps"@en ;
    skos:memberList ( wf:skill-assessment wf:goal-setting wf:career-planning ) .
```

Figure 68:SKOS collections.

"Job search skills" gathers Résumé writing and Interview preparation for display, and "Career planning steps" holds an ordered sequence: skill assessment, then goal setting, then career planning. A collection is not a substitute for skos:broader or skos:narrower; it carries no inference and no hierarchy, and it serves navigation and display only. For a reader, a collection is a labeled bundle—a menu heading or a facet in a search sidebar. For a machine, it is a set to iterate over through skos:member, one that asserts no broader or narrower relation, so a reasoner never mistakes the grouping for hierarchy.

### *Integration with classification systems*

A concept can carry an integration code for the systems it feeds, using skos:notation, keeping a foot in an existing classification scheme while it lives in the thesaurus.

```
@prefix rdf:    <http://www.w3.org/1999/02/22-rdf-syntax-ns#> .
@prefix rdfs:   <http://www.w3.org/2000/01/rdf-schema#> .
@prefix skos:   <http://www.w3.org/2004/02/skos/core#> .
@prefix skosxl: <http://www.w3.org/2008/05/skos-xl#> .
@prefix wf:     <https://contextually.com/workforce#> .

wf:job-readiness skos:notation "WF.JR" ;
    skos:note "Internal classification code for job-readiness services"@en .
```

Figure 69: SKOS notation.

### *Mapping between vocabularies*

A thesaurus connects beyond itself through the mapping properties. We can point a concept out to a public reference, and we can align our scheme with a partner's without either side giving up its structure.

The closeMatch to DBpedia's Résumé record anchors our concept to a public description. Across schemes, exactMatch declares the same concept in both, closeMatch a near equivalent, and relatedMatch, an associative link. These mappings let a query or a retrieval system travel from our vocabulary to another without a custom integration. This is also where the doorway triple from Chapter 3 is honored: Financial capability closeMatches an outside financial literacy vocabulary, so the two schemes read as one connected space, and financial literacy is joined to the workforce development thesaurus through both associative and mapping relations.

```
@prefix rdf:     <http://www.w3.org/1999/02/22-rdf-syntax-ns#> .
@prefix rdfs:    <http://www.w3.org/2000/01/rdf-schema#> .
@prefix skos:    <http://www.w3.org/2004/02/skos/core#> .
@prefix skosxl: <http://www.w3.org/2008/05/skos-xl#> .
@prefix wf:      <https://contextually.com/workforce#> .
@prefix shock:  <https://shock.org/taxonomy/> .

# to the Chapter 3 Bee Taxonomy (shock:) – the doorway from the taxonomy chapter
wf:financial-capability skos:closeMatch   shock:FinancialLiteracy .
wf:budgeting-basics      skos:exactMatch   shock:Budgeting .
wf:credit-management     skos:relatedMatch shock:FinancialPlanningBasics .
wf:workforce-development skos:closeMatch   shock:WorkforceDevelopment .

# public linked-data resources (DBpedia)
wf:workforce-development skos:closeMatch <http://dbpedia.org/resource/Workforce_development> .
wf:resume-writing        skos:closeMatch <http://dbpedia.org/resource/Résumé> ,
                                         <http://dbpedia.org/resource/Curriculum_vitae> .

# name-authority pointers to the ILO (an agent, not a concept)
wf:workforce-development-scheme rdfs:seeAlso
    <http://viaf.org/viaf/133287293> ,
    <http://id.loc.gov/authorities/classification/KJE5062.I68> .
```

Figure 70: SKOS mapping between concept schemes.

## *Validating the thesaurus*

A thesaurus is only as trustworthy as its structure, and SKOS has a quality checker built for this: qSKOS, a set of criteria for the mistakes SKOS vocabularies tend to make—concepts with no relations, cycles in the hierarchy, associative links that duplicate the tree, labels that collide, missing documentation. The easiest way to run it is SKOS Play, a free web tool that reads a Turtle file and returns a qSKOS report.[13]

Upload the file at skos-play.sparna.fr/play/, choose the validation path, and read the report grouped by criterion. A clean run of the Workforce development thesaurus returns no errors, no warnings, and no informational flags, with every concept carrying a definition or scope note. Both tools are open source: SKOS Play at github.com/sparna-git/skos-play, and the qSKOS engine it runs at github.com/cmader/qSKOS.[14]

---

[13] qSKOS is an open-source quality-assessment tool for SKOS vocabularies. Mader, Christian. *qSKOS: Vocabulary Quality Assessment Tools*. GitHub, github.com/cmader/qSKOS. Accessed 19 July 2026. Its quality criteria are described in Mader, Christian, et al. "Finding Quality Issues in SKOS Vocabularies." *Theory and Practice of Digital Libraries*, edited by Panayiotis Zaphiris et al., Lecture Notes in Computer Science, vol. 7489, Springer, 2012, pp. 222–33.

[14] Francart, Thomas. *SKOS Play!* Sparna, skos-play.sparna.fr. Accessed 19 July 2026.

Two of qSKOS's checks shape how we wrote the associative links above. The first, valueless associative relations, flags a skos:related link between two siblings—concepts under the same parent—because the shared parent already ties them together. That is why the financial-to-career bridge is drawn child to child, budgeting basics to career planning, rather than between the branch tops. The second, unidirectional related concepts, flags a skos:related asserted in only one direction; because the property is symmetric, we state both halves of every pair.

Collections are the one part of the model kept out of the validated file. A skos:Collection is not a concept—it groups by membership, not hierarchy—so a concept-level validator that imports it as a concept reports it as an orphan and is left as undocumented. Those flags describe the import, not a fault in the vocabulary, so the collections are omitted or ignored through validation and the core validates clean. The same file can be round-tripped through the taxonomy tool from Chapter 3: a faithful import and export, concepts and relations intact, is its own proof that the vocabulary is well formed and portable.

---

## Thesauri in the wild

The Workforce development thesaurus is small by design. The vocabularies that run the world's libraries, museums, governments, and research systems are built using the same SKOS framework, only at a larger scale, demonstrating what a mature thesaurus becomes.

The Getty Art & Architecture Thesaurus (AAT) organizes the language of art, architecture, and material culture—tens of thousands of concepts with preferred and alternate terms, hierarchy, and scope notes—and the Getty publishes it as SKOS linked open data for anyone to reference.[15] The Library of Congress Subject Headings (LCSH), the backbone of subject cataloging in American

---

[15]Getty Research Institute. Art & Architecture Thesaurus (AAT). J. Paul Getty Trust, getty.edu/research/tools/vocabularies/aat/; published as linked open data at getty.edu/research/tools/vocabularies/lod/.

libraries for over a century, is published as SKOS/RDF through the Library of Congress linked data service, each heading a dereferenceable URI.[16]

In the European Union, EuroVoc is a multilingual thesaurus covering the activities of the EU across dozens of languages, maintained by the Publications Office and distributed as SKOS so legal and legislative systems can index documents consistently across borders.[17] In agriculture, AGROVOC—maintained by the Food and Agriculture Organization of the United Nations—gathers tens of thousands of concepts in many languages and publishes them as SKOS linked open data, a shared reference hub for food and farming data worldwide.[18] And in medicine, the National Library of Medicine's Medical Subject Headings (MeSH) is the controlled vocabulary that indexes the biomedical literature in PubMed, organized as a thesaurus of descriptors, qualifiers, and entry terms and available in RDF.[19]

Each of these carries the same three relationships built throughout this chapter—equivalence, hierarchy, and association—and each does the same job: by giving people and machines one agreed, disambiguated vocabulary to point at. The Workforce development thesaurus is a small member of that family.

---

## Knowledge infrastructure and the thesaurus

Category discovery operates through semantic networks. Related concepts are discovered through URI-based relationship traversal rather than keyword similarity.

This URI-based approach transforms how AI systems interact with knowledge. RAG systems retrieve by semantic concept matching over URI relationships instead of by keyword overlap. LLMs learn through training data, the explicit semantic relationships between concepts, beyond text alone,

[16] Library of Congress. Library of Congress Subject Headings. LC Linked Data Service: Authorities and Vocabularies, id.loc.gov/authorities/subjects.html.

[17] Publications Office of the European Union. EuroVoc: The EU's Multilingual Thesaurus. op.europa.eu/en/web/eu-vocabularies/eurovoc.

[18] Food and Agriculture Organization of the United Nations. AGROVOC Multilingual Thesaurus. FAO, agrovoc.fao.org.

[19] National Library of Medicine. Medical Subject Headings (MeSH). U.S. National Library of Medicine, nlm.nih.gov/mesh/.

which improves understanding and lowers hallucinations; when many labels share a single URI, the thesaurus serves as a primitive kind of NLP.

Knowledge integration lets different organizational AI systems share and build on each other's models through URI-based concept alignment, supported by mapping relations. Entity recognition is strengthened, as NER systems link entities to authoritative URI-based concepts instead of ambiguous text strings. And question answering improves, since a system can lean on the semantic relationships between query and knowledge base concepts, a step up from question-answer banks mapped to SQL.

## Conclusion

A thesaurus serves AI systems in several ways. It enhances training data: a well-structured SKOS thesaurus improves training data quality, so that in place of raw text about "job programs," the data carries explicit relationships, résumé writing to job readiness to workforce development, which helps a model grasp how terms relate on top of what they mean. It optimizes retrieval and RAG: when a user asks about "interview preparation," the system leans on skos:related to pull relevant context on résumé writing and job readiness, while skos:broader and skos:narrower tell it when to zoom in or out. And it supports RIG (Retrieval Interleaved Generation): systems that use retrieval to influence generation at several points across the query and prompt journey can use SKOS hierarchies to guide search and response, with the semantic relationships helping determine which retrieved passages are significant and how they shape the output.

The SKOS thesaurus supports real applications in three ways. For vector-database integration, SKOS preferred and alternative labels improve embedding quality and the semantic relationships guide similarity, so concepts joined by skos:related carry higher similarity scores; a SKOS structure can also serve as a category backbone for a vector database, inserting a human-in-the-loop into decisions about categories and hierarchy that otherwise sit with the machine.

For query expansion, a search for "career planning" widens through skos:related to concepts such as "goal setting" and "skill assessment," while skos:altLabel and skos:hiddenLabel let one URI answer to a concept's synonyms and misspellings, so "CV writing" finds "Résumé writing." For concept classification, the taxonomic structure tags new content: a document about "résumé writing" picks up broader concepts such as "job readiness" and "workforce development," and because SKOS supports these relations, inference should be leveraged in the classification logic.

Our Workforce development model now uses virtually every SKOS element. The concept scheme is the overall vocabulary container; concepts are the individual services and terms; labels are the preferred, alternative, and hidden forms on each concept. Hierarchical relations, broader and narrower, create the taxonomic structure, while associative relations connect concepts across branches. Mapping relations connect to external and partner vocabularies; collections group related concepts, and ordered collections arrange them in sequence. And documentation, including definitions, scope notes, examples, and change histories, carries the human-readable context throughout.

This isn't relegated to the halls of academia—it's a practical knowledge foundation that makes AI systems smarter, more reliable, and more transparent.

SKOS provides an excellent foundation, and it is meant to be a stepping stone. As your workforce development knowledge matures, you might graduate to OWL for formal classes, axioms, and constraints that let a reasoner derive new facts from the concept graph you have built here. Your SKOS foundation makes that transition smooth and protects the modeling work you have already done. That is where the next chapter begins, with ontology.

A knowledge graph is a network of real-world entities, people, places, concepts, and the typed relationships between them, stored so that both humans and machines can traverse and reason over the connections. Where a thesaurus organizes terms, a knowledge graph connects the things those terms stand for, along with facts about them; Chapter 6 walks through a knowledge graph in full.

The concept graph you've built with SKOS is the essential scaffolding upon which robust AI applications stand. AI systems are only as good as their context, and SKOS gives you the tools to make that context explicit, machine-readable, and semantically rich.

Your journey from candidate concepts to a full thesaurus mirrors the evolution of AI itself: from simple rule-based systems to sophisticated, context-aware intelligence.

And just as AI does, your concept graph will continue to evolve, learn, and improve.

CHAPTER 5

# Ontology

What is an ontology?

An ontology is a formal, explicit, and shared model of a domain that defines classes of entities, the properties that characterize them, and the relationships between them. Unlike informal vocabularies or classification schemes, an ontology expresses knowledge using a set of strict, machine-readable logical axioms and facts.

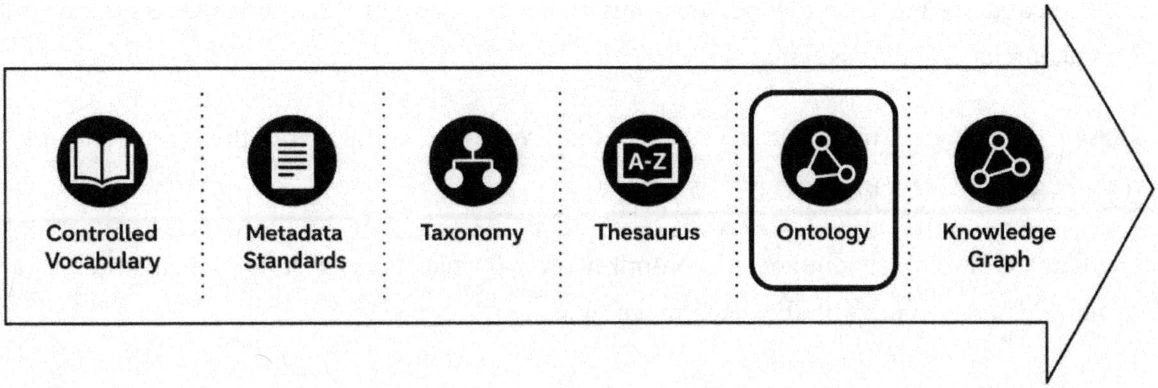


Figure 71: The Ontology Pipeline framework.

By explicitly defining categories (classes), their properties, and the constraints between them, ontologies enable computer systems and software agents to process the underlying meaning of the data and draw logical inferences. The level of expressiveness varies depending on the need. Some domains require the full logical machinery of OWL. Others are well served by RDFS-based models that define clear class hierarchies, domain and range constraints, and property structures. Both are ontologies. What distinguishes an ontology from other knowledge structures is the commitment to formally modeling what exists in a domain and how things relate, in terms that machines can interpret and act on.

What's not an ontology?

**A flat list of keywords** is not an ontology. A product category tree without defined classes or semantic relationships is not an ontology.

**A JSON config file** is not an ontology.

**A database schema**, however well-designed, is not an ontology, because it describes how a specific system stores data, not what kinds of things exist in a domain independent of any system.

**Controlled vocabularies** provide standardized terms for describing resources. A list of approved terms is not a model of a domain. It is a tool for consistent reference within a model.

**Taxonomies** organize concepts into hierarchical structures. A taxonomy is a skeleton. Add SKOS to that taxonomy and you've started building the nervous system. An ontology is a skeleton with musculature and a nervous system.

**Thesauri** are graph-structured data stores that represent entities and their relationships. A knowledge graph *uses* an ontology. It is not one.

The bar for ontology is ontological commitment, a formal model of a domain's structure and meaning. The bar scales with the domain's complexity.

All that work depends on the foundation laid here: a clear understanding of what an ontology is, what it is not, and why the distinction has been so difficult for the field to settle. There's a whole lot of loose terminology and inflated claims that are important to clarify, so we can discuss ontologies without the market baggage they carry. Precision is not pedantry, but a prerequisite for true clarity.

The domain we will model is workflow management at a midsize technology company—the kind of place where 1,100 employees, multiple product lines, human specialists, AI agents, and automated pipelines all operate inside the same processes—and where the process knowledge that coordinates all of them has become dangerously fragmented, hard to find, and even harder to trust.

We will use open standards as building materials: PROV-O, FOAF, Dublin Core, DCAT, Schema.org, and RDF/RDFS. OWL to provide the framing. Almost every element will be borrowed from existing standards and traced to its source. Every custom element will be justified, labeled, and documented. The result will be a solid, logically valid ontology model to support workflows at our fictitious mid-size company: Special Solutions.

## Before we get started

To build functional and useful ontologies, it is important to further understand the history of ontology in the context of information science and AI. Because ontologies have emerged as the sought-after brass ring in the AI race, they have become confusing as marketing copy has gotten ahead of the discipline of building ontologies. There is confusion around the concept, the terminology, the technology stack—all of it. This confusion is worth noting because it has become a barrier to entry. Understanding the causes of this confusion is the first step toward working productively with ontologies.

## Why the confusion exists

If you have spent any time in the semantic technology space, you have had some version of this experience. You read an article that says an ontology must be expressed in OWL. You read another that says any RDF model with classes and properties qualifies. A third article says a taxonomy is a kind of ontology. A fourth says an ontology is a knowledge graph with extra steps. A vendor at a conference will call their product category tree an "ontology-powered AI solution." Two textbooks contradict each other on where the boundary falls.

You are not confused because you are missing something. You are confused because the field is flooded with conflicting messaging and too many domain experts regaling audiences with different, partial versions of the truth. This mixed messaging has real consequences—for practitioners trying to build, for organizations trying to invest, and for AI systems that increasingly depend on formally structured knowledge to perform reliably.

So let's step back for a moment to take a look at the big picture (and history). Let's trace the concept of ontology from philosophy to its contemporary application in computer science. We'll look at the core building blocks of the Semantic Web, examining which standards qualify as ontologies and which do not (a surprisingly interesting question). Then, I'll introduce the Ontology Pipeline and the well-known ontology spectrum as complementary frameworks for understanding where ontologies fit within the broader landscape of knowledge infrastructure.

Let's first examine some of the common misperceptions around ontologies because the confusion surrounding them has identifiable sources.

---

## Ontology is philosophizing

The word ontology is borrowed from philosophy, and the borrowing can lean toward imprecision. In philosophy, ontology (lowercase, no article) is a branch of metaphysics—the study of what exists and what categories of being there are. It is a field of inquiry. When computer scientists adopted the term in the early 1990s, they turned it into a countable noun: *an* ontology, meaning a specific formal model of a domain.

The philosophical baggage is never fully detached. Some people hear "a formal model" and others hear "the study of existence," and the two pull in different directions. For our purposes, information science ontologies are mostly deterministic by nature, while philosophical ontology invites an open deliberation on the nature of things.

## The field lacks institutional standardization

Ontology engineering sits at the intersection of philosophy, library science, information science, artificial intelligence, computer science, and data engineering—six disciplines that use different vocabularies, train different intuitions, and publish in different journals. There is no governing body that arbitrates what "ontology" means across these communities.

But there *is* an institutional standardization based on communities of practice, which is often ignored or overlooked. The W3C governs open ontology standards and reference documentation, with working groups and open protocols designed to ensure that ontology standards are interoperable and machine-readable.

## The Semantic Web stack is not a relic of the past

The Semantic Web may seem like a relic—an unrealized vision from a different era of the internet. Why should practitioners care about a project that never achieved mainstream adoption?

Because ontologies and their related standards are not adjacent to the Semantic Web. They *are* the Semantic Web.

The Semantic Web—sometimes called Web 3.0—was proposed by Tim Berners-Lee, the inventor of the World Wide Web, as an extension of the existing web. Not a replacement, an *extension*. The foundational principles that ontology engineering depends on—URIs as global identifiers for things, RDF as a universal data model for expressing meaning as triples, namespaces for disambiguating terms across independent systems, and linked data for connecting knowledge across organizational boundaries—are components of the Semantic Web architecture.

Every standard we work with today from SKOS to RDFS and OWL to PROV-O was developed within this framework and published through the W3C as part of a coherent, layered engineering vision. To dismiss the Semantic Web as a failed experiment is to dismiss the infrastructure your ontology (and your LLM) is built on.

## Ontology as a marketing concept

Because of the confusion around what an ontology is and is not, marketers and hungry VCs have swooped in to capitalize on the term. Without clear boundaries, the ontology concept has been manipulated and appropriated to reference database schemas, flat lists of terms, a YAML config file, and even a mission or values statement. You can't blame them. The word "ontology" conjures images of a professor with a pipe, reading a book by the fireside. In other words, it evokes scholarly trust.

## It's a model, it's a language, it's an expression

An ontology is a formal model of a domain. OWL is the Web Ontology Language. SKOS is defined *as* an OWL ontology. So "ontology" refers simultaneously to the thing you build, the language you build it in, and the specification that defines some of your building materials. This circular terminology is one of the steepest barriers to entry. This confuses many people, leaving them unsure of what to use, where, and when.

## We don't see the problem

Ontologies solve a problem most engineers were never taught to see. Software and data engineers are trained to think about structures, schemas, pipelines, and algorithms. Neither discipline systematically trains practitioners to think about what kinds of things exist in a domain and how they formally relate, which is the problem ontologies solve. When engineers encounter ontologies for the first time, they reach for the nearest familiar analogy, such as a database schema, an API contract, a class hierarchy, and each breaks down in different but important ways.

## A brief history

The word "ontology" predates computer science by roughly two and a half millennia. Its roots are Greek: *ontos* (being) and *logos* (study of). Aristotle's *Categories*, written in the fourth century BCE, is among the earliest systematic attempts to enumerate the fundamental types of things that can be said to exist: substances, quantities, qualities, relations, places, times, positions, states, actions, and affections. When Aristotle asked, "What are the fundamental categories of being?" he was doing something that modern ontology engineers do every day—deciding what kinds of things a system needs to know about, and how those things relate.

The philosophical tradition that runs from Aristotle through medieval scholastics, through Leibniz's dream of a *characteristica universalis*—a formal language capable of expressing all human knowledge—through Kant's categories of understanding, and into 20th-century analytic philosophy, is the direct ancestor of computational ontology.

The term migrated into computer science in the early 1990s, most influentially through Tom Gruber's 1993 definition: An ontology is "a formal, explicit specification of a shared conceptualization."

Every word in that definition does real work.

**Formal** means machine-readable and logically structured. **Explicit** means the commitments are stated, not implied. **Specification** means there is a defined model, not a loose collection. **Shared** means it is intended for use by a community, not a private notation. **Conceptualization** means it represents a way of thinking about a domain—a model of what exists and how it is organized.

Gruber's work at Stanford during that period was part of a larger DARPA-funded effort to enable independently-developed AI systems to share data, models, and knowledge without sharing data schemas or formats. The insight was that interoperability required a *semantic* agreement—an agreement about what things mean—rather than a structural agreement about how data is stored. This is the same insight that drives the Semantic Web, and it is the reason ontologies matter for AI today.

## Ontologies are symbolic AI

Ontologies are symbolic AI. Symbolic AI represents knowledge through formal structures: defined concepts, explicit relationships, and logical rules that machines can reason over. That is precisely what an ontology does. When an ontology declares that a Person is a subclass of Agent, that two classes are disjoint, or that a property is transitive, it is encoding knowledge as symbols with formal semantics—the defining characteristic of the symbolic tradition in artificial intelligence.

The current AI landscape is dominated by neural networks, which excel at pattern recognition but operate as black boxes. This means current models cannot explain their reasoning, cannot guarantee logical consistency, and struggle without massive amounts of training data. Recent research in neurosymbolic AI, including work published in *IEEE Access* on ontology-based neural networks, demonstrates that ontologies address these limitations. When domain ontologies serve as the symbolic backbone of a neural system, they make predictions interpretable by connecting outputs to human-understandable concepts; they reduce data requirements by encoding prior knowledge that the network does not have to learn from scratch; and they enable formal reasoning that statistical models cannot perform on their own. While the neural network perceives, the ontology reasons. This is why ontologies shape the formal knowledge infrastructure that AI systems require, to move from pattern-matching to genuine understanding.

## The Semantic Web and the problem it solves

The World Wide Web, as Sir Tim Berners-Lee originally built it, is a system for linking documents. HTML tells a browser how to display a page. Machines store, route, and render this content, but they do not understand it. An HTML page about a recipe can display "2 cups flour" to a human reader who knows what flour is, what a cup measures, and what flour's role is in baking. The machine rendering that page knows that a string of characters should appear in a certain font at a certain position. That is all.

This limitation prevents powerful things. You cannot ask the Web for all dessert recipes without citrus ingredients unless someone has manually tagged every recipe accordingly. You cannot merge two recipe databases without writing custom scripts to align every field and resolve every naming inconsistency. Every act of cross-system understanding requires human engineering.

Berners-Lee's vision—articulated publicly in a landmark 2001 *Scientific American* article with James Hendler and Ora Lassila—was to extend the Web with a layer of machine-readable data where meaning could be formally expressed, shared across systems, and reasoned over by software agents. The W3C adopted this vision: "The Semantic Web provides a common framework that allows data to be shared and reused across application, enterprise, and community boundaries."

A December 2007 follow-up *Scientific American* article, 'The Semantic Web in Action," illuminates progress and successes in ontology and RDF adoption, featuring corporate adoption and use cases. But it notes that in spite of adoption and successes, "Researchers in these disciplines face tremendous data-integration challenges at almost every stage of their work." Sound familiar? This is the ecosystem for which the ontologies were designed. And to understand ontologies, you need to understand the building blocks of this ecosystem.

## The Resource Description Framework (RDF)

RDF is the foundational data model of the Semantic Web. Everything in this landscape is built with RDF, so it is worth understanding the standard clearly. RDF is not itself a knowledge graph; it is the data model a knowledge graph is usually built from. RDF gives you the atomic unit—the triple—and the rules for combining triples into a graph. A knowledge graph is what you get when you use RDF to represent a whole domain of entities and relationships at scale. RDF is the grammar; the knowledge graph is the architecture that enables the coalescence of the vocabulary, metadata, and ontology, into one, cohesive knowledge system.

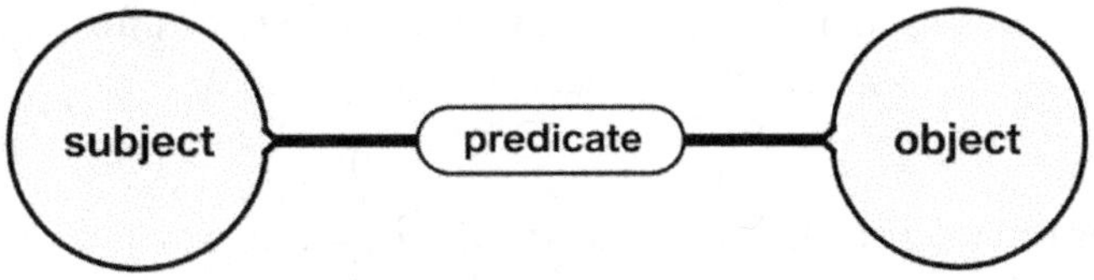


Figure 72: RDF represents information as triples: subject, predicate, object.

RDF represents information as triples: subject, predicate, object. Every triple is a statement. A collection of triples forms a directed graph. That is the entire data model.

The key component is the Uniform Resource Identifier (URI). In RDF, resources are identified by URIs, which means every node and every edge in an RDF graph can be globally and unambiguously identified. This is critical. When you want to say something about a lemon on the Semantic Web, you need a URI that identifies the lemon—not a web page *about* lemons. The URI identifies the thing, not the document describing the thing.

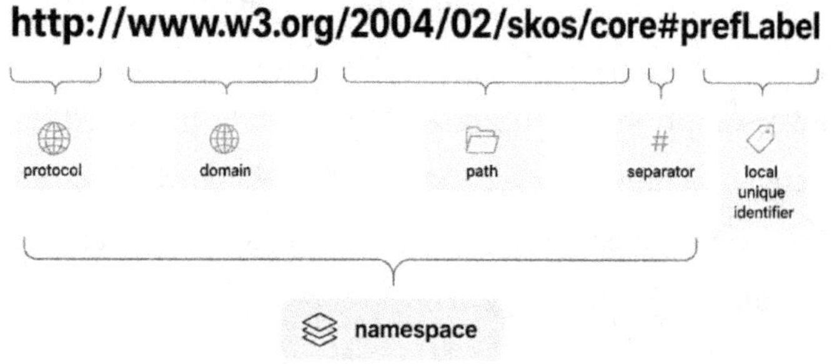


Figure 73: SKOS URI for prefLabel.

Berners-Lee proposed four Linked Data principles that flow from this design, turning isolated datasets into a connected web of knowledge:

1. Use URIs as names for things.
2. Use HTTP URIs so that people can look up those names.
3. When someone looks up a URI, provide useful information, using the standards (RDF*, SPARQL to query).
4. Include links to other URIs so that they can discover more things.

RDF can be serialized in multiple formats, including RDF/XML, Turtle, N-Triples, JSON-LD, and others. These are surface syntax. A triple expressed in Turtle is the same triple in JSON-LD and is the same statement, but it is rendered differently. Choosing between formats is an implementation decision.

RDF itself is not an ontology. It is the grammar in which ontologies and many other things can be expressed. RDF makes no claims about what exists. It provides a universal structure for making statements.

## RDFS is the first step toward semantics

RDF Schema (RDFS) adds a vocabulary for describing the structure of RDF data. You can define classes of resources with RDFs. With rdfs:Class, you can state that one class is a subclass of another. With rdfs:subClassOf, you can declare domains and ranges for properties. And with rdfs:subPropertyOf, you can establish property hierarchies.

An RDFS-aware processor can make real inferences. If you state that ex:Person is a subclass of ex:Agent, and that ex:Alice is of type ex:Person, the processor infers that ex:Alice is also of type ex:Agent. That is a genuine inference—a new fact derived from a formal model. The semantic commitment is there and can be reasoned over, which qualifies the representation as ontological and semantic. But more to come on those qualifiers later.

RDFS has limitations. It cannot express that two classes are disjoint, that a property is transitive, or define cardinality constraints. For many domains, these limitations require stricter constraints. For many others, RDFS provides exactly the level of expressiveness the domain requires.

## RDFa: The embedding syntax

You don't hear much about RDFa these days. RDFa is the specification most likely to be confused with the other two, thanks to the shared prefix. RDFa is not a data model or a schema language. It is an embedding syntax—a way to annotate HTML documents with structured data. When you see attributes like vocab, typeOf, and property in HTML tags, that is RDFa. It is a delivery mechanism for getting structured data into web pages. We see RDFa used with Schema.org, an ontology designed primarily for web discovery and SEO but now used for so much more than the web.

## OWL: Logical machinery

The Web Ontology Language (OWL) is where the Semantic Web stack reaches its full expressive power for domain modeling. OWL is grounded in description logics—decidable fragments of first-order logic, designed to balance expressiveness against computational tractability.

An OWL ontology is a formal data model that represents knowledge explicitly through a set of strict logical axioms and facts. It defines a domain using three main components:

- **Classes:** Categories representing sets of individuals (instances) that share common characteristics.
- **Object properties:** Relationships that link individuals to other individuals or classes.
- **Datatype properties:** Relationships that link individuals or classes to literal data values, like text strings or numbers.

Unlike simpler vocabularies, an OWL ontology allows for comprehensive semantic modeling. Enforcing specific constraints and rules enables systems to process data and automatically detect logical inconsistencies.

OWL provides capabilities that RDFS cannot. Class constructors let you define new classes through logical operations, such as intersections, unions, and complements. Property characteristics let you declare that a relationship is transitive, symmetric, or functional. Cardinality constraints specify how many values a property can or must have. Disjointness axioms declare that two classes cannot overlap.

These capabilities are essential for domains that need them: healthcare, legal systems, complex supply chains, and scientific research. OWL enables automated reasoning, inconsistency detection, and classification at a level of rigor that nothing else in the stack can match.

But OWL is a tool for building ontologies. It is not what *makes* something an ontology. OWL comes in several profiles, such as OWL EL, OWL QL, OWL RL, and OWL DL, each with different trade-offs.

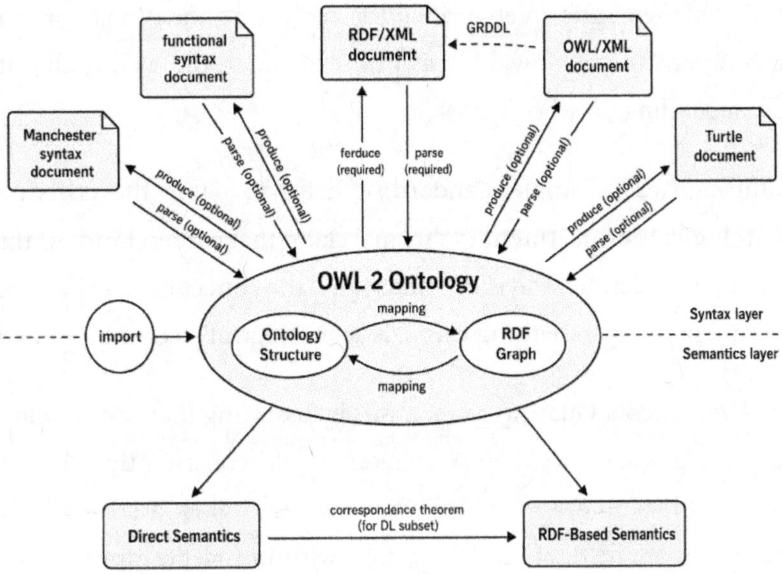


Figure 74: The structure of OWL 2.

| Profile | Focus | Typical Use Case | Complexity |
|---|---|---|---|
| EL | Large class hierarchies | Medical terminologies (SNOMED) | Polynomial-time |
| QL | Large instance data | Data integration, SQL access | $AC^0$ (LOGSPACE) |
| RL | Efficient rule reasoning | Rule engines, RDF data | Polynomial-time |
| DL | Maximum expressivity | Complex, small-med domains | High (N2EXPTIME) |

Figure 75: Key differences.

The existence of these profiles is a lesson in engineering pragmatism: No single level of expressiveness serves all contexts.

---

## Are these ontologies?

This is where things get interesting—and where the unsettled terminology becomes most visible.

We've established that Semantic Web principles are the foundations for ontologies and the standards that accompany them. Now, let's visit how the question "Is this an ontology?" produces different answers, depending on who you ask.

Before walking through each sample standard, it helps to name the criterion we are actually evaluating. An **ontological commitment** is a formal claim that certain kinds of things exist and that they relate to each other in defined ways. In philosophy, the concept traces back through Quine and Aristotle—when a theory says something exists, it is ontologically committed to that thing.

In information science, Nicola Guarino refined this by asserting that "an ontological commitment is an agreement to use a shared vocabulary coherently and consistently, where the terms refer to defined categories of things in a domain." This is the test. When a standard defines classes and asserts that those classes are distinct kinds of things with formal relationships between them, it is making ontological commitments. It is saying: *This is what exists here, and this is how it is organized.* The question for each standard below is not whether it uses OWL syntax. We are looking for ontological commitment—whether it commits to describing a model of what exists, using Semantic Web principles.

Let's look at some common standard vocabularies and ontologies expressed in RDF. By the end of this exercise, we will have a better idea of what makes for an ontology, while gaining visibility into a nice variety of commonly used standards.

---

## Semantic standards and ontological commitment

**Dublin Core** (prefix DC) has evolved into three distinct layers, all available at a single reference point. The Dublin Core Element Set (DCES) is the original 15 metadata elements, published as a recognized standard in 1998, as a flat, minimal vocabulary for resource discovery.

**Qualified Dublin Core**, introduced in 2000, extends that flat set with refinements. For example, the element DC:date extended coverage with the qualifiers dateCreated, dateIssued, and dateModified. Coverage splits into Spatial and Temporal, while DC:relation branched into hasPart, isVersionOf, replaces, and a dozen others.

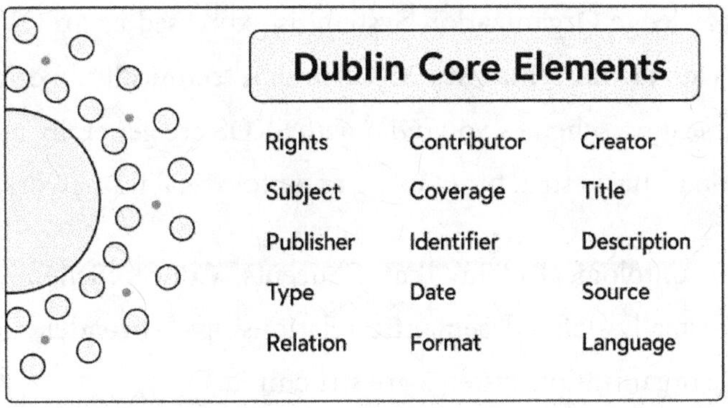


Figure 76: The 15 Dublin Core elements.

The guiding principle is the "Dumb-Down Rule," which states that any application that does not understand a qualifier can ignore it and still treat the value as the broader element. Qualified Dublin Core also added three elements not in the original 15—audience, provenance, and rightsHolder (not pictured)—to serve communities whose metadata needs had outgrown the base set.

The **DCMI Metadata Terms** redefined the full vocabulary in 2008—the original 15 elements plus the qualified refinements—as RDF properties under the namespace http://purl.org/dc/terms/, following Semantic Web principles and standards. DCMI Metadata Terms also introduced more than 20 **RDF classes**: agent, agentClass, licenseDocument, jurisdiction, linguisticSystem, periodOfTime, physicalResource, provenanceStatement, standard, and others—that serve as formal domains and ranges for the properties. These classes are defined using rdfs:Class and rdfs:subClassOf, which means Dublin Core is no longer a flat metadata vocabulary. It has class hierarchies, subproperty relationships, and domain and range constraints.

Under a strict OWL-only definition, Dublin Core is not an ontology. But through the lens of what Dublin Core commits to—that Agents and Locations and Jurisdictions are distinct kinds of things, that the relationship between a licenseDocument and a rightsStatement is a formal subclass relationship—it is making genuine ontological claims about the structure of the resource description domain.

*Dublin Core makes ontological commitments*
*while also adhering to Semantic Web standards.*

**SKOS**, the Simple Knowledge Organization System, is expressed as an OWL ontology. It defines classes and properties with formal semantics. SKOS itself is technically an ontology. But the thesauri, taxonomies, and classification schemes you *build with* SKOS are generally not ontologies—they are knowledge organization artifacts structured using an ontological framework.

**SKOS** commits to the ontological claim that Concepts, ConceptSchemes, and Collections are distinct classes with formally defined semantic relationships—broader, narrower, related—that govern how knowledge organization systems are structured.

---

*SKOS makes ontological commitments and adheres to Semantic Web standards.*

---

**FOAF** (Friend of a Friend) is technically expressed as an OWL ontology. It defines classes and properties with formal domain and range constraints. It makes substantive claims about social reality—that persons and organizations are distinct kinds of agents, and that online identity is connected to but distinct from the person. FOAF qualifies as a lightweight but genuine ontology.

**FOAF Core**

- Agent
  - Person
  - name
  - title
  - img
  - depiction (depicts)
  - familyName
  - givenName
  - knows
  - based_near
  - age
  - made (maker)
  - primaryTopic (primaryTopicOf)
- Project
  - Organization
  - Group
  - member
- Document
- Image

**Social Web**

- nick
- mbox
- homepage
- weblog
- openid
- jabberID
- mbox_sha1sum
- interest
- topic_interest
- topic (page)
- workplaceHomepage
- workInfoHomepage
- schoolHomepage
- publications
- currentProject
- pastProject
- account
- OnlineAccount
- accountName
- accountServiceHomepage
- PersonalProfileDocument
- tipjar
- sha1
- thumbnail
- logo

Figure 77: Friend of a Friend (FOAF) Ontology.

**FOAF** commits to the ontological claim that Persons and Organizations are distinct kinds of Agents, that online accounts are ontologically connected to but distinct from the people who hold them, and that social relationships like "knows" have formal domains and ranges.

*FOAF makes ontological commitments while following Semantic Web standards.*

**PROV-O**, the Provenance Ontology, is unambiguously an ontology, and no framework disagrees. It provides a formal model for representing who created something, how it was derived, and what activities produced it. It is organized around three core classes—Entity, Activity, and Agent—with disjointness axioms, qualified patterns, and formal constraints. PROV-O matters because provenance is foundational to trust. In an era of AI-generated content and complex data pipelines, the ability to formally represent where something came from is an infrastructure requirement.

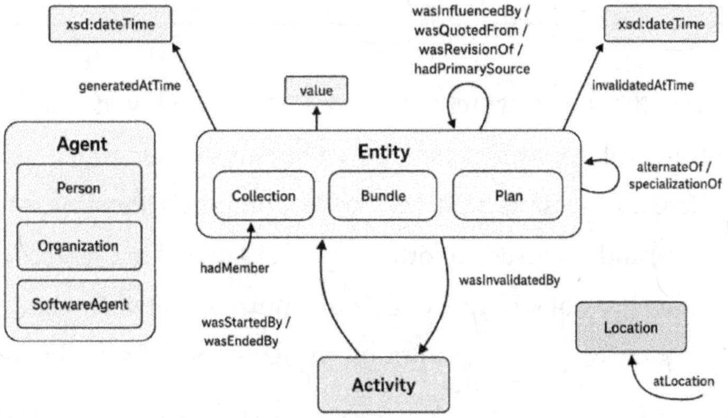


Figure 78: Snapshot from PROV-O.

**PROV-O** commits to the ontological claim that the provenance universe consists of exactly three disjoint core classes—Entities, Activities, and Agents—and that derivation, generation, and attribution are formally constrained relationships among them, with qualified patterns that support full logical reasoning.

*PROV-O makes ontological commitments and follows Semantic Web standards.*

**DCAT**, the Data Catalog Vocabulary, sits on the threshold, and many ontologists think it is not an ontology. DCAT defines classes and properties with domain and range constraints, but lacks disjointness axioms, cardinality constraints, and class constructors. DCAT is more structured than Dublin Core and less formal than PROV-O. When DCAT distinguishes a Dataset from a Distribution, it echoes the FRBR model in library science—the distinction between abstract works and physical manifestations.

These commitments matter because they formalize a model for the data publishing domain, enabling catalogs from different organizations—governments, research institutions, international bodies—to interoperate without custom integration work. DCAT describes datasets and asserts a shared understanding of what a dataset *is* and how it relates to its distributions, services, and catalog records— and that assertion is an ontological one.

---

*DCAT makes ontological commitments while adhering to Semantic Web standards.*

---

**Schema.org** is arguably the most widely deployed structured vocabulary on the web. Does Schema.org make ontological commitments? Unambiguously, yes—at a scale that dwarfs most formal ontologies. Schema.org asserts that the world comprises Persons, Organizations, Events, Products, Creative Works, and hundreds of other types, organized in hierarchical relationships. But it does not enforce cardinality constraints, define disjointness between classes, or support formal inference. Schema.org is ontologically ambitious in scope and formally modest in expression. Ramzee

Nonetheless, **Schema.org** commits to the ontological claim that the world contains Persons, Organizations, Events, Products, Creative Works, and hundreds of other types, organized in hierarchical subclass relationships, making it one of the broadest ontological commitments on the web, even without formal inference support.

---

*Schema.org asserts ontological commitment*
*while following Semantic Web standards.*

---

These standards illuminate a real question in the field: ***Where does vocabulary end and ontology begin?***

We can assume that if a model makes ontological commitments and follows Semantic Web standards, then it is an ontology. Let's build on this bold assertion by looking at ontologies through the lens of The Ontology Spectrum and the Ontology Pipeline to better understand what makes an ontology an ontology.

---

## The spectrum and the pipeline

### *The Ontology Spectrum*

The Ontology Spectrum is a framework that originated from a 1999 AAAI panel on ontologies. The panelists, Gruninger, Lehman, McGuinness, Uschold, and Welty, found that they encountered many forms of specifications that different people called ontologies.

Deborah McGuinness refined the discussion into a visual continuum, published in her 2003 chapter "Ontologies Come of Age," that maps knowledge structures along a gradient of semantic expressiveness. The spectrum ranges from controlled vocabularies and glossaries at the lightweight end, through thesauri and informal hierarchies, to strict subclass hierarchies with properties and value restrictions, and finally to richly axiomatized logical models at the heavyweight end.

The Ontology Spectrum recognizes that meaning is not binary; something does not jump from "no semantics" to "full semantics" in a single step. A catalog of terms carries some meaning. A thesaurus with synonym relationships carries more. A strict hierarchy with property constraints carries more still. A formally axiomatized model with disjointness, inverse relationships, and first-order logic carries the most.

But here is the detail that gets lost almost every time the Spectrum is cited— McGuinness drew a line on it. She did not say everything on the continuum is an ontology. She defined explicit minimum criteria for what she called a "simple ontology"—a finite controlled vocabulary, an unambiguous interpretation of classes and their relationships, and strict hierarchical subclass relationships.

Catalogs, glossaries, thesauri, and informal hierarchies like Yahoo's category tree all sit to the *left* of that line. They are on the spectrum. They are not ontologies, even by the spectrum's own terms.

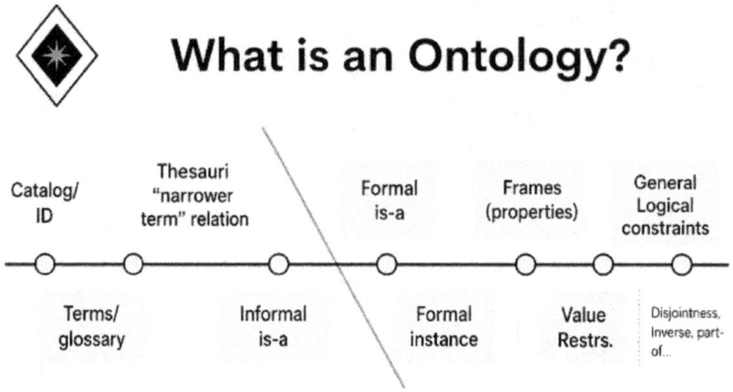


Figure 79: Deborah McGuinness's original Ontology Spectrum, 2003.

McGuinness then distinguished features that are typical but not mandatory —properties, instances, value restrictions—from features that are desirable but not mandatory: disjointness axioms, arbitrary logical relationships, inverse, and part-whole relationships. The spectrum is a tool for understanding where a given knowledge structure sits and what capabilities it provides.

The Ontology Spectrum becomes problematic not in what McGuinness describes, but in how it has been applied. Because the Spectrum shows a *continuum*, it has been misread as implying that everything on the continuum is an ontology of varying weight. That reading strips the framework of its own boundary. It is equivalent to citing a maturity model and claiming that every team at level one is already doing what the model measures.

The Ontology Spectrum was designed to classify and locate. It was not designed to flatten meaningful distinctions between engineering stages that require fundamentally different skills, tools, and standards.

## *The Ontology Pipeline*

The Ontology Pipeline—a methodology developed through years of semantic engineering practice—asks a different question. The spectrum asks, "Where does this artifact sit?" The Pipeline asks, "How do you build from where you are to where you need to be?"

The Ontology Pipeline describes the systematic process of constructing knowledge infrastructure through defined stages: controlled vocabularies, metadata schemas, taxonomies, thesauri, ontologies (*where we are now*), and knowledge graphs. Each stage produces a distinct deliverable with its own structure, standards, and engineering value.

The Pipeline insists on calling each stage by its own name, because the current moment in industry discourse has a specific pathology. "Ontology" is being applied indiscriminately to flat keyword lists, product category trees, JSON config files, and any structured artifact dressed up for a pitch deck.

If a SKOS taxonomy is already an ontology (just a lightweight one), an organization that has built a taxonomy may believe it has "done" ontology work and can proceed to building AI systems that require formally modeled domain knowledge. It cannot. A taxonomy categorizes. An ontology—whether expressed in RDFS and/or OWL—models the semantic structure of a domain: what exists, how things relate, and what those relationships mean.

If the Pipeline stages are clearly named, the gap is visible and can be planned for. If everything is an ontology of some weight, the gap disappears in the language, even though it persists in the infrastructure—and that invisible gap is where projects fail. The spectrum tells you where you are. The Pipeline tells you how to build. We are interested in both building and semantic expressivity.

---

## The scenario

Special Solutions builds enterprise infrastructure and automation software. It has 1,100 employees across data, engineering, operations, legal, product, human resources (HR), finance, and a growing AI systems team. Like most companies of this size, it has accumulated a thicket of workflows over the years of growth. Some are documented in wikis, some live only in the institutional memory of long-tenured employees, and, increasingly, some are executed, partially or entirely, by AI agents and automated pipelines.

This last point is important. Special Solutions' workflows now involve three categories of actors: human specialists who make judgment calls and approvals, AI agents that perform analysis, classification, and drafting tasks, and automated software pipelines that handle deterministic execution. These three types have very different accountability structures, delegation rules, and audit requirements. The ontology model will need to account for the three workflow types, making the distinctions clear. Leadership wants to make this process knowledge queryable. They want to answer questions like:

- What are all the steps in the release process, and in what order do they execute?
- Who—or what—is responsible for approving a production deployment?
- Which steps in each workflow are executed by AI agents, and which require a human decision?
- What artifacts does the design review produce, and what systems or agents consume them downstream?
- Which workflows haven't been reviewed or updated in 12 months?
- What happens when the VP of Engineering is unavailable during an escalation—and can an AI agent act in a delegation chain?
- Which workflows involve both engineering and legal, and at what steps do they intersect?
- What datasets does the quarterly business review consume, and which AI agents processed them?

Beyond these business requirements, these questions can be part of the formal specifications of the ontology. Understanding ***what*** we want our ontology to answer takes us into the first and most important design discipline in ontology engineering.

---

## Ontology design heuristics

### *Competency questions: The ontology's contract*

A competency question (CQ) is a natural-language question that the ontology, when combined with real instance data, must be able to answer. The concept was formalized by Gruninger and Fox in 1995, and it remains the most practical tool in ontology engineering, with reasons worth expanding upon and understanding.

First, competency questions define ***scope.*** An ontology is not a database schema that tries to capture everything about a domain. It is a model that represents aspects of the domain and is expected to answer a specific set of questions.

Everything the ontology needs to model is implied by its competency questions. And, of equal importance, everything the ontology ***does not*** need to model is also defined by competency questions. Explicit exclusions prevent scope creep. So, when you decide that your workflow ontology does not need to answer, "What is the salary band of the person filling the Release Manager role?", you have made a principled modeling decision that eliminates an entire concern from the design. Competency questions define the scope of an ontology—what to include and what not to include.

Second, competency questions are also *acceptance criteria*. When the ontology can answer every question in its competency set, it is complete for its intended scope. This is the ontological equivalent of a passing test suite. When a question fails—when the SPARQL query returns nothing or returns the wrong thing—you have found a gap in the model. The question tells you where to dig and where the ontology model falls short of serving its design and purpose.

Third, competency questions are a *communication tool*. Domain experts who cannot read RDF or SPARQL can engage with and evaluate competency questions to ensure that the objectives and design of the knowledge graph are sufficient for domain coverage. The question set becomes the shared contract between those who understand the domain and those who formalize it. Before writing a single triple, you should be able to sit down with a domain expert and walk through every question, getting confirmation that, yes, these are the things the organization needs to know about its own processes.

Now, look at the Special Solutions leadership questions using the CQ lens. "Which steps in a given workflow are executed by AI agents, and which require a human decision?" immediately implies that the model must distinguish among human agents, AI agents, and software systems—not just as different individuals, but as different *classes* with different behavioral and accountability rules. "Can an AI agent act in a delegation chain?" implies that delegation must be modeled at the level of roles, not persons, and that the model must be able to express constraints on which kinds of agents can fill which roles. None of this would have been obvious from an informal requirements document.

---

*The CQs surface what questions the ontology must answer*
*before a single modeling decision is made.*

---

This is the right order of operations: questions first, model second. Every class, property, and axiom defined must trace back to at least one competency question it helps answer. If you cannot point to a question that justifies a modeling decision, that decision is likely unnecessary—and unnecessary complexity in an ontology is not neutral. It accumulates as technical debt, making the model harder to reason about, explain, and maintain.

---

*We will adopt and adapt the leadership questions as our competency questions,*
*which naturally shapes requirements,*
*telling us what we must model for our ontology.*

---

## *Design heuristics principles*

Competency questions define *what* to model, while design heuristics guide you through *how* to model. These are design principles derived from decades of ontology engineering practice that exist as shared ontology design best practices.

### Heuristic 1: Reuse before you invent

Every term you define from scratch is a term the Semantic Web does not already know about. It can create an island. Every term you borrow from an existing standard is a bridge to every other system that uses that standard. Before defining any class or property, search the existing ontology landscape, particularly the W3C standards, which include ontologies such as PROV-O, FOAF, Dublin Core, DCAT, SKOS, Schema.org, and domain-specific registries such as Linked Open Vocabularies, for terms that meet your needs.

---

*The goal of ontology engineering is not to produce a comprehensive custom vocabulary. It is to define the minimal set of custom terms needed to connect existing standards to your specific domain.*
*A well-designed domain ontology is mostly assembly.*

---

**Heuristic 2: Separate roles from agents**

This is the most violated heuristic in organizational ontologies, and violating it reliably breaks the model within months of deployment. "Release Manager" is a role—a function, a set of responsibilities, a position in a process. "Maria Gonzalez" is an agent, a person who fills that role right now. If you conflate these two things by making a person directly responsible for a workflow step, you have built a model that must be updated every time someone changes jobs, goes on leave, or leaves the company. Separate them.

*Model steps as pointing to roles; model roles as pointing to agents. When personnel change, you update the role-to-agent binding—one triple. You never touch the workflow structure.*

This heuristic extends naturally to AI agents. A "Risk Analysis Agent" is a role, a function that requires an automated risk assessment capability. Which specific AI system fills that role today, which model version it runs, and when it was last updated are all properties of the agent-role binding, not of the workflow step. This separation allows the ontology to survive the rapid churn of AI system deployments without requiring constant restructuring of the process model itself.

**Heuristic 3: Use SKOS for classification, RDFS/OWL for commitment**

This distinction trips up nearly every ontology engineer at some point in their career. When you make statements in RDFS—declaring a class, asserting a subclass relationship, or specifying the domain and range of a property—you are making *commitments*. These are formal claims about the structure of a domain that carry logical consequences. When you write rdfs:subClassOf, you are asserting that every instance of the subclass is also an instance of the parent class or superclass. When you declare rdfs:domain on a property, you are asserting that anything that appears as the subject of that property *must* belong to that class.

*Ontological commitments are not cosmetic.*
*A reasoner, or even a simple RDFS inference engine, will act on commitments and produce new inferences. Incorrect commitments produce incorrect inferences.*

SKOS concepts, by contrast, are organizational—they provide labels, hierarchies, and associative relationships for human navigation and controlled-vocabulary classification, and they can also be used for inference. A skos:broader relationship between two concepts means that instances of the narrower concept inherit characteristics from the broader one. It is a signal for browsing, indexing, and logical assertion.

*Use SKOS for classifying things—workflow categories, artifact types, capability tags—where overlapping or dual classification is legitimate.*
*Use RDFS classes and properties for things where membership and structure have logical consequences that should flow automatically from your ontology.*

**Heuristic 4: Domain and range are inferential, not restrictive**

This is one of the most common sources of unexpected reasoning behavior when building with RDFS—and the behavior carries forward unchanged into OWL, which simply adds more powerful machinery on top of the same foundation.

In RDFS, rdfs:domain and rdfs:range are not constraints. They are *inference rules.* When you declare that the domain of assignedRole is workflowStep, you are not preventing other things from using assignedRole. You are making a formal commitment—in the RDFS sense—that *if something uses* assignedRole, *it must be a* workflowStep. The inference engine does not check the type of the subject before allowing the triple to exist. The engine reads the triple and infers the type.

This is a priority in domain ontology design before introducing any OWL axioms. If you attach assignedRoleTo an approvalGate—which you intend to do—the engine will not flag an error. It will infer that approvalGate is a workflowStep. In a well-modeled domain ontology, that inference is correct because approvalGate is already declared to be a subclass of workflowStep. The domain declaration and the subclass hierarchy agree, and the inference is sound.

But if you accidentally attach assignedRole to a workflowArtifact, the engine will infer that the artifact is a workflowStep; it will not flag an error. The modeling mistake disappears silently into a new, incorrect type assertion. When OWL reasoning is later applied, that spurious type assertion can propagate further, corrupting downstream inferences in ways that are difficult to trace back to their source.

This is how modeling errors hide in domain ontologies. The relation looks legitimate, but the inferences are incorrect. To manage these types of errors, populate a test ABox early, and run an RDFS-aware inference engine over it before you ever introduce OWL axioms. The errors that surface at the RDFS level are the cheapest to fix.

**Heuristic 5: Model for the open world**

RDF operates under the open world assumption. If a fact is not present in your dataset, the system does not treat its absence as evidence that it is false. It treats it as unknown. This shapes every structural decision you make in both RDFS and the minimal OWL vocabulary we are using here.

RDFS gives you the backbone: classes, subclass hierarchies, and property declarations with domain and range. What it does not give you is any mechanism for saying that something is *wrong* when a class instance is missing a property.

The bare-minimum OWL vocabulary we are working with adds a small number of precisely scoped commitments on top of that RDFS foundation.

- owl:ObjectProperty and owl:DatatypeProperty clarify the nature of your property relations—whether a property links a resource to another resource, or to a literal value.
- owl:FunctionalProperty restricts a property so that a given resource can have at most one value for it.
- owl:InverseOf declares that two properties are the same relationship in opposite directions.
- owl:disjointWith declares that two classes are mutually exclusive—that nothing can simultaneously be a member of both.

These are the commitments available to us, and none of them introduces cardinality. There is no mechanism here to assert that a :workflow *must* have at least one :hasStep. That kind of minimum-count restriction belongs to OWL's fuller axiom set, which we are deliberately not using.

*The heuristic, then, is to add a structural commitment only if a violation of that commitment would represent a real logical error in your domain.*

owl:disjointWith is appropriate when something genuinely cannot be two things at once. owl:FunctionalProperty is appropriate when a resource genuinely can have only one value for a property at a time.

We care about this because these are ontological claims, not data quality rules. We are modeling what exists and how things relate to each other. As in the natural world, relationships have constraints that manifest as rules for logical reasoning and inference.

**Heuristic 6: Document as you build, not after**

Documentation is a design discipline. Every ontology must have it, and the time to write it is when you are making the modeling decision—not when the ontology is finished, and certainly not when someone else is trying to use it.

An undocumented class is an ambiguous class. "Agent" means something different in FOAF, in PROV-O, in insurance contracts, and in AI systems. Without an explicit rdfs:comment that defines what :AIAgent means in *this* ontology—what it includes, what it excludes, how it differs from prov:SoftwareAgent and foaf:Agent—the term will be misread by every engineer and possibly machine who encounters it. Misinterpretation in an ontology propagates as semantic errors throughout every downstream system that consumes the data.

Use rdfs:label to give the class its canonical human-readable name. Use rdfs:comment to write the definition. Definitions include what the class covers, what it excludes, and where it sits relative to any adjacent terms in external vocabularies you are aligning against.

My disciplined approach to design documentation is simple:

- Write the label and the definition before writing the axioms.
- If you cannot write a clear definition, you do not yet understand the concept well enough to model it.

Difficulty writing the comment is diagnostic—it tells you that the class boundary is still unclear in your own thinking, and that an axiom written now will be encoding confusion rather than knowledge.

## The three-box architecture as design process

**The CBox comes first**, which surprises most people who expect to start with classes and properties. The CBox is the administrative and governance layer. These are the ontology declarations, metadata, namespaces, license, version information, documentation conventions, and controlled vocabularies you will use to classify things.

Building the CBox first forces two important disciplines. It forces you to commit to a namespace URI that you actually control and maintain, preventing the most common governance failure in ontology engineering—URIs that resolve to nothing. And it forces you to think about documentation standards before you start building the model, which means documentation is woven in from the beginning rather than retrofitted at the end.

**The TBox comes second,** where we model the classes. Within the TBox, we build the class hierarchy and classes before the constraints, properties, and instances. The class hierarchy tells you what things *are*, while the properties tell you how things *relate*.

The constraints describe what combinations are logically required or forbidden. Getting this order right prevents a common mistake: engineers add constraints before they have established the full hierarchy, and then discover that a constraint they added early on conflicts with a subclass relationship they realize they need later.

**The ABox comes third,** not last—it serves as a design validation step. Before deploying an ontology, build a representative set of ABox instances that exercises every class, every property, and every constraint available in the TBox. Load this test ABox into a reasoner alongside the TBox, and check two things: first, that the reasoner produces no inconsistency—no class has been made empty and no individual simultaneously satisfies two disjoint classes. Second, ensure that the reasoner produces the *expected* inferences—subclass relationships should trigger the right inheritance. Validate that every transitive property closes correctly and that every functional property enforces uniqueness.

If the reasoner does not represent the intended properties, relations, and constraints, you have found either a modeling error or an implicit assumption you did not realize you were making. Either way, fixing it now is dramatically cheaper than fixing it after the ontology is in production.

These three disciplines—competency questions for scope, design heuristics for quality, and the three-box sequence for process—are the basics of ontology design and engineering.

Soon, we will walk through all three disciplines applied to a real problem. For now, we will establish the ontology design heuristics, our use of OWL, and the CBox or SKOS-controlled vocabulary.

---

## Building our workflow ontology framework

Before the first triple, we need to be clear about the utility of OWL in our ontology. OWL is the framing (not the structure) in this exercise. Think of it as the steel frame of a building. It holds everything in place and gives the whole thing integrity, but it is not the walls, the rooms, or the plumbing. That work is done by RDFS and the open standards we borrow.

RDFS lets you define classes, properties, subclass hierarchies, domain and range constraints, and human-readable labels and comments. That is most of what an ontology needs. OWL will add a specific and limited set of things on top.

First, we have the formal declaration that a resource is an ontology (owl:Ontology). Next, we introduce the explicit distinction between object properties and datatype properties (owl:ObjectProperty, owl:DatatypeProperty).

We implement a small set of logical constraints with inverse relationships(owl:inverseOf) and functional properties (owl:FunctionalProperty).

We also express class disjointness (owl:disjointWith). We use exactly these things and nothing else.

Because we are using an OWL framework, you may wonder about the difference between owl:Class and rdfs:Class. They represent the same basic concept—a category of things—but owl:Class enables logical constraints on class membership. These logical constraints include disjointness declarations, property restrictions, and constructed classes. We use owl:Class throughout this ontology because we need a reasoner to enforce the disjointness between Roles and Agents and between AIAgents and HumanAgents. Without owl:Class, those disjointness declarations have no logical force.

### *Step 1: Competency questions*

Each competency question translates into a specific set of modeling needs. Working through this translation systematically is what makes the TBox coherent and purpose-built.

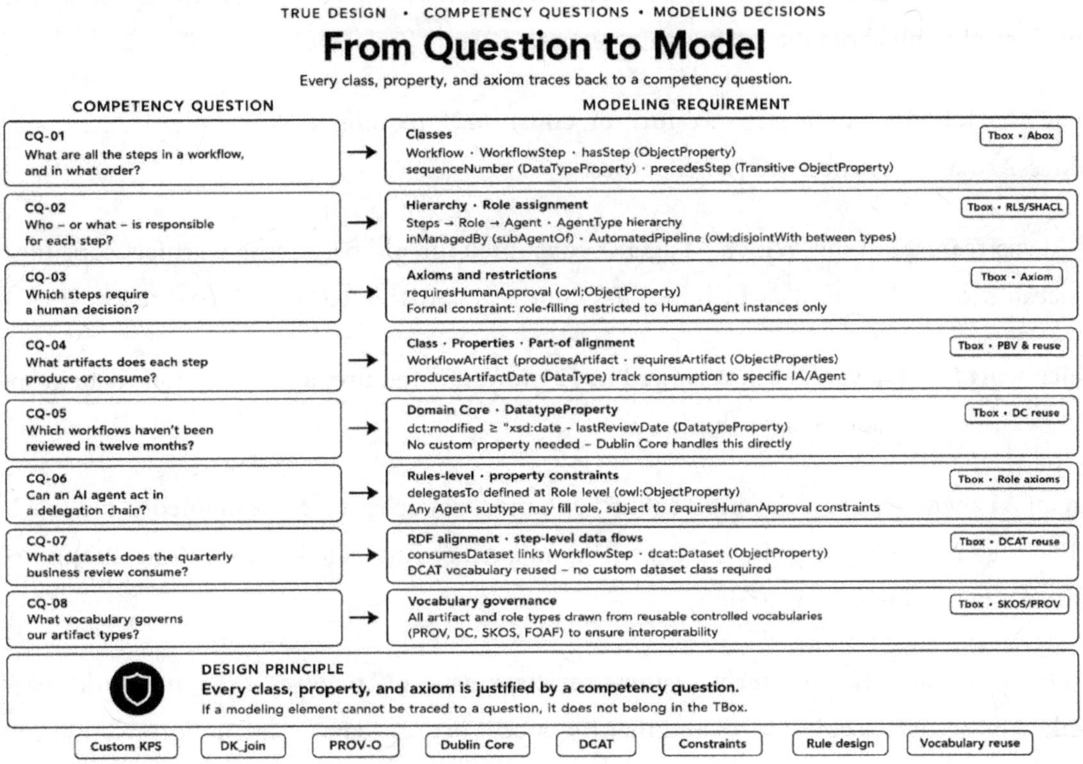


Figure 80: From question to model.

**"What are all the steps in a workflow, and in what order?"** requires a Workflow class, a WorkflowStep class, a hasStepRelationship between them, and a way to express sequence—either a sequence number property or a step-ordering relationship. We will use both a numeric sequence property for simple ordering queries and a transitive precedesStepProperty for full ordering-chain reasoning.

**"Who or what is responsible for each step?"** requires that we model responsibility through a role, not through a person or agent directly. This is heuristic two applied. Steps point to Roles; Roles point to Agents. We also need the model to distinguish among human agents, AI agents, and automated pipelines, because the accountability and audit rules differ for each. This implies an AgentType hierarchy.

**"Which steps require a human decision?"** requires that the model express a constraint on role-filling. Some roles can only be filled by human agents. This is an axiom, not just a property. It is a formal logical claim about the relationship between a class of roles and a class of agents.

**"What artifacts does each step produce or consume?"** requires a WorkflowArtifact class and producesArtifact / requiresArtifact properties.

The downstream question **"Which AI agents consumed them?"** requires that artifact consumption be traceable to specific agents, which PROV-O's prov:wasAttributedTo handles directly.

**"Which workflows haven't been reviewed in 12 months?"** requires a modification -date property. Dublin Core's dct:modified does this for us.

**"Can an AI agent act in a delegation chain?"** requires that delegatesTo be defined at the role level, and that the model allow any kind of agent—human, AI, or automated—to fill a role, subject to any requiresHumanApproval constraints.

**"What datasets does the quarterly business review consume?"** requires that some workflow steps be linked to dcat:Dataset instances and that the model express data-consumption relationships at the step level.

Every modeling decision traces back to one of these questions. Therefore, every class, property, and axiom is justified.

### *Step 2: Shopping for standards*

Survey what exists before defining a single custom term. The key sources for this domain are PROV-O, FOAF, Schema.org, Dublin Core, and DCAT.

**PROV-O**

PROV-O is the backbone of this ontology. It was designed precisely to model processes, activities, agents, and provenance. Its three core classes map directly onto our domain.

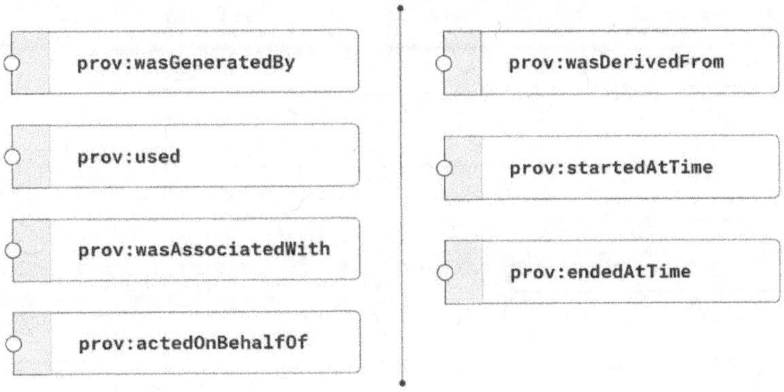


Figure 81: The PROV-O Ontology.

- prov:Plan is the superclass for Workflow. A plan is defined as "a set of actions intended by agents to achieve goals."
- prov:Activity is the superclass for WorkflowStep. Activity is defined as "something that occurs over a period and acts upon or with entities."
- prov:Entity is the superclass for WorkflowArtifact.

PROV-O also gives us a rich set of ready-made relationships. The elements selected from PROV-O cover most of what we need to express process execution and artifact lineage.

**FOAF—Friend of a Friend**

FOAF is a vocabulary for describing people, their relationships, and their online presence. This ontology provides the foundational agent and person classes that anchor the human side of the AgentType.

foaf:Agent is the superclass of anything capable of acting in the world. In FOAF's own definition, an agent is anything that can do things. We use it as the root of our agent hierarchy, from which :HumanAgent, :AIAgent, and :AutomatedPipeline all descend. Using foaf:Agent as the root means any system that understands FOAF can reason about our agent classes without custom knowledge of our vocabulary.

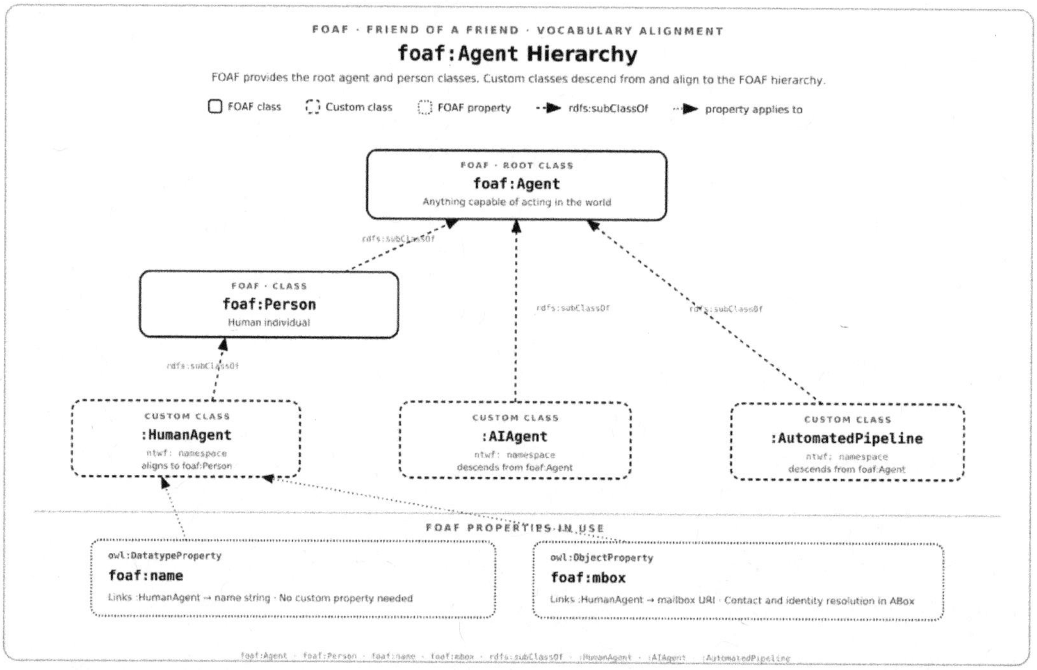


Figure 82: Agent hierarchy.

foaf:Person is a subclass of foaf:Agent representing a human individual. We align :HumanAgent with foaf:Person to inherit its semantics and connections to the broader Linked Data ecosystem, where foaf:Person is one of the most widely used class terms.

foaf:name is a datatype property linking an agent or person to a name string. We use it in preference to defining a custom name property. There is no reason to reinvent it.

foaf:mbox is a property linking a person to a mailbox URI. It is used for contact and identity resolution of human agents in the ABox.

### Schema.org

Schema.org is a collaborative vocabulary maintained by Google, Microsoft, Yahoo, and Yandex, designed for web-scale semantic markup. It provides organizational and software semantics that FOAF does not cover at the required level of specificity.

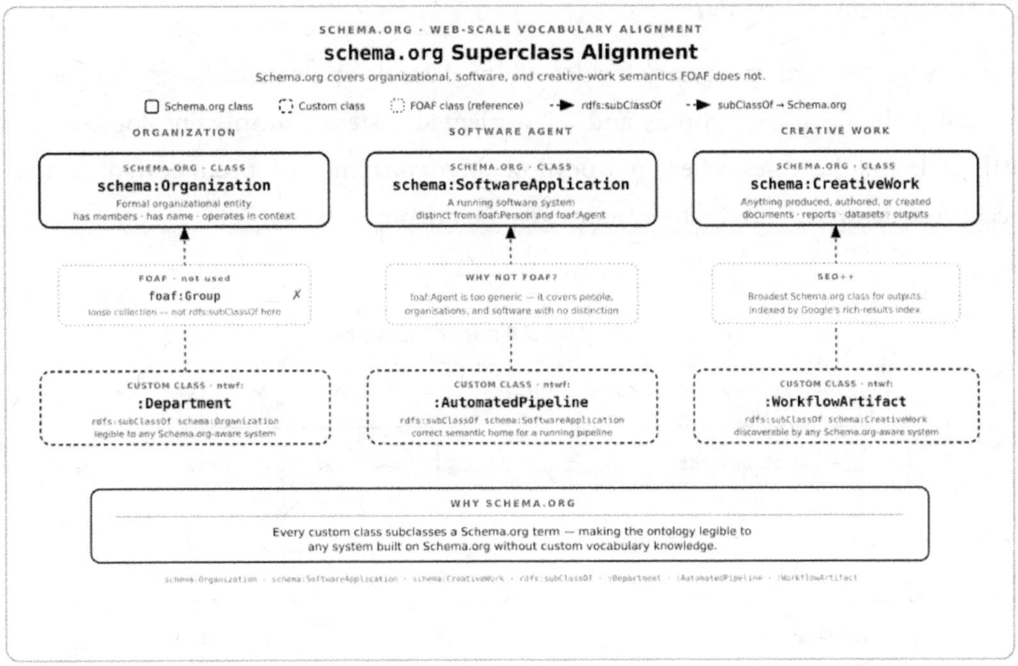


Figure 83: Superclass alignment.

schema:Organization is the superclass we use for departments. Where FOAF offers foaf:Group, a loose collection of agents, schema:Organization carries formal organizational semantics: it has members, a name, operates in a context, and is understood by every major search engine and data consumer built on Schema.org. We subclass it with our custom :Department class, meaning that every department in the workflow graph is automatically recognized as an organization by any Schema.org-aware system.

schema:SoftwareApplication is the superclass we align to automated pipeline agents. An automated pipeline is not a person and not a generic agent; it is a running software system. schema:SoftwareApplication gives that class its correct semantic home and distinguishes it cleanly from foaf:Person and foaf:Agent in systems that consume both vocabularies.

schema:CreativeWork is a complementary superclass for workflow artifacts. schema:CreativeWork is Schema.org's broadest class for anything that is produced, authored, or created, including documents, reports, datasets, and outputs of any kind. Aligning :WorkflowArtifact to it means our artifacts are discoverable and interpretable by any system built on Schema.org's vocabulary, including search engines that index structured data.

### DCAT—Data catalog vocabulary

DCAT is a W3C standard vocabulary for describing datasets and data catalogs, designed to enable interoperability between data portals and data-oriented systems. In this ontology, it handles the data-artifact layer: the cases where a workflow step consumes or produces something that is specifically a structured dataset rather than a general document or output.

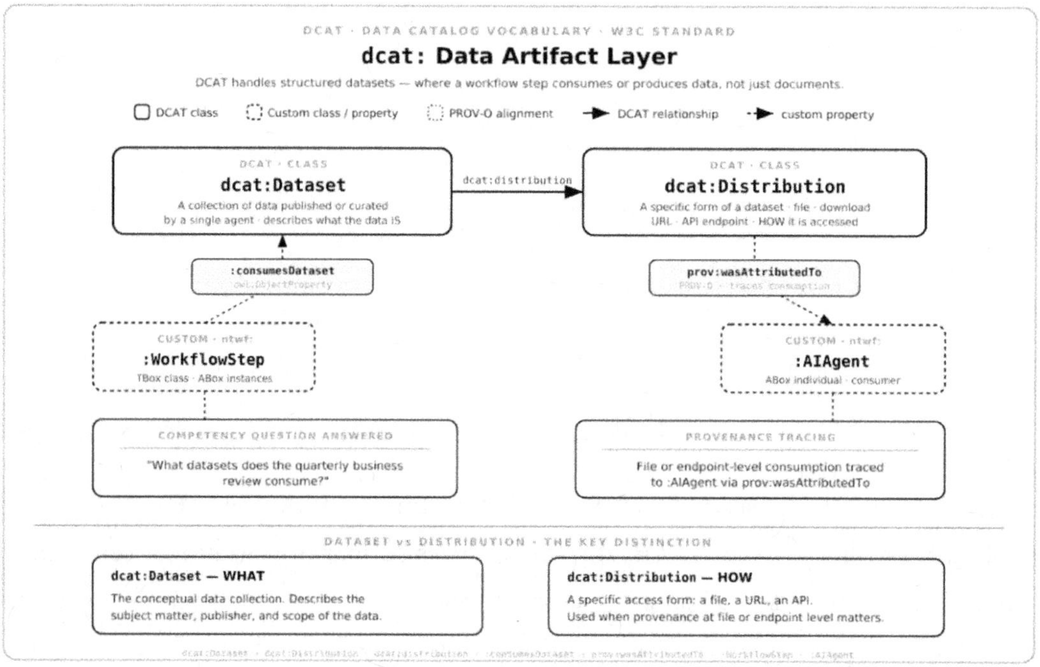


Figure 84: Data artifact layer.

dcat:Dataset represents a collection of data published or curated by a single agent. We link: WorkflowStepInstances to dcat:Dataset individuals via the consumesDataset property when a step takes a dataset as its input. This is what makes the competency question, "What datasets does the quarterly business review consume?" answerable without a custom dataset class.

dcat:Distribution represents a specific available form of a dataset: a particular file, a download URL, an API endpoint. Where dcat:Dataset describes what the data is, dcat:Distribution describes how it is accessed. We use it when provenance at the file or endpoint level is required, particularly for AI agent consumption tracing via prov:wasAttributedTo.

**Dublin Core—DCMI terms**

Dublin Core Metadata Initiative terms dct: and dcterms: provide the metadata layer for the ontology itself and for individual resources within it. Every descriptive annotation that is not about domain logic—titles, descriptions, dates, identifiers, rights, creators—comes from Dublin Core. We use the dcterms: namespace throughout, which is the fully defined terms namespace with formal range declarations, rather than the legacy dc: namespace.

- dct:title is a name given to the resource. It is used on the ontology declaration itself and on individual workflow and artifact instances that require a human-readable title.

- dct:description is an account of the resource. It is used in the ontology declaration and in class and individual annotations, where rdfs:comment addresses the technical definition and dct:description addresses the broader contextual purpose.

- dct:creator is the entity responsible for making the resource. It is used in the ontology declaration to identify the authoring team and in artifact individuals to identify the agent that produced them.

- dct:created is the date of creation of the resource, typed as xsd:date. It is used in the ontology declaration and for ABox individuals whose creation date is part of the audit record.

- dct:modified is the date on which the resource was most recently changed. This is what makes the competency question, "Which workflows haven't been reviewed in 12 months?" answerable. We attach dct:modified to workflow individuals and query against it. No custom property is needed.

- dct:identifier is an unambiguous reference to the resource within a given context. It is used when a workflow or artifact has an external identifier—a ticket number, a document ID, a system reference—that must be carried in the graph alongside the URI.

- dct:type is the nature or genre of the resource. It is used to classify artifact individuals by type—report, dataset, decision record—drawing from a controlled vocabulary in the CBox.

- dct:license is a legal document granting official permission to use the resource. It is used on the ontology declaration to assert the terms under which the ontology may be reused.

- dct:rights is a statement about the rights held in and over the resource. It is used for artifact individuals whose rights information is part of the administrative record, distinct from the ontology's license.

### The complete ontology

Below is our complete list of ontologies and vocabularies being used. When using other standard ontologies, note that we do not use every element of each ontology listed. We use only what we need to assemble a coherent and descriptive representation of our ontology design. For Special Solutions' custom ontology elements, we have created the namespace:

@prefix ntwf: <https://ontology.specialsolutions.example.com/workflow#>

| Ontology Standard | What it Provides |
|---|---|
| **PROV-O** | prov:Plan, prov:Activity, prov:Entity, prov:Agent, and 8 provenance properties |
| **FOAF** | foaf:Person, foaf:Agent, foaf:name, foaf:mbox, foaf:member |
| **Schema.org** | schema:Organization, schema:SoftwareApplication, schema:CreativeWork |
| **Dublin Core** | dct;title, dct:description, dct:creator, dct:created, dct:modified, dct:identifier, dct:type |
| **DCAT** | dcat:Dataset, dcat:Distribution, dcat:accessURL, dcat:mediaType |
| **Custom** | 8 classes, 12 object properties, 5 datatype properties |

Table 14: Ontology standards.

There will be eight classes, 12 object properties, and five data properties in the Special Solutions custom ontology design and build. The NTWF ontology will address gaps in coverage that open standard ontologies do not.

### Namespaces

Beyond the complete ontology, we also must represent the syntax and languages employed as namespaces. Before we write our RDF or define our ontology, we begin with a preamble listing the namespaces for everything we use. This is how we set the stage:

@prefix owl: http://www.w3.org/2002/07/owl# .

@prefix rdf: http://www.w3.org/1999/02/22-rdf-syntax-ns# .

```
@prefix owl:    <http://www.w3.org/2002/07/owl#> .
@prefix rdf:    <http://www.w3.org/1999/02/22-rdf-syntax-ns#> .
@prefix rdfs:   <http://www.w3.org/2000/01/rdf-schema#> .
@prefix xsd:    <http://www.w3.org/2001/XMLSchema#> .
@prefix dct:    <http://purl.org/dc/terms/> .
@prefix dcat:   <http://www.w3.org/ns/dcat#> .
@prefix prov:   <http://www.w3.org/ns/prov#> .
@prefix foaf:   <http://xmlns.com/foaf/0.1/> .
@prefix schema: <https://schema.org/> .
@prefix skos:   <http://www.w3.org/2004/02/skos/core#> .
@prefix ntwf:   <https://ontology.specialsolutions.example.com/workflow#> .
```

Table 15: Namespaces and prefixes

We are ready to consider what to do with our SKOS-controlled vocabulary now that we have our ontology design framework. How will the taxonomies or thesauri be referenced or integrated into the ontology, if at all?

## *Step 3: The CBox—concepts*

The CBox is not the ontology. It precedes it.

In the Ontology Pipeline framework, the CBox refers to the controlled vocabulary layer—the SKOS structures built during the earlier phases of the pipeline: the controlled vocabularies, taxonomies, and thesauri that establish the organizational categories, preferred labels, and hierarchies of a domain before any formal logical commitment is made. If you have followed the pipeline, this work is already done. The CBox is what you built before you were building an ontology.

The CBox brings clarity to the ontology and serves as the business vocabulary. skos:prefLabel and skos:altLabel establish the canonical human-readable names for concepts and their acceptable variants. Skos:definition and skos:scopeNote record what a concept means and where its boundaries lie. skos:notation provides machine-readable codes where needed. Together, these annotations do something the TBox cannot do alone—they make the vocabulary legible to the humans who will maintain it, query it, and extend it.

The CBox taxonomy also carries its own inferential weight, which is often under-appreciated. A skos:broader hierarchy is not a logical subsumption as it does not trigger the kind of inheritance reasoning that rdfs:subClassOf does. But SKOS does define a weak form of transitivity via skos:broaderTransitive and the associated closure rules.

A reasoner or SPARQL query that traverses skos:broaderTransitive will walk the full hierarchy upward from any concept, which is sufficient for many classification and navigation tasks without requiring a full OWL reasoner. This is the inference the CBox provides on its own terms: hierarchical reachability, not class membership.

**Integrating the CBox into the ontology**

The pipeline eventually forces the question, "Which SKOS concepts need to become ontological commitments, and which can remain organizational categories?"

Not all CBox concepts need to be represented in the ontology. Many concept categories—workflow status values, artifact type tags, capability labels—serve their purpose as SKOS concepts alone. They organize and filter; they do not need a reasoner to enforce membership rules or inheritance. Leave those in the CBox and reference them from the ontology via skos:inScheme or alignment properties.

But some CBox concepts do need to become TBox or ABox elements, and those crossings require ontology design decisions. The two mechanisms are distinct.

To promote a SKOS concept to a TBox class, you declare it as an owl:Class or rdfs:Class and carry its SKOS labels forward as RDFS annotations:

```
ntwf:ApprovalGate a owl:Class ;
 rdfs:subClassOf ntwf:WorkflowStep ;
 rdfs:label "Approval Gate"@en ;
 rdfs:comment "A workflow step that requires explicit authorization
 before the workflow may proceed."@en ;
 skos:exactMatch ntwf:concept/ApprovalGate .
```

The skos:exactMatch link preserves the relationship back to the CBox concept, keeping the vocabulary and the ontology aligned without merging them. The class now participates in RDFS inference—rdfs:subClassOf is active—while the SKOS concept continues to serve the controlled vocabulary layer.

To promote a SKOS concept to an ABox individual, you assert it as a named instance of a class:

```
ntwf:statusDraft a ntwf:WorkflowStatus ;
 rdfs:label "Draft"@en ;
 skos:prefLabel "Draft"@en ;
 skos:inScheme ntwf:WorkflowStatusScheme .
```

Here, the concept becomes a concrete individual in the graph, typed against a class in the TBox, while retaining its SKOS label structure for human readability and vocabulary management.

**The SKOS-XL route**

There is a second integration path that avoids splitting labels between two vocabularies: SKOS-XL. Where standard SKOS treats labels as plain literals —skos:prefLabel "Approval Gate"@en—SKOS-XL reifies labels as first-class resources using skosxl:Label. This means a label can carry its own properties, including rdfs:subClassOf alignments, OWL annotations, or provenance metadata.

```
ntwf:ApprovalGate skosxl:prefLabel ntwf:label/ApprovalGate .
ntwf:label/ApprovalGate a skosxl:Label ;
 skosxl:literalForm "Approval Gate"@en ;
 dct:created "2026-01-15"^^xsd:date ;
 rdfs:isDefinedBy ntwf:WorkflowOntology .
```

SKOS-XL is the right choice when labels need to be citable, versioned, or aligned to external class structures independently of the concept they name. It adds overhead—every label becomes a resource requiring its own URI and assertions—so use it selectively for terms where label provenance and alignment are critical, rather than across the entire vocabulary.

The practical rule for the Ontology Pipeline is this: Build the CBox first, keep it intact, and integrate into the TBox and ABox only what needs the inferential machinery of RDFS and OWL. The CBox does not disappear when the ontology is built. It becomes the vocabulary layer that sits atop it, providing the labels and classifications over which the ontology reasons.

It's important to cover the CBox at this point, as it has already been modeled and, in some cases, may already be in use. We want to think through how we will use our CBox during the design heuristics phase so we can plan how we will integrate our controlled vocabulary. Also, the controlled vocabulary, whether a taxonomy or a thesaurus, is well-defined, with ready-to-use concepts that may be allocated to the TBox and/or ABox.

Leveraging the work that has already been done, the CBox is a semantic artifact that is a critical consideration for translating the ontology into human-readable concepts with definitions. It is far more difficult to communicate with stakeholders and users without the CBox, and we need the CBox for the bridge it builds.

---

## The complete ontology design framework

The ontology design methodology presented here—competency questions for scope, design heuristics for quality, three-box sequencing for process—produces something specific and valuable: a model where every element is *justified*, every constraint is *intentional*, and every borrowed term is a *bridge* to a larger ecosystem.

The competency questions are what keep the model honest. Every class and property traces back to a question it helps answer. Everything else has been left out. An ontology built without this discipline will grow until it collapses under its own weight or becomes so general that it answers nothing specific well.

The design heuristics are what keep the model clean. Separating roles from agents means the workflow structure survives personnel changes and AI system upgrades. Using SKOS for classification means the model avoids OWL disjointness constraints where dual classification is legitimate. Documenting as you build means the model is adoptable by engineers who didn't write it.

The three-box sequence is what keeps the model consistent. Building the CBox foundation first—namespace, metadata, documentation conventions—means governance is built in from the start.

The goal is not a perfect ontology. We are building a correct ontology for its stated scope, documented well enough to be extended, connected to the Semantic Web broadly enough to be useful beyond the organization that built it, and formal enough to support real reasoning over real data.

Now, the custom ontology elements are in place to complete the NTWF workflow ontology, and we are ready to test the ontology against data.

At this point, we have every custom term in the NTWF vocabulary: nine classes, 13 object properties, and five datatype properties. For each one, we align the competency question(s) it serves. Based on a standards survey, the NTWF custom ontology elements address gaps in ontology coverage, thereby articulating the design rationale for the custom elements.

Two principles govern every decision here. A custom term is justified only when the standards survey returns no adequate results. And the label and comment are written before the axioms—if a definition cannot be stated clearly, the concept boundary is not yet understood well enough to model. Difficulty writing the comment is diagnostic, as that difficulty is a signal to stop and think, not to proceed and model what cannot be defined.

---

## The metadata layer

Before we declare our first class, it is worth explaining how the metadata layer fits into the NTWF architecture. The metadata architecture deserves its own explanation. Because it appears in all three boxes, it is the primary integration surface with the organization's existing systems and the layer most misunderstood as purely documentary.

Metadata in the NTWF ontology is not a single thing in a single place. It serves a different function in each box, and understanding which box a given metadata statement belongs in determines whether it is queryable, inferable, or administrative. Also, incorporating a metadata schema such as Dublin Core substantiates organizational metadata through its ontological backbone.

You may be wondering, why not just use the CBox to represent organizational metadata? The CBox carries metadata about the ontology itself and houses controlled vocabularies and thesauri. The CBox vocabularies can also function as tagging suites to explicitly describe documents and assets.

However, we must use a standard such as Dublin Core, which is specifically oriented to capture metadata or data about data. And often, we leverage organizational metadata, represented in all three boxes: TBox, CBox, and ABox.

The owl:Ontology declaration at the top of the TTL (Turtle) file exists in the CBox: dct:title, dct:creator, dct:created, dct:license, owl:versionInfo. This is metadata about the knowledge artifact, rather than the domain it describes. It answers questions like, "Who owns this ontology?", "What version is it?", and "Under what terms can it be reused?" A reasoner does not act on it. It exists for governance, discovery, and documentation.

The TBox contains metadata as property declarations—the Dublin Core properties that the ontology makes available for describing individuals. When the TBox establishes that workflows may carry dct:title, dct:description, dct:modified, and dct:identifier, it is not asserting values. It is declaring the vocabulary available for describing instances. The range of dct:modified is xsd:date. That range declaration is a TBox commitment, and a reasoner acts on it. If something carries dct:modified, the reasoner knows the value is a date literal.

The ABox carries metadata as assertions on specific individuals. When ss:workflow-production-deployment is given dct:title "Production Deployment Workflow" and dct:modified "2026-01-15"^^xsd:date, those are ABox triples. These are instance-level facts about a specific workflow. This is where metadata becomes queryable data.

Clarifying how metadata is integrated into our ontology highlights an operational reality. CBox metadata is for humans and governance systems. TBox metadata declares what descriptions are possible and constrains their types. ABox metadata is the actual descriptive declaration that SPARQL queries run against. Confusing the three levels is why people sometimes build ontologies in which metadata exists in documentation comments but cannot be queried because it was written at the CBox level when it should also exist at the ABox level.

The reason NTWF uses Dublin Core for descriptive metadata rather than defining custom properties is not just reuse for its own sake. Dublin Core's dcterms: namespace carries formal range declarations that are active in an RDFS-aware environment. They produce inferences, not just documentation.

More importantly, Dublin Core is the metadata interchange standard across a wide range of library systems, public repositories, data catalogs, and content management systems built over the last 25 years. A ntwf:Workflow individual that carries Dublin Core metadata is immediately legible to any system that understands Dublin Core, without that system knowing anything about NTWF. This is what makes the metadata layer an integration surface, critical for connecting organizational data systems and for building knowledge infrastructures.

---

## Metadata as integration

Special Solutions already has metadata in other systems. Workflow documents are stored in a document management system, with creation dates, owners, and version numbers. Datasets consumed by workflows are registered in a data catalog with titles, publishers, and access URLs. Employees who fill roles have records in an HR system carrying names, email addresses, and department affiliations. Tickets and change records in the engineering system carry identifiers, descriptions, and modification timestamps.

The metadata layer in the NTWF ontology is the surface where all those existing records can be joined to the graph without requiring a migration. Because ntwf:Workflow is a subclass of schema:CreativeWork and declares Dublin Core properties for its metadata, a workflow record from the document management system can be expressed as an NTWF individual by asserting its existing Dublin Core values. The document system does not need to know about PROV-O. The ontology does not need to know about the document system's internal schema. The Dublin Core properties are the shared contract.

The same logic applies to datasets. dcat:Dataset individuals carry dct:title, dct:modified, dct:publisher, and dcat:distribution. When ss:dataset-risk-metrics-q1-2026 is declared as a dcat:Dataset in the NTWF ABox, it can be populated from the organization's existing data catalog feed with no custom transformation because both the catalog and the ontology use DCAT and Dublin Core. The metadata does not need to be re-entered. It only needs to be referenced.

*This is the integration model: The ontology declares the structure and the relationships, the operational systems carry the metadata values, and the shared standards vocabulary is the bridge between them.*

## Building the classes

The nine classes form two distinct groups. The first models the workflow structure itself: Workflow, WorkflowStep, ApprovalGate, and WorkflowArtifact. The second models the actors and organizational context: Role, HumanAgent, AIAgent, AutomatedPipeline, and Department.

The two groups connect through properties, not through inheritance. Keeping the workflow structure classes and the actor classes logically separate is what makes the role-agent separation heuristic structurally enforceable rather than merely advisory.

### *ntwf:Workflow*

The competency question, "What are all the steps in a workflow, and in what order?" requires a class that represents the workflow itself as a first-class entity—not a container node, but a named individual with its own identity, metadata, and queryable properties.

The standards survey leads immediately to PROV-O's prov:Plan. A plan is a set of actions or steps intended by agents to achieve a goal. That captures the semantics needed here: A workflow at Special Solutions is a plan with a purpose, a defined sequence of steps, and a specific intended outcome. ntwf:Workflow is declared as a subclass of prov:Plan. Every workflow individual is therefore also a plan, which means any system that understands PROV-O can reason about Special Solutions workflows without knowing the NTWF vocabulary.

The second alignment is to schema:CreativeWork. Workflows contain documents—they are written, versioned, owned, and need to be discoverable. The dual alignment prov:Plan for process semantics and schema:CreativeWork for document semantics, reflects the dual nature of a workflow: It is both a process specification and an organizational record.

The metadata layer for workflows comes entirely from Dublin Core. dct:title, dct:description, dct:created, dct:modified, and dct:identifier cover the complete administrative metadata requirement without any custom properties. dct:modified is what makes the stale-workflow competency question answerable—no custom property needed. This is the metadata layer doing its most immediate business—enabling a compliance query across the entire workflow graph by using a date field that already exists in the document management system, expressed through a standard property.

### *ntwf:WorkflowStep*

Three competency questions operate at the step level:

- Which steps are executed by AI agents?
- What artifacts does each step produce?
- In what order do the steps execute?

Steps must therefore be first-class entities—individually addressable, individually queryable, individually typed—not anonymous nodes hanging off a workflow.

CLASS · TBOX · GROUP A – WORKFLOW STRUCTURE

**ntwf:WorkflowStep**

TBox | prov:Activity

```
ntwf:WorkflowStep
    a owl:Class ;
    rdfs:subClassOf prov:Activity ;
    rdfs:label     "Workflow Step"@en ;
    rdfs:comment
        """An atomic, individually addressable unit of work within a workflow.
        Steps are first-class entities: individually typed, individually queryable,
        individually sequenced. Not anonymous nodes hanging off a workflow.
        prov:Activity supplies execution timestamps and agent-association
        properties at no custom cost."""@en .
```

*CQ01 · CQ03 · CQ04 · prov:Activity supplies prov:startedAtTime, prov:endedAtTime, prov:wasAssociatedWith*

Figure 85: ntwf:WorkflowStep.

The standards survey produces prov:Activity. A PROV-O activity is something that occurs over a period of time and acts upon or with entities. Every workflow step satisfies this definition. The PROV-O alignment supplies prov:startedAtTime and prov:endedAtTime for execution timestamps, prov:wasAssociatedWith for agent linkage, and prov:used and prov:generated as additional artifact-tracing predicates—all without requiring custom properties.

### *ntwf:ApprovalGate*

The competency question "Who is responsible for approving a production deployment?" implies something more than a regular workflow step. An approval gate is a decision point at which workflow execution blocks until a designated authority explicitly authorizes its continuation. It is categorically different from a step that an AI agent or pipeline executes; it is a checkpoint with accountability, an escalation path, and a time threshold.

ntwf:ApprovalGate is declared as a subclass of ntwf:WorkflowStep. Because approval gates are a specialization of workflow steps, they inherit everything true of steps: They have sequence positions, they carry ntwf:requiresHumanApproval, they produce artifacts, and they appear in ntwf:hasStep chains in correct sequence order alongside non-gate steps. No special handling is required in workflow structure queries. The distinctiveness of a gate is expressed through its type and through the additional property ntwf:escalationThresholdHours, whose domain declaration encodes the constraint that this property applies only to gates.

One practical note: ntwf:ApprovalGate individuals are explicitly double-typed in the ABox as both ntwf:ApprovalGate and ntwf:WorkflowStep. Without the explicit ntwf:WorkflowStep type, SPARQL queries asking ?step rdf:type ntwf:WorkflowStep will miss approval gate individuals at endpoints that do not materialize RDFS subclass entailments, which is the common case in production deployments. The explicit double-typing costs one triple per individual and prevents a silent query gap.

### *ntwf:WorkflowArtifact*

The artifact traceability competency question "What artifacts does each step produce, and what agents consumed them downstream?" requires that artifacts be independently addressable and provenance-traceable.

The standards survey produces prov:Entity. A PROV-O entity is a physical, digital, or conceptual thing with some fixed aspects at a point in time. The PROV-O alignment gives prov:wasGeneratedBy to link an artifact to its producing step, prov:wasAttributedTo to link it to its responsible agent, and prov:wasDerivedFrom to express lineage when one artifact is downstream of another. The second alignment is schema:CreativeWork, which makes artifacts discoverable by any system built on the Schema.org vocabulary. None of these requires custom properties.

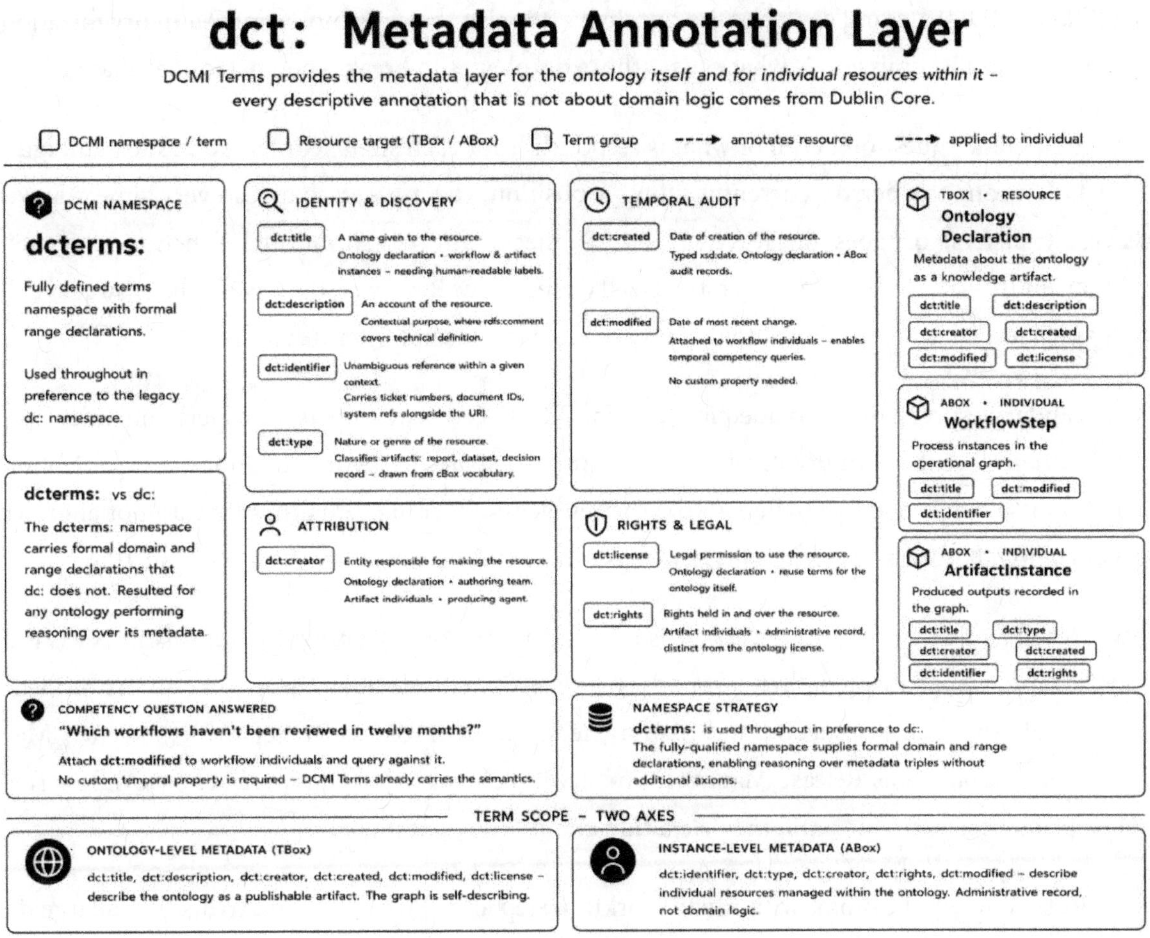


Figure 86: Metadata annotation layer.

Artifact metadata follows the same Dublin Core pattern as workflow metadata. dct:title provides a human-readable name. dct:created records when the artifact was produced. dct:identifier carries the external reference—the ticket number, document ID, or system reference—that links the graph individual back to the operational system where the artifact lives. This is the metadata layer functioning as a join key—the dct:identifier on an artifact individual is what allows a downstream system querying the graph to retrieve the full artifact record from the document management system without that system needing to speak RDF.

### *ntwf:Role*

This class is the structural center of the ontology. It is also the class most omitted in organizational ontologies, and its omission is what causes those ontologies to break when personnel change.

The competency question "Who or what is responsible for each step?" contains a hidden ambiguity. If "who" means the person currently filling a position, the answer changes every time someone leaves, transfers, or goes on leave. If "who" means the organizational function that holds responsibility—the Release Manager, the Legal Compliance Reviewer, the CFO—the answer is stable across personnel changes. The ontology must model the second interpretation.

The standards survey finds no adequate match. PROV-O's prov:Role is a property qualifier, not a class. It describes the capacity in which an agent participates in an activity, not the organizational function itself. Schema.org's schema:Role carries web-publishing semantics that do not align with organizational process accountability. The custom ntwf:Role class is therefore fully justified.

ntwf:Role has no external superclass. It is a root class for organizational functions in NTWF. Its logical work is done through three properties: ntwf:assignedRole links a step to a role, ntwf:filledBy links a role to its current agent, and ntwf:ownedBy links a role to its department. When Maria Gonzalez is replaced as Release Manager, one ntwf:filledBy triple is updated. The workflow steps, the approval gate structure, and the delegation chain—none of it changes.

ntwf:Role is declared disjoint with ntwf: WorkflowStep and ntwf:WorkflowArtifact. In a large data import or a poorly structured query, something typed as a role could accidentally appear where a step or artifact is expected. The disjointness declarations cause a reasoner to flag those cases as inconsistencies rather than letting them propagate silently.

### *ntwf:HumanAgent • ntwf:AIAgent • ntwf:AutomatedPipeline*

These three classes are treated together because their design rationale is inseparable. The competency question "Which steps are executed by AI agents, and which require a human decision?" requires the model to distinguish among the three categories of actor at the class level—not as a data annotation, but as a structural commitment that carries logical consequences.

This is critical for capturing accountability chains. Human agents have legal standing in organizational processes. AI agents produce probabilistic outputs that may require human review. Automated pipelines produce deterministic outputs according to predefined rules. These are not cosmetic differences. They determine which steps can be automated, which require oversight, which carry legal accountability, and which appear in delegation chains.

ntwf:HumanAgent subclasses both foaf:Person and prov:Agent. The FOAF alignment provides it with the full person vocabulary—name, email, organizational affiliation—and the social graph semantics of the most widely deployed person class in Linked Data. Human agents are the only agent type that may fill roles where ntwf:requiresHumanApproval is true.

ntwf:AIAgent subclasses prov:SoftwareAgent. PROV-O defines software agents as running software that may be attributed to humans. That is the correct semantic home for an AI agent in a workflow context. The custom class imposes the organizational constraint that AI agents carry a model version—a string captured in ntwf:modelVersion—which makes AI-produced artifacts auditable at the version level.

ntwf:AutomatedPipeline subclasses both prov:SoftwareAgent and schema:SoftwareApplication. The dual alignment distinguishes it from ntwf:AIAgent in Schema.org-aware systems: A software application is a deterministic running system, whereas an AI agent carries probabilistic output semantics that Schema.org does not express, but PROV-O accommodates.

Without these declarations, a data entry error or a poorly structured import could result in an individual being typed as two of these classes, and downstream queries would return inconsistent accountability information without any system flagging the error. With the disjointness declarations, a reasoner reports the inconsistency immediately.

### *ntwf:Department*

The competency question "Which workflows involve both Engineering and Legal, and at what steps do they intersect?" requires departments to be first-class entities, not string labels on agents. A string label cannot be queried structurally. You cannot command, "Give me all workflows where the set of departments owning roles includes both Engineering and Legal" if department membership is a literal annotation rather than a typed URI reference.

ntwf:Department subclasses schema:Organization. Schema.org's Organization class carries formal institutional semantics and is more precise than FOAF's foaf:Group, which is defined loosely as a collection of agents. The property ntwf:ownedBy links roles to departments, and because both are typed individuals, the path ntwf:assignedRole / ntwf:ownedBy is traversable in a single SPARQL property path expression.

---

## Building the properties

Thirteen object properties and five datatype properties connect the nine classes and link them to external standard individuals. Every property is declared with an explicit domain and range. Where a property is functional, the declaration is explicit. Where two properties are inverses, both are declared. Where a property is transitive, the declaration carries logical weight that the reasoner acts on.

### *The workflow structure properties*

ntwf:hasStep is the structural spine. It links a Workflow to the workflowSteps it contains. Its inverse, ntwf:isStepOf, enables navigation from step to workflow. Neither property encodes order; sequence is handled separately by two complementary mechanisms.

ntwf:sequencePosition is a functional datatype property carrying an integer. It supports positional queries: Give me step three, give me all steps in order. It is declared functional because a step has exactly one position in a given workflow's sequence.

ntwf:precedesStep is an object property declared owl:TransitiveProperty. It expresses the ordering relationship between steps directly. The transitivity declaration is necessary, as a reasoner acting on it infers that if Step A precedes Step B and Step B precedes Step C, then Step A precedes Step C. The ABox asserts four explicit ntwf:precedesStep triples for the five-step production deployment workflow. After OWL-RL closure, all 10 non-adjacent pairs are present in the graph—including Step 1 preceding Step 5, which was never asserted.

ntwf:workflowStatus links a workflow to a SKOS concept from the ntwf:workflowStatusScheme. It is declared functional—a workflow has exactly one current status. Like ntwf:hasCapability below, this bridges the CBox vocabulary with the TBox, without promoting status concepts to OWL classes, which is the correct approach when overlapping or provisional classification is legitimate.

### *The role-agent decoupling properties*

ntwf:assignedRole links a WorkflowStep to the role responsible for it. Declared as an owl:FunctionalProperty, this property details and represents that a step is designed with exactly one responsible role. A step with two ntwf:assignedRole values represents an ambiguous accountability assignment. The functional declaration causes the reasoner to flag this—specifically, it merges the two roles via owl:sameAs, which is detectable and reveals the modeling error.

ntwf:filledBy links a Role to its current agent. Its range is prov:Agent, which covers all three NTWF agent subclasses through inheritance. This is the change-management triple. It is the one thing in the model that changes when personnel change, when an AI system is upgraded, or when a process transitions from human to automated execution. The workflow steps, the role definitions, the artifact structure—none of it is touched. One ntwf:filledBy triple is updated.

ntwf:ownedBy links a role to its owning department. It is declared functional—each role has exactly one owning department. This is the property that makes cross-departmental intersection queries answerable.

ntwf:delegatesTo links a role to its fallback role in an escalation chain. The chain in the production deployment ABox runs from Release Manager to VP Engineering to CTO. The full chain is traversable in SPARQL via the ntwf:delegatesTo+ property path operator.

ntwf:hasCapability links a role to a SKOS concept from the ntwf:AgentCapability scheme. This is the CBox connecting to the TBox. The controlled vocabulary for capabilities is defined in the CBox as an SKOS scheme, and roles reference it via this property, with skos:Concept as the range. It bridges the two layers without requiring capability terms to be modeled as OWL classes.

### *The artifact tracing properties*

ntwf:producesArtifact and ntwf:requiresArtifact connect steps to the artifacts they generate and consume. Both are aligned to PROV-O properties—prov:generated and prov:used respectively—but defined as custom properties to provide the domain and range specificity that SPARQL queries against NTWF classes require. The inverse of ntwf:producesArtifact is ntwf:isProducedBy, which enables navigating from an artifact back to its producing step.

ntwf:consumesDataset is defined separately from ntwf:requiresArtifact because dcat:Dataset individuals carry metadata—distribution format, access URL, catalog entry, modification date—that generic ntwf:WorkflowArtifact individuals do not. Keeping the two properties distinct preserves the DCAT semantics for dataset individuals and allows queries to target dataset consumption specifically. This is the property that makes CQ8 answerable.

### *The datatype properties*

Five datatype properties carry literal values that the object property layer cannot express.

ntwf:sequencePosition carries the integer ordinal position of a workflow step. It is functional; each step has exactly one position in its workflow's sequence.

ntwf:requiresHumanApproval carries the boolean flag marking whether a step requires a human agent as its role-filler. The explicit boolean on every step—rather than inferring it from the step's type—means a single FILTER on this property answers the human-vs-AI step query without joining against the agent type hierarchy.

ntwf:modelVersion carries the AI model version string for an ntwf:AIAgent individual. Its domain is ntwf:AIAgent. This domain declaration carries inferential weight: If this property is accidentally applied to a ntwf:HumanAgent, a reasoner will infer that the human is an AI agent, rather than flagging an error.

*This is Heuristic 4. Domain and range are inference rules, not constraints. The test ABox, run through a reasoner before production deployment, is what catches this class of error.*

ntwf:stepDurationMinutes carries the expected duration of a workflow step in minutes. It is not declared functional. A step may carry multiple duration estimates for different execution contexts.

ntwf:escalationThresholdHours carries the integer number of hours that may elapse on a pending ntwf:ApprovalGate before the ntwf:delegatesTo chain activates. Its domain is ntwf:ApprovalGate. Like ntwf:modelVersion, the domain declaration is an inference rule: If this property appears on a step not explicitly typed as ntwf:ApprovalGate, a reasoner will infer the gate type rather than reject the triple.

### *The instance namespace of ss:*

Until now, every term in this series has carried the ntwf: prefix. That prefix belongs to the ontology vocabulary—the classes, properties, and axioms that define the structure of the domain. But the vocabulary and instance data are two distinct things, so distinct that they deserve separate namespaces.

The ntwf: namespace is a schema namespace. It is where the organization's reusable, generalizable knowledge lives—the definitions that apply to every workflow Special Solutions will ever model. The ABox is something else: It is the population of specific, named individuals that instantiate those definitions. Maria Gonzalez is not a vocabulary term. The Production Deployment Workflow is not a class. These are organizational facts about a particular company at a particular time, and they belong in a dedicated namespace that reflects the declaration of these facts.

The ss: prefix—declared as @prefix ss: https://data.specialsolutions.example.com/instances/ is the instance namespace. Its URI pattern follows a deliberate convention: ss:workflow-production-deployment, ss:agent-maria-gonzalez, ss:role-release-manager.

The base URI signals that these are data resources, not schema resources, and the local name uses a type-hint followed by a human-readable slug. This pattern makes URIs legible to engineers reading the Turtle directly while remaining globally unambiguous as identifiers.

Separating the schema namespace from the instance namespace is an architectural decision that impacts operational workflows. It means the vocabulary can be versioned, published, and reused across systems without dragging along the specific personnel, workflows, and artifacts of any one deployment. Another organization wanting to adopt the NTWF ontology vocabulary would import ntwf: and populate their own instance namespace with their own individuals. The schema is shared infrastructure. The instances are local facts. Keeping them in separate namespaces keeps that boundary enforced in the graph itself.

### *The ABox: Instance data for the workflow*

The three-box architecture assigned the ABox a specific role in the design process: populate a representative set of instances before deployment, load them alongside the TBox into a reasoner, and confirm two things: that the reasoner produces no inconsistencies and that the reasoner produces the expected inferences.

The ABox becomes integral to the validation instrument.

The production deployment workflow at Special Solutions exercises every class, every object property, and every datatype property in the TBox. It involves five steps, three agent types, six roles, five artifacts, one DCAT dataset, and one approval gate.

The three agent types appear together in the same workflow, which reflects the various workflows at Special Solutions.

ss:agent-maria-gonzalez and ss:agent-james-okafor are ntwf:HumanAgent individuals carrying foaf:name and foaf:mbox.

ss:agent-risk-ai is an ntwf:AIAgent carrying ntwf:modelVersion "risk-classifier-v2.4.1."

ss:agent-ci-pipeline is an ntwf:AutomatedPipeline carrying schema:name—not foaf:name, because FOAF's name property is appropriate for persons, not for software systems.

This separation of concerns is critical. When writing SPARQL queries that retrieve agent names across all three types, use COALESCE(?foafName, ?schemaName) to handle both patterns cleanly.

Six roles are declared within NTWF. Each points to an agent via ntwf:filledBy, to a department via ntwf:ownedBy, and to one or more CBox capabilities via ntwf:hasCapability. Three of the six form an explicit delegation chain:

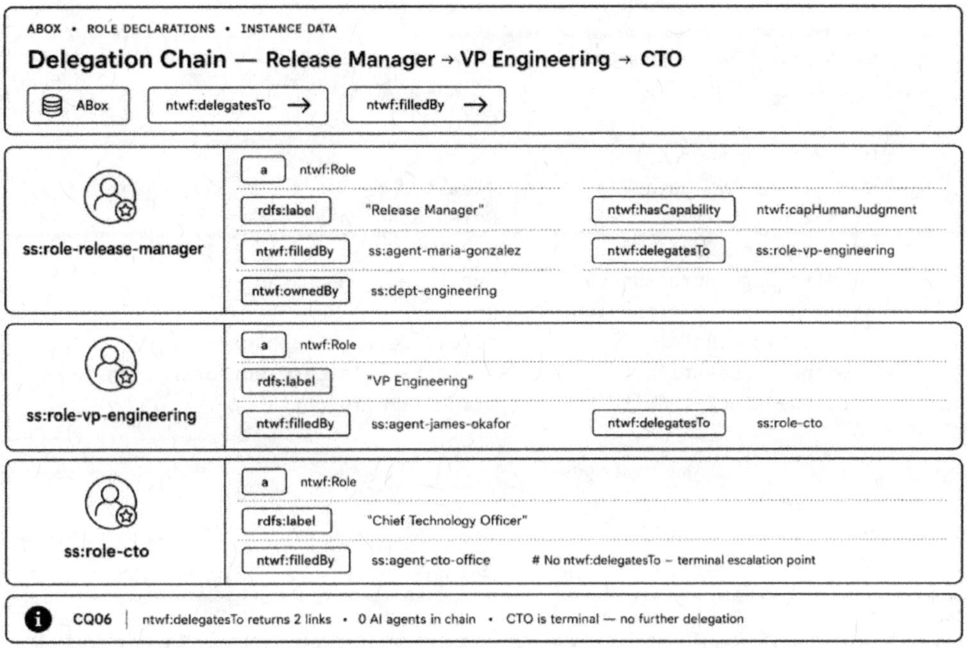


Figure 87: Release Manager.

The workflow individual carries its full Dublin Core metadata header, and each is asserted as ABox triples:

dct:title
dct:description
dct:created
dct:modified
dct:identifier

These values already exist in the document management system, expressed through the standard vocabulary that both systems share.

The dct:identifier value maps directly to the workflow's ticket reference in the engineering system. The dct:modified value is what the system uses when it asks which workflows are stale.

Step 3, the Release Approval Gate, is explicitly double-typed:

ABOX · APPROVALGATE · EXPLICIT DOUBLE-TYPE · INSTANCE DATA

**Release Approval Gate — step 3 of 5**

ABox | explicit double-type | ntwf:ApprovalGate + ntwf:WorkflowStep

```
ss:step-release-approval
    a ntwf:ApprovalGate , ntwf:WorkflowStep ;      # explicit double-type
    rdfs:label                    "Release Approval Gate" ;
    ntwf:sequencePosition         3 ;
    ntwf:requiresHumanApproval    true ;
    ntwf:escalationThresholdHours 24 ;
    ntwf:assignedRole             ss:role-release-manager ;
    ntwf:producesArtifact         ss:artifact-release-authorization ;
    prov:wasAssociatedWith        ss:agent-maria-gonzalez .
```

CQ02 · Double-typing costs one extra triple and prevents silent SPARQL gaps at non-entailing endpoints

Figure 88: Release approval gate.

The ordering chain is expressed as four asserted ntwf:precedesStep triples. After OWL-RL reasoning on the transitive property, all 10 non-adjacent pairs are present in the graph. The validation framework confirms three specific long-range inferences: Step 1 precedes Step 3, Step 1 precedes Step 4, and Step 1 precedes Step 5—none of which was asserted.

The five artifacts form a provenance chain.

Each is attributed to the agent that produced it via prov:wasAttributedTo, linked to its producing step via prov:wasGeneratedBy, and linked to its upstream source via prov:wasDerivedFrom. Each artifact also carries dct:title and dct:identifier as ABox metadata—the title for human readability, the identifier as the join key back to the document management system.

The chain runs from risk report through legal clearance, through release authorization, through deployment log, to post-deployment report.

Four prov:wasDerivedFrom links trace the full lineage.

## The metadata layer at work: A business use case

The most immediate, valuable business use of the metadata layer requires no custom properties at all. It demonstrates how descriptive logic and metadata combine to answer questions that no individual operational system can answer on its own.

The competency question "Which workflows haven't been reviewed or updated in 12 months?" is answered entirely by dct:modified on ntwf:Workflow individuals:

That query is executable the moment workflow individuals carry dct:modified values from the document management system. No custom property, new class, or ontology change is necessary.

Now, let's extend the scenario. Special Solutions needs to know not just which workflows are stale, but which involve AI agents executing steps, as those pose the highest compliance risk when the workflow documentation is out of date. That query joins the metadata layer with the accountability structure:

SPARQL · CQ03 + CQ05 · COMPOUND · THREE-LAYER JOIN

**Stale Workflows with AI-Executed Steps**

`CQ03 + CQ05` `dct:modified` `ntwf:AIAgent` `three-layer join`

```
# Joins the metadata layer (dct:modified from document management system),
# the structural layer (ntwf:hasStep → ntwf:WorkflowStep),
# and the accountability layer (ntwf:assignedRole → ntwf:filledBy → ntwf:AIAgent).
# No bespoke integration code. One query across three operational systems.

SELECT ?wf ?title ?modified ?stepLabel ?agentName WHERE {
    ?wf      rdf:type           ntwf:Workflow .
    ?wf      dct:title          ?title .
    ?wf      dct:modified       ?modified .
    FILTER (?modified < "2025-03-01"^^xsd:date)
    ?wf      ntwf:hasStep       ?step .
    ?step    rdfs:label         ?stepLabel .
    ?step    ntwf:assignedRole  ?role .
    ?role    ntwf:filledBy      ?agent .
    ?agent   rdf:type           ntwf:AIAgent .
    ?agent   foaf:name          ?agentName .
}
```

`Metadata layer: dct:modified from DMS` `Structural layer: ntwf:hasStep chain` `Accountability layer: role → AIAgent type` `Zero bespoke integration code`

Figure 89: State workflow with AI-executed steps.

No system that stores workflows as documents and AI agent assignments in a separate ticketing system could produce that result without a bespoke integration written specifically for that pair of systems. The ontology presents it as a standard query because the metadata, structural, and accountability layers are all expressed in the same graph.

The dct:modified date from the document management system, the step-to-role-to-agent chain from the workflow definition, and the agent type classification from the ontology are all first-class graph nodes connected by typed properties. They are queryable together because they share a URI space and a vocabulary.

This is where descriptive logic becomes visible to organizational stakeholders. A class hierarchy is an abstraction. A disjointness axiom is invisible to most users. But a query that returns every stale workflow where an AI agent is executing a step and the compliance documentation hasn't been reviewed is a business question, answered automatically by a machine across a live graph. The metadata layer provides the descriptive logic with organizational traction. The dates, titles, identifiers, and provenance values in the ABox are what transform inference chains from logical constructs into auditable, actionable results.

---

## Validating the model

The validation framework runs against the TTL file in Python using rdflib and owlrl. It is organized into four suites. The result is 104 tests, all passing.

Suite 1 loads the raw TTL with no inference applied and confirms that the vocabulary is present, complete, and correctly declared. All nine classes are checked for their owl:Class declaration and all 12 subclass alignments to external standards. All 13 object properties are verified as owl:ObjectProperty. All four functional properties carry their owl:FunctionalProperty declaration. The transitive property is confirmed. Both inverse pairs are checked. All five disjointness pairs are verified. The two CBox schemes and all four status concepts are present.

Suite 2 applies the OWL-RL reasoner and confirms that the TBox axioms produce the expected logical consequences. The baseline graph has 433 asserted triples. The graph expands to more than 800 after OWL-RL closure.

The suite checks 23 specific inferences; the workflow individual is typed as both prov:Plan and schema:CreativeWork. All three human agent individuals are typed as foaf:Person and prov:Agent. The AI agent is typed as prov:SoftwareAgent. The automated pipeline is typed as schema:SoftwareApplication. All five artifacts are typed as prov:Entity. The transitive step ordering chain is confirmed at three non-adjacent pairs. The two inverse property pairs are confirmed by checking inferred triples in the reverse direction.

Suite 3 runs each of the eight competency questions as a SPARQL query and confirms the results. CQ1 returns five steps in order. CQ2 returns one approval gate, assigned to the Release Manager role, filled by Maria Gonzalez. CQ3 returns two AI-executed steps and two human-required steps. CQ4 returns five step-artifact pairs and four lineage links. CQ5 confirms dct:modified is present and queryable; this is the metadata layer's most direct contribution to the competency question set.

CQ6 returns a two-link delegation chain with zero AI agents in it. CQ7 returns one workflow involving both Engineering and Legal, with exactly one Legal-owned step. CQ8 returns one dataset-consuming step, the Q1 2026 Risk Metrics dataset, processed by the Risk Analysis-AI agent.

Suite 4 is the most instructive. It injects deliberate errors and confirms the model responds correctly. Adding ntwf:AIAgent typing to a ntwf:HumanAgent individual produces a detectable disjointness violation—owl-rl does not implement the owl:disjointWith → owl:Nothing rule directly, so detection requires a SPARQL query that finds individuals simultaneously satisfying two mutually exclusive classes. This is the correct production detection pattern.

Assigning two roles to one step via the functional ntwf:assignedRole property causes the reasoner to assert owl:sameAs between the two roles, revealing the double-assignment as a logical anomaly. Applying ntwf:modelVersion to a ntwf:HumanAgent silently infers that the individual is a ntwf:AIAgent—the domain inference fires exactly as Heuristic 4 predicts—and the compound effect of inferred ntwf:AIAgent plus existing ntwf:HumanAgent produces a detectable disjointness violation. The clean ABox produces zero inconsistencies.

Suite 4 does something no amount of description about Heuristic 4 can accomplish. It shows, with a running test, exactly what happens when a domain declaration is violated. The domain declaration on ntwf:modelVersion does not prevent the error. It produces a wrong inference that is detectable only if you are running a reasoner and looking for it. Understanding the difference between that behavior and a constraint that rejects the triple is a practical matter that determines whether modeling errors propagate undetected into production data.

---

## NTWF ontology coverage

Every term in the NTWF ontology traces back to at least one competency question. Every custom term exists because the standards survey returned no adequate results. The ontology vocabulary is small by design—nine classes, 13 object properties, five datatype properties—because the open standards supply most of what the model needs.

What the ontology does not define is important to note. It does not define its own person class because FOAF provides it. It does not define its own metadata properties because Dublin Core provides them. It does not define its own dataset class because DCAT provides it. It does not define its own provenance properties because PROV-O provides them. The absence of custom terms in these areas is the result of the standards survey and the reuse heuristic applied consistently.

The NTWF prefix marks the vocabulary boundary. Every ntwf:term is either a bridge to an existing standard or a gap-filler where no bridge existed. The metadata layer—Dublin Core properties spread across all three boxes—is the bridge that makes the ontology an integration surface rather than an isolated formal model. It is what connects the descriptive logic of the TBox to the operational systems where the organization's data already lives.

Figure 90 shows the full NTWF ontology file, with example instance data represented within.

---

*The day an ontology is deployed is the day it starts to drift.*

---

The domain changes, the organization changes, and AI systems are integrated, upgraded, and retired. New competency questions emerge that the original model cannot answer. Old competency questions may become irrelevant. Personnel move, leave, or retire, and reorgs happen—all part of the day-to-day of a typical technology organization. The NTWF ontology, so carefully built and validated, now has to survive contact with an organization that will not hold still.

This is where ontology governance steps in. Governance is the engineering discipline that keeps an ontology coherent across states of change. It is neither documentation nor a wiki page. It is a set of processes, ownership structures, versioning conventions, and change management protocols that determine who can change what, when, and how—and what happens when something breaks.

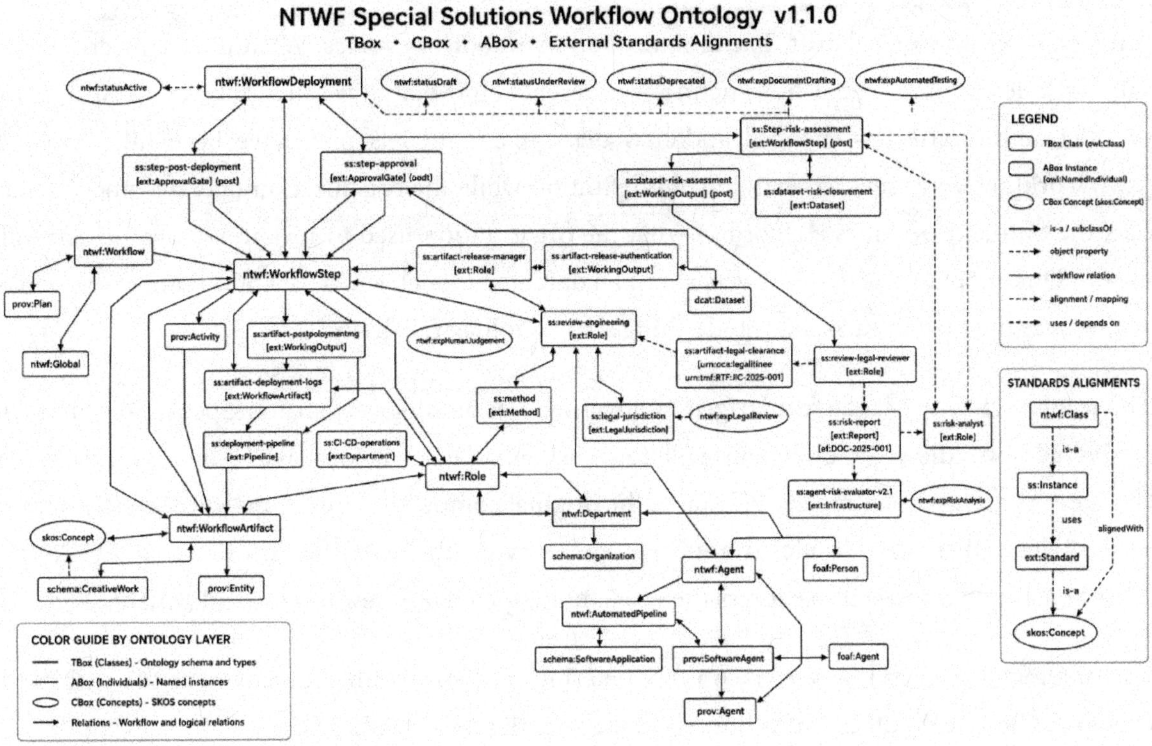


Figure 90: Full NTWF ontology file.

---

## Governance

### *Why ontologies decay*

> *An ontology is not exactly software, but it has the same failure mode as software—it rots when it is not maintained.*

The rot is subtler and harder to detect than a failing test suite or a broken build pipeline, which is why it is more dangerous.

The NTWF ontology deployed at Special Solutions will encounter at least four categories of change that governance must handle.

The first is terminological drift. The organization's vocabulary evolves. What the engineering team called a "release" in 2024 may be structurally different from what they call a "release" in 2026, as the product architecture has changed and new deployment models may have been introduced. If ntwf:Workflow continues to carry the old definition while the organization operates under a new one, the ontology becomes a record of what the organization used to mean, not what it currently means. Queries return correct answers about an outdated model, which is worse than no answers at all, because the trust of each stakeholder hinges on ontology reliability.

The second category of change managed by governance is ontology expansion. Special Solutions will always add workflows—new teams will form while others will dissolve. Amid organizational changes, AI agents are introduced for tasks the original competency questions never contemplated. The HR department may decide it wants to model its own onboarding workflows using NTWF. The AI systems team may want to express the evaluation pipeline for new model deployments.

For ontology expansion, governance must determine whether either deployment fits within the existing TBox without modification, or whether the new workflows require new terms or modifications to existing terms because the classes are scoped too narrowly. New TBox and CBox class definitions may require expanded representations to properly account for how these facts will be represented.

The third category of change managed by governance is external dependency change. NTWF leverages the open, W3C standard ontologies, including PROV-O, FOAF, Dublin Core, DCAT, and Schema.org. These are living standards. PROV-O is stable; it has not changed since 2013. Schema.org publishes new versions regularly, adding and deprecating ontology elements. DCAT underwent a major revision from Version 2 to Version 3, introducing new classes and deprecating others. If our NTWF ontology uses ontology elements that are deprecated by Schema.org, that usage remains valid in existing data—URIs do not disappear—but the semantic alignment has shifted, and documentation must be updated.

Versioning of open ontologies can be easily handled through a simple ontology rework, with governance accounting for changes and assuming ownership of the deprecated classes, properties, or relations. For example, this solution takes a deprecated FOAF element, such as foaf:name, and prepends a prefix to assign it to the NTWF ontology.

This simple solution modifies foaf:name to become ntwf:name. This means that the namespace and prefix have changed. The ontology edit would thereby trigger a versioning of the ontology, and a reconciliation relation, to declare that foaf:name is OWL:sameAs—> ntwf:name. The result is simple and clean, with proper representation, description, and reconciliation throughout. We could get fancier, but this suffices for now.

---

*The URI for each instance of a thing serves as the unique identifier for that thing. Therefore, the change in prefix and representation must consider any alteration to prefixes and URIs, so that the ontology and data modeled remains consistent and accurate. If an ontology fails to capture these changes, SPARQL queries and APIs risk failing and the ontology itself may degrade.*

---

The fourth category of change, and the one that is most consequential for current practitioners, is AI system turnover. The NTWF ontology models AI agents as first-class individuals with ntwf:modelVersion identifiers. That design decision was made to account for AI systems' evolution and churn as model versions are updated, agents are replaced with more capable systems, and task assignments shift. Humans and AI systems must respond to a rapidly evolving technology landscape, maintaining some modicum of consistency and continuity in data representation and description. Ontology governance anticipates change and is prepared to absorb the ontology's change management processes without corrupting the graph.

### *Ownership*

An ontology without an owner will not survive its first year. Ownership is the first governance requirement, and it is where most organizational ontology efforts fail. Without clear ownership, there is no authority for the ontology as an artifact.

*Ownership has two distinct dimensions that are frequently conflated: stewardship and authority.*

A steward is responsible for the ontology's health. They monitor for drift, track external dependency updates, field user questions, maintain documentation, and ensure the validation suite stays current. Stewardship is ongoing maintenance work. At Special Solutions, the steward role is naturally held by whoever owns the engineering knowledge infrastructure—the team or individual responsible for the ontology tooling and data systems.

Authority is the power to approve changes to the CBox, ABox, and TBox. A steward can identify that a change is needed, while the authority decides how and where it is made. In organizational terms, authority over the TBox, ABox, or CBox should sit with the function that owns the domain the ontology models. For NTWF, that is the workflow governance function, the people responsible for how Special Solutions defines and enforces its operational processes.

The distinction matters because changes to the TBox and ABox are ontological commitments. Changing a class definition, adding a new subclass, or modifying a property's domain or range will all affect what the reasoner infers, which in turn changes which queries return, and thus downstream decisions made by systems. A steward who can make TBox or ABox changes without authority review is a single point of failure for the entire knowledge graph's semantic integrity.

The practical minimum for a working governance structure is a named steward with documented responsibilities, a named authority with defined approval scope, and a change log that records every TBox and ABox modification, along with its rationale. None of this requires a committee, although best practice is to support two distinct roles: Steward and Authority. For a smaller organization—fewer than 500 people—a single person can hold both roles. The base requirement is that the roles exist, are known, and are exercised.

### *Versioning*

The CBox declares and maintains the version metadata for the NTWF ontology and is declared in our ontology as owl:versionInfo. That field is the anchor for a versioning discipline that makes the ontology survivable across states of change.

The practice in ontology engineering is semantic versioning, adapted from software, like MAJOR MINOR PATCH. The mappings are straightforward. A patch version increment—1.1.0 to 1.1.1—covers documentation corrections, label clarifications, and comment updates. The formal model is unchanged. Any system that loaded 1.1.0 will behave identically with 1.1.1.

A minor version increment—1.1.0 to 1.2.0—covers additive changes: new classes, new properties, new CBox concepts. Existing terms are unchanged. Systems that loaded 1.1.0 will continue to function correctly against 1.2.0; they simply will not use the new elements until they are updated to do so. Therefore, backward compatibility is preserved.

A major version increment—1.1.0 to 2.0.0—signals a breaking change. A class has been removed or renamed. A property's domain or range has changed in a way that invalidates existing ABox triples. A disjointness axiom has been added, making previously valid individuals inconsistent. Any system using the previous version must be explicitly updated and re-validated.

*Major version changes are rare in stable ontologies and should be treated as significant engineering events with migration planning.*

NTWF is currently at version 1.1.0. The most likely near-term version events are minor increments as Special Solutions adds new workflow types and the HR and AI teams extend the vocabulary. The governance discipline is to ensure that every version event is a deliberate decision that is documented and communicated widely.

There is an important nuance in ontology versioning that catches practitioners off guard: versioning the ontology file is not sufficient. The ABox must be versioned separately because it represents dynamic data representations or instance data and therefore changes more frequently.

Because the TBox houses our defined classes and is typically much smaller than the ABox, changes occur less frequently, especially with deliberate governance. The ABox changes continuously—new workflow individuals are added, ntwf:filledBy triples are updated as personnel change, dct:modified values are refreshed as workflows are reviewed. These ABox changes fall under the guise of operational data management, not ontology governance. Conflating the two is a common source of confusion about what "changing the ontology" means.

The clean separation dictates that TBox changes are governed, while data operations govern ABox changes. The versioning discipline applies to both, but through different mechanisms.

### *Change management*

Every TBox change request should move through a defined process. The specifics of that process scale with organizational size, but the logic is fixed.

A change request begins with a stated need tied to a competency question—either an existing question the model is currently failing, or a new question the organization needs to answer. A change request that cannot be anchored to a competency question is a signal that the requester has not yet thought through what the change is meant to support. Sending it back for clarification is necessary for ontological hygiene.

The change request then proceeds to an impact assessment, which leverages our competency questions, SPARQL query engine, ontology reasoner, CBox, and domain coverage model featured in the taxonomy series. We use all the listed levers and artifacts to determine which existing triples would become inconsistent if this change is made. What inferences would change? What queries would return different results? Do we represent all the necessary metadata and taxonomy elements in our CBox and domain coverage model?

The validation framework is the instrument for this assessment. Re-run the test suite with the proposed change applied and observe to see what breaks. If the suite was built correctly, gaps in ontology coverage and representation should surface, and the possible impact of proposed changes will be visible.

The steward may be authorized to approve and deploy minor changes. Authority review is required, however, for changes that modify existing elements or vocabularies or add disjointness constraints. The change is documented in the change log, including the competency question that motivated it, the terms affected, the release version number, and the date.

For the specific case of AI system changes—when ntwf:modelVersion is updated because a new model version has been deployed, or when a step transitions from ntwf:AIAgent to ntwf:HumanAgent execution—the governance decision is to determine if the change is a data operation or a modeling change.

Updating ntwf:filledBy to point from an old AI agent individual to a new one is a data operation—no term changes, no inferences change, and only one triple changes.

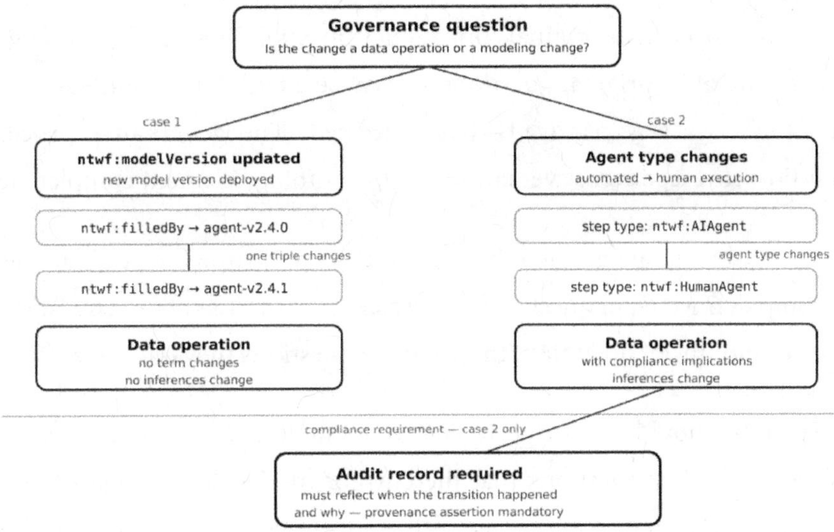


Figure 91: Governance question.

Changing the agent type of a step from ntwf:AIAgent to ntwf:HumanAgent—when a task that was automated is assigned to a human for execution—is a data operation with compliance implications, because the audit record must reflect when that transition occurred and why.

The PROV-O provenance structure built into NTWF gives governance a powerful tool here. Because every step is typed as prov:Activity and artifacts carry prov:wasAttributedTo, the ontology can record not only the current state of agent assignments, but the history of changes. However, this requires one additional practice. When a ntwf:filledBy triple is updated, the old triple should not be deleted.

Instead, it should be timestamped and retained in a named graph or replaced with a versioned triple that carries the validity period. The question, *"Which AI agent was executing this step on March 1, 2026?"* is only answerable if the history of agent assignments is preserved in the graph. Deletion discards provenance, thereby erasing traces and chains of custody.

## Competency questions as a governance instrument

Pulling competency questions across the phases of ontology design, development, validation, and deployment yields consistent, intentional ontology frameworks that closely mirror software development frameworks.

An ontology that can answer all its original competency questions is a healthy ontology. An ontology that cannot answer one of its original questions—because a term was modified, a property's range was narrowed, or a class was removed—has regressed. The governance process must track competency question coverage across versions, not just ontology element completeness.

Equally important is what happens when the organization outgrows the original questions. Special Solutions' leadership defined eight questions at the start of this series. Those questions were correct at the time. After 12 months of operation, there will be questions they did not anticipate.

The governance process should include periodic reviews (at least quarterly), where the competency question set is revisited. New questions that the current model cannot answer are scope change requests. Old questions that are no longer relevant are candidates for deprecation. A question that the model should be able to answer but for which it returns incorrect results, is a defect and must be addressed rigorously to fix what is broken.

This review cycle is what makes an ontology a living system rather than a snapshot or static artifact. Without it, the model drifts away from the domain it was built to describe, and the degradation is invisible until a query returns an answer that a domain expert knows is wrong.

## Ontologies and AI

The relationship between ontologies and AI systems is not one-directional, and understanding the bi-directionality is instrumental to how ontologies and AI systems work symbiotically.

In one direction, ontologies serve AI. A well-governed ontology is an infrastructure that AI systems consume and understand logically. It provides structured, formally typed, semantically consistent data that statistical models cannot produce completely on their own. This is the direction most practitioners encounter first: using an ontology to improve the quality of inputs to a language model. Extended uses include retrieval-augmented generation (RAG), output constraints using controlled vocabularies, and ontology-derived reasoning substrates to improve model accuracy when working with unstructured text.

In the second direction, AI can contribute handsomely to ontologies. Language models can assist in ontology development—drafting definitions, suggesting alignments, generating candidate terms from domain text, and proposing competency questions from requirements documents. This direction is newer, less mature, and requires careful thought about where human judgment is irreplaceable.

LLMs are especially useful when a basic ontology framework or seed ontology is used to derive new ontology elements to support ontology expansion. Humans build the initial framework and competency questions—preparing the canvas, points of orientation, initial competency questions and domain modeling. AI is particularly useful for ontology scaling when it has a solid ontology foundation and framework.

Both directions are of equal importance. Practitioners who understand only the first will underutilize AI in their knowledge engineering workflows. Practitioners who understand only the second—who believe a language model can build a sound ontology without human governance—will produce formally invalid, semantically inconsistent models that fail under reasoner scrutiny.

### *How AI systems consume an ontology*

The NTWF ontology, when deployed and populated with ABox data, provides three distinct consumption surfaces for AI systems. ss: is our prefix for our ABox or instance data and is representative of our data graph.

The first is structured retrieval. A language model with access to the NTWF graph can answer organizational questions by querying the graph directly, rather than retrieving from unstructured documents. When an AI assistant is asked, *"Who approves the production deployment, and who is their escalation backup?"*, a SPARQL query against the graph returns a precise, typed answer:

ss:role-release-manager —> **filled by** ss:agent-maria-gonzalez —> **with** ntwf:delegatesTo —> **pointing to** ss:role-vp-engineering —> **filled by** ss:agent-james-okafor. Notice that retrieval did not come from document text, thereby reducing–if not eliminating–hallucination risk. We have removed any ambiguity about what "approves" means. The ontology's formal semantics make the answer trustworthy because the data is well-defined and semantically structured.

This is the most immediate value of a knowledge graph for language model applications—reducing the surface area where hallucination can occur. A language model that fills in organizational facts from training data or document retrieval produces probabilistic outputs. A language model querying a governed knowledge graph is retrieving formal assertions. This is critical when working with compliance-sensitive applications.

The second consumption surface is controlled vocabulary grounding. The NTWF CBox defines concept schemes for workflow status, artifact types, and agent capabilities. When a language model is generating structured outputs—filling in workflow metadata, classifying a new artifact type, assigning a capability tag to a role— grounding those outputs against the CBox ensures they use canonical terms rather than invented synonyms.

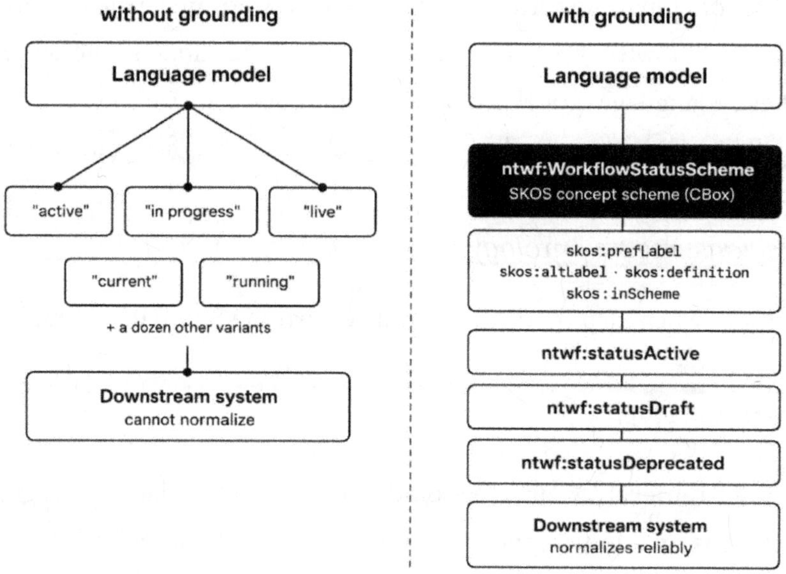


Figure 92: With or without grounding.

A model that has access to ntwf:WorkflowStatusScheme when classifying workflow status will return ntwf:statusActive, ntwf:statusDraft, or ntwf:statusDeprecated. A model without that grounding will return whatever label feels right in context, which may be "active," "in progress," "live," "current," "running," or a dozen other variants that a downstream system cannot normalize.

Controlled vocabulary grounding is not a new idea; it predates language models by decades, rooted in library science and document management practice. What is new is the scale and the mechanism. A large language model can apply a controlled vocabulary to large volumes of unstructured text faster than any human curation process, provided the vocabulary is formally defined and machine accessible. The SKOS structure of the NTWF CBox, with skos:prefLabel, skos:altLabel, skos:definition, and skos:inScheme, is exactly the format required by vocabulary-grounding systems.

The third consumption surface is inference-augmented context. The OWL-RL reasoner is run to materialize inferences before serving a language model a set of triples as context for any specific question. These inferences give the model the closed graph reasoning paths. Rather than simply asserting facts, the AI model is served everything that is logically entailed by the TBox.

When the LLM is asked about agent accountability for a workflow step, the ontology goes beyond the explicit ntwf:filledBy triple, extending to the inferred foaf:Person type for human agents, the inferred prov:SoftwareAgent type for AI agents, and the complete transitive ordering chain for step sequences. The model reasons over a richer, more coherent picture of the domain based upon the ontology and the reasoner's derived inference.

Ontologies are critical for driving accurate, reliable reasoning, since language models are not reliable logical reasoners. While an LLM can appear to reason—they will often produce correct-looking outputs for simple logical patterns—they do not guarantee logical consistency, and they do not maintain a formal model of what is true. The logical consistency guarantee comes from the reasoner, not the LLM, when the reasoning substrate is the ontology and the model is consuming materialized inferences.

The LLM's contribution is natural language interpretation and generation. The ontology's contribution is formal correctness. This is where we see *neurosymbolic AI* come to life—*neuro* derived from the LLM and *symbolic* coming from the ontology.

## *AI contributes to ontology development*

The second direction—AI contributions to ontology construction—requires more careful treatment because the failure modes are less obvious.

Language models are useful for several specific tasks in the ontology development pipeline. They are good at generating candidate competency questions from domain documents. Given Special Solutions' engineering handbook, a model can produce a list of questions the handbook implies—questions about escalation, artifact ownership, and AI agent accountability—that an ontology engineer can evaluate, filter, and add to the formal competency question set. This is accelerated discovery, not modeling. The engineer still evaluates every candidate.

Language models are proficient at drafting rdfs:label and rdfs:comment values. Given a class name and its context in the ontology, a model can produce a candidate definition that captures what the class covers, what it excludes, and where it sits relative to adjacent terms. This draft definition is the starting point for the human-written definition, not a replacement for it. The engineer or ontologist reads it critically, identifies scope errors, and rewrites where necessary. The model saves time on the initial draft while the engineer ensures correctness.

For ontology building, LLMs can suggest alignment candidates from external standard ontologies, as we modeled earlier.

Given a custom class definition, a model familiar with PROV-O, FOAF, and Schema.org can propose candidate classes and superclasses: "*This looks like it might subclass* prov:Plan." Naturally, the engineer or ontologist must formally evaluate LLM suggestions for ontology elements. LLM suggestions are helpful for ontology standards surveys and design assistance, but the final modeling decisions should always rest in the hands of ontologists or ontology engineers.

Where language models are not useful—and where practitioners have been commonly burned—is in generating axioms, disjointness declarations, or property domain and range assignments, absent of human review. These are the decisions that carry logical consequences. An incorrectly placed domain declaration produces incorrect inferences that propagate through every query that touches those triples. A disjointness axiom was added based on a model's intuition that "*These seem like different kinds of things*" may be formally incorrect for the domain and cause legitimate TBox individuals to be flagged as inconsistent.

> *The discipline is simple to state, but requires constant enforcement—language models generate candidates; humans make commitments.*

A competency question is a commitment about what the ontology must answer. A class definition is a commitment about what the class covers. An axiom is a commitment with logical consequences. These all require human judgment, domain knowledge, and accountability, which a language model does not possess. In other words, have a human-in-the-loop (HITL) throughout all stages and phases of ontology design and construction.

## The NTWF graph as an AI system registry

One of the most valuable extensions to the NTWF ontology—and one that emerges directly from its existing structure—is the utility of the ontology graph as an AI system registry. This is possible, thanks to the decisions already made.

The NTWF ontology models AI agents as first-class individuals with ntwf:modelVersion, typed as prov:SoftwareAgent, assigned to roles through ntwf:filledBy, and producing artifacts that carry prov:wasAttributedTo relations and provenance links. Everything required to register an AI system in the graph already exists in the ontology.

An AI system registry cannot provide rich, logical, and descriptive context, whereas an ontology can. The ontology contains all of the qualities and requisites for contextual understanding. For example, a row in a database table that records risk-classifier-v2.4.1 was deployed on 2026-01-10 is a fact in isolation. An ntwf:AIAgent individual in the NTWF ontology, connected through ntwf:filledBy to the role it fills, through ntwf:assignedRole to the workflow steps it executes, through prov:wasAttributedTo to every artifact it has produced, is a fact in a semantic network.

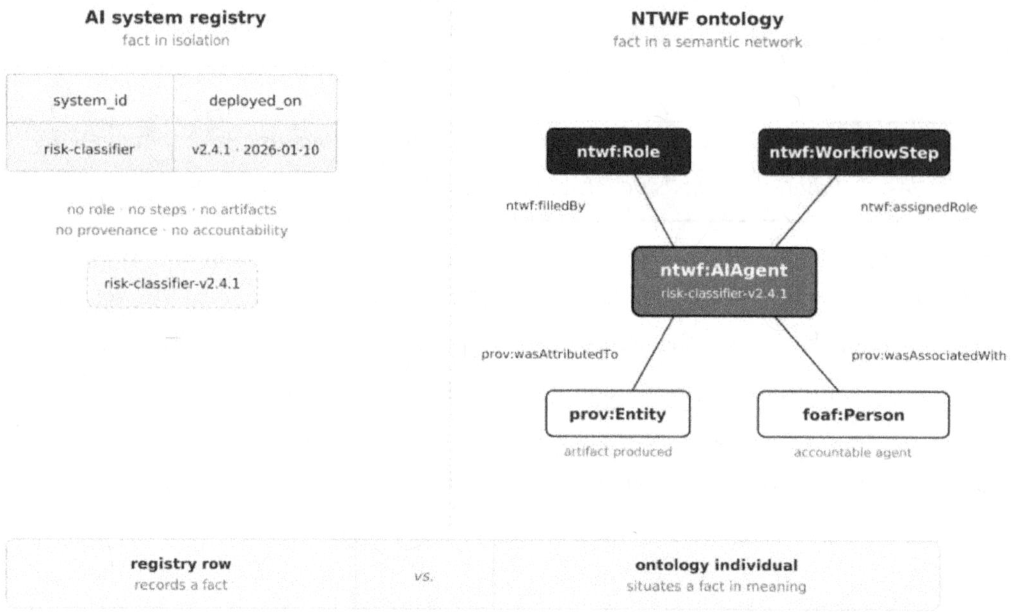


Figure 93: Facts in isolation versus semantic network.

The question "What is the blast radius of upgrading risk-classifier from v2.4.1 to v2.5.0?" becomes a graph traversal: find all artifacts attributed to this agent, find all downstream steps that consume those artifacts as inputs, find the roles and agents responsible for those downstream steps, and find the workflows containing all of them. The impact assessment is rendered thanks to a SPARQL query. Without the ontology, it is a manual exercise that risks missing nuances and dependencies.

Here's where the metadata layer's integration surface works to enable fact-finding at an operational scale. Because ntwf:AIAgent individuals carry Dublin Core metadata alongside their ontological type assertions, the ontology individual can be populated from the AI system registry feed—whatever system manages model versions, deployment records, and evaluation results—through the shared vocabulary. The registry does not need to know about PROV-O and the ontology does not need to know about the registry's internal schema. The Dublin Core properties are the shared contract, adding context through the relationships between ontology elements and the description encoded within.

## Ontology is the ground truth

There is a threshold in knowledge infrastructure maturity that organizations cross when they stop treating the ontology as a documentation artifact and start treating it as the authoritative source for organizational facts.

At Special Solutions, that threshold is crossed when the first AI system is deployed that makes routing decisions based on the graph. When the deployment pipeline queries ntwf:filledBy to determine who receives an approval notification—rather than reading from a spreadsheet maintained by the operations team—the ontology's correctness becomes an operational dependency. A stale ntwf:filledBy triple produces incorrect query results and sends the approval notification to the wrong person, or to no one at all. This threshold is the goal.

*Ontologies are built to be used, and the highest-value use is as a live, queryable source of organizational truth that operational systems can depend on.*

But crossing the threshold fundamentally changes the governance requirements. When an ontology exists solely as documentation without governance, a stale triple becomes an accuracy issue. When the ontology is infrastructure, a stale triple is an operational failure. The governance processes described earlier—stewardship, change management, versioning, and competency question review—are designed for organizations that have crossed or are approaching this threshold.

The change management protocol for ntwf:filledBy triples becomes a critical path process. When Maria Gonzalez leaves the Release Manager role, the triple must be updated before the first deployment that needs her approval. Governance defines the process, who is responsible for triggering the change process, and what the SLA is. The answer depends on the organization. But generally, the design of the NTWF ontology makes the answer straightforward to implement. There is exactly one triple to update per role-agent assignment, and the role-agent decoupling heuristic ensures that updating it does not require touching the workflow structure. The governance overhead of maintaining a live organizational ontology is minimized because of the modeling decisions made in Part Two. Good design makes governance tractable.

## RAG over structured graphs

Without jumping too far ahead, let's set the scene for how retrieval augmented generation (RAG) works using ontologies. A knowledge graph represents an architecture, with its star players being the taxonomy, thesaurus, ontology, metadata schemas, and a reasoner. When we talk about querying a knowledge graph, we are mostly talking about querying the ontology. With this understanding, let's explore how to leverage RAG using a knowledge graph, while keeping the ontology, a reasoner, and SPARQL queries in mind.

The current dominant approach to using knowledge graphs with language models is RAG. In its most common form, RAG retrieves chunks of unstructured text—paragraphs from documents, passages from wikis—and supplies chunks as context to a generation model. The model produces outputs grounded in retrieved text rather than solely in training weights.

The limitation of text-chunk RAG for organizational knowledge is that it retrieves representations of facts, not the facts themselves. A paragraph from a workflow document describing who is responsible for approving a production deployment is a natural-language assertion that requires the model to parse, interpret, and decide whether to trust it.

A ntwf:assignedRole triple linking the release approval gate to the release manager role, with a ntwf:filledBy triple linking that role to the current release manager, is a formal assertion that a query engine can return with certainty.

Structured graph RAG—sometimes called GraphRAG—uses the graph as the retrieval substrate rather than text chunks. Given a query about organizational accountability, the system generates a SPARQL query, runs it against the knowledge graph, and supplies the returned triples as structured context to the generation model. The model receives precise, formally typed facts rather than probabilistic text chunks. The outputs are more accurate, more consistent, and more auditable because the source of each fact is a named triple in a governed graph rather than a fragment of a document.

The NTWF ontology is designed to accommodate this pattern. The URI naming convention for ABox instance data—ss:workflow-production-deployment, ss:role-release-manager, ss:agent-maria-gonzalez—produces human-readable identifiers that a generation model can interpret and cite. The Dublin Core metadata on every individual provides the natural-language labels and descriptions that give graph context its intelligibility. The provenance structure means every fact can be traced to its source.

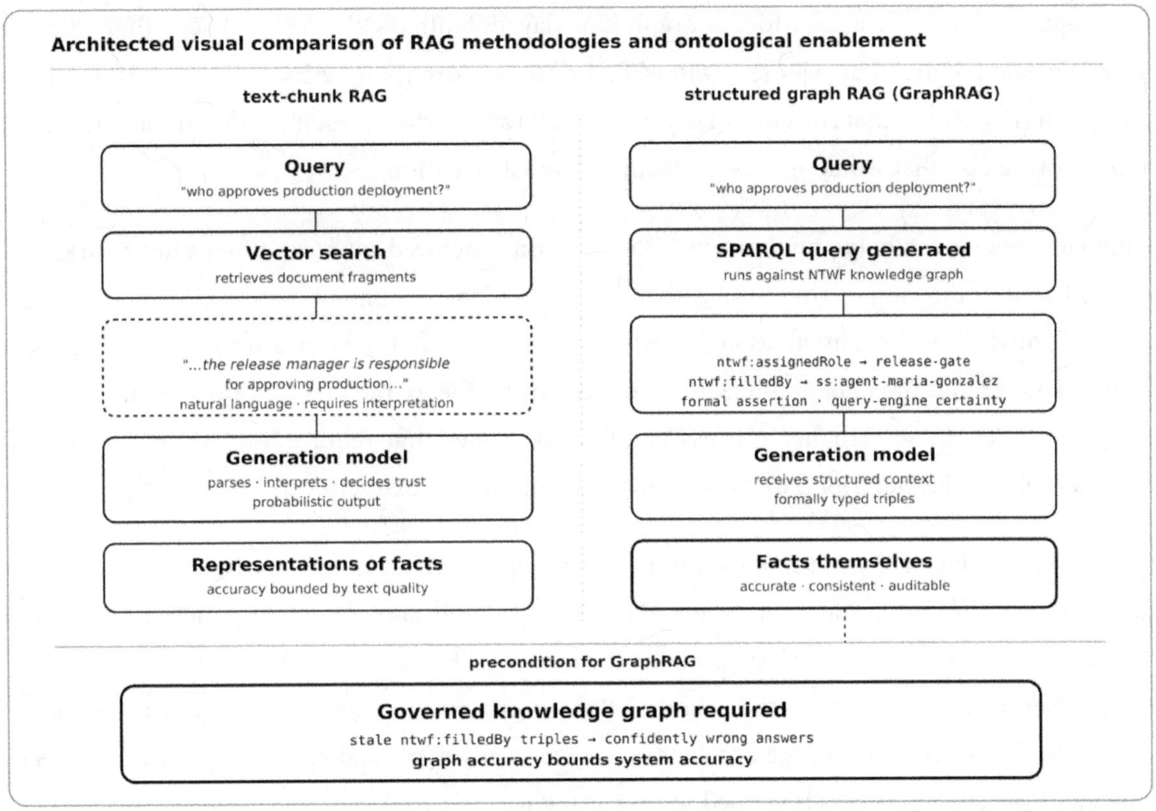


Figure 94: RAG methodologies and ontological enablement.

What GraphRAG requires that text-chunk RAG does not is a governed, knowledge graph. A knowledge graph with stale ntwf:filledBy triples or deprecated workflow individuals will produce confidently wrong answers when queried. The accuracy of a structured RAG system is bounded by the accuracy of the graph it queries, which is why governance is a precondition for deploying AI systems against the graph.

## AI-assisted ontology maintenance

The maintenance loop—monitoring for drift, updating the ABox, reviewing the competency question set—is where AI systems can provide the most practical assistance to knowledge engineers.

Language models with access to the graph can flag potential staleness. A query that identifies ***ntwf:Workflow*** individuals whose ***dct:modified date*** is more than 12 months old is the staleness query. An AI assistant that runs this query periodically and surfaces results to the steward automates a monitoring task that would otherwise require manual attention.

Language models can help populate the ABox from unstructured sources. When a new workflow is documented in the engineering wiki, a model can parse the document and propose a set of ABox triples— ntwf:Workflow, ntwf:hasStep, ntwf:assignedRole—that the steward reviews and approves before loading into the data graph. The model performs the extraction, and the steward performs the validation. The governance process handles the triples that require human judgment, while automation handles the triples that constitute straightforward extractions.

Language models can also assist in identifying gaps in competency question coverage. Given a set of questions posed by organizational stakeholders that the graph cannot currently answer, a model can classify them into three categories: questions the existing TBox could answer if the right ABox data were present; questions that require a minor TBox extension; and questions that require a structural change to the model. This triage accelerates the steward's work and ensures that the appropriate change management process is applied to each category.

What AI systems cannot do is decide whether a proposed TBox change preserves the semantic integrity of the model. That requires an understanding of what the existing terms mean, the proposed change impact, and whether the inference consequences are consistent with the domain. It requires running the validation framework and evaluating whether the 104-test suite still passes. It requires asking whether the change introduces a disjointness violation, an unintended domain inference, or a property range inconsistency. These are engineering judgments that rely upon formal knowledge and the accountability that human engineers hold.

## Ontology as organizational memory

Our exploration of ontology began with a problem statement that is all too familiar to those working with AI, data, and technology.

> *Ontology is simultaneously the most powerful and the most misunderstood technology in the knowledge infrastructure landscape.*

The confusion has led to organizations that cannot distinguish between a taxonomy and an ontology, and to systems that visually resemble knowledge graphs but cannot reason.

Organizations that treat ontology engineering as a database schema exercise may build structures that appear to be valid models but cannot be queried, maintained, or extended for lack of a standards-based logical descriptive ontology.

Most people love bubbles on a page, where entities are represented in relation to one another. We use visuals of graphs to assist with ontology adoption and organizational communication, in addition to assisting with ontology design. The actual bubbles and arrows on a screen are communicating the story, as told by the ontology. Without the ontology, you simply have bubbles and arrows on a screen. The ontology is the engine room where organizational memory is built and maintained, allowing it to persist over time and space.

Handle the ontology with care, attending to ontology governance. Augment ontology construction and expansion with the help of AI rather than relegating all responsibilities to a machine. Ontology design, construction, and governance are about modeling, describing, and representing a world or reality, where facts are established and property relations fill in the gaps, so context can flourish. The human element will always be necessary because ontologies are about modeling knowledge. Humans (not machines) own knowledge, and so ontologies are about humans modeling the world with all six senses, and are therefore an act of knowledge ownership and stewardship.

## Conclusion

The NTWF workflow ontology is not a large model. It is composed of nine classes, 13 object properties, and five datatype properties. The custom ontology is small by design; it exists to add custom ontology elements and to work well with existing standard ontologies. The open standard ontologies—PROV-O, FOAF, Dublin Core, DCAT, Schema.org—do their fair share of descriptive and logical work.

The governance discipline ensures that the model stays correct and aligned, as the domain changes. The versioning convention ensures that breaking changes are deliberate and traceable. The stewardship structure ensures that someone is responsible when the ontology drifts.

The AI integration patterns—structured retrieval, controlled vocabulary grounding, inference-augmented context, GraphRAG—transform the validated ontology from a formal model into operational infrastructure. The ontology is kept current and patterns are trustworthy because of ontology governance.

This is what the Ontology Pipeline builds toward: a live, governed, queryable source of organizational knowledge that operational systems and AI systems can depend on. The pipeline stages—controlled vocabulary, taxonomy, thesaurus, ontology, and knowledge graph—each produce something valuable on their own. Together, they produce something the organization could not build any other way: a formal, explicit, shared, and continuously maintained model of what the organization knows about its own processes, actors, and artifacts.

An ontology is not a database schema, nor is it a taxonomy with extra steps. It is certainly not a marketing concept or a JSON config file with philosophical aspirations. An ontology is a formal model of a domain, built with shared, interoperable standards, governed by people who understand what the ontology means, and used by systems that depend on its correctness.

That is what you have built and now you must keep it alive.

CHAPTER 6

# Knowledge Graph

The term knowledge graph has been applied to an enormous range of artifacts—from a lightly annotated property graph to a fully axiomatized semantic architecture with formal reasoning and provenance tracking at every layer. The diverse range of things that assume the label 'knowledge graph' reflects a deeper confusion stemming from treating knowledge graphs as a product category rather than as a way of describing an architecture.

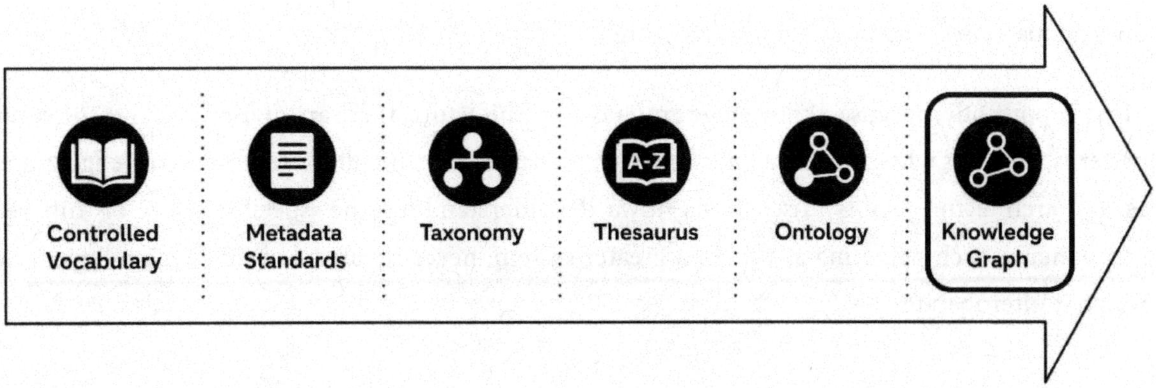


Figure 95: The Ontology Pipeline framework.

A product has walls and doors. A product is a finished thing with fixed boundaries—you buy it, install it, and use it as delivered. An architecture is not a thing you buy; it is a purposeful arrangement of components: vocabulary, ontology, knowledge base, metadata schemas, reasoner, and—depending on the use case—NLP pipelines, vector retrieval, and graph analytics. What makes a knowledge graph a knowledge graph is the composition—the way those components work in relationship to one another to represent a domain, its entities, and the logical rules governing what can be asserted and inferred. You can acquire any individual component off a shelf but the architecture is what gets built.

The definition of a knowledge graph is still widely contested, but the research literature has been working toward a more concrete definition to address the lack of consistency across marketplaces and disciplines. A useful formulation from the ACM's survey on knowledge graph construction defines a knowledge graph as a semantic graph where nodes represent concepts and edges represent relationships, drawing on background knowledge about those concepts and relations. Including background knowledge is instrumental in moving the definition of a knowledge graph beyond a collection of facts toward facts organized within a formal model, connected to a knowledge base, and used to encode what facts mean. That formal model is the ontology.

This chapter examines knowledge graphs as architectures. First, we'll define the architecture and its components, survey the broader landscape of graph patterns, and focus on the three most common RDF-based architectures across industries. Then, we'll examine each of the three predominant architectural patterns in depth, explaining the utility of each graph type and its associated use cases. Finally, we'll address how organizations select and implement a specific architecture given their domain, use cases, and existing infrastructure.

Most importantly, because a knowledge graph is an architecture, there are myriad graph architecture patterns, which is why defining a knowledge graph can be so difficult. Accepting knowledge graphs as an architecture shifts discussions toward understanding the specific roles of different components, each operating as part of a greater system, never isolated from the technologies with which it interoperates.

---

## A knowledge graph is an architecture

The first thing to establish is what defines a knowledge graph. A knowledge graph is an architecture—a purposeful arrangement of components that together represent a domain of entities, the relationships among them, and the rules governing how those entities and relationships may be described and reasoned over. Why architecture and not model? A model is a single representation—

one schema, one ontology, one diagram. A knowledge graph is not one representation; it is the coordinated arrangement of several—vocabulary, ontology, knowledge base, and often a reasoner and a retrieval layer—each doing a distinct job. "Architecture" describes that composition and the relationships among the parts, which is exactly what "model" fails to capture.

The defining characteristic is that the graph encodes not just data but meaning. This includes typed entities known as classes, semantically defined relationships, a conceptual model expressed as a vocabulary or taxonomy, and a formal logical model that makes the graph's assertions machine-interpretable and subject to inference and reasoning.

This is the distinction Hogan et al. drew when they defined a knowledge graph as "a graph of data intended to accumulate and convey knowledge of the real world, whose nodes represent entities of interest and whose edges represent relations between these entities."[20] It is the distinction Ehrlinger and Wöß sharpen when they specify that a knowledge graph must include an ontology as its backbone, the formal model that makes inference possible and that separates a knowledge graph from a database that merely uses a graph data structure.[21]

When we frame a knowledge graph as an architecture rather than a product, we can better understand its capabilities relative to an organization's needs and use cases. For example, an organization that acquires a graph database and loads data into it has not built a knowledge graph. The knowledge graph emerges from the composition of its components in relationship to one another. The sections that follow describe each component and its distinct function within that composition.

---

*A knowledge graph is an architecture—a purposeful arrangement of components that together, represent a domain, the relationships within it, and the logical rules that govern how it may be reasoned over.*

---

[20] Noy, N., Gao, Y., Jain, A., Narayanan, A., Patterson, A., & Taylor, J. (2019). Industry-scale knowledge graphs: Lessons and challenges. *Communications of the ACM*, 62(8), 36–43.

[21] Ehrlinger, L., & Wöß, W. (2016). Towards a definition of knowledge graphs. Proceedings of the SEMANTICS 2016 Conference, Posters and Demos Track.

## Knowledge graph architecture components

Knowledge graph architectures share a common set of possible components. Not every architecture uses every component. Which components are present, how they are implemented, and how they interact with one another define the character of a specific knowledge graph. Each component, in turn, beginning with the vocabulary and ontology layers, is related but distinct. The components are frequently collapsed incorrectly into a single identifying concept.

## Taxonomies and thesauri as a conceptual model

The conceptual model of a knowledge graph comprises its vocabulary, which is a controlled set of terms, concepts, and relationships that describe the domain in human-intelligible language. Vocabularies establish what items exist in the domain, what they are called, how they relate hierarchically and associatively to one another, and how synonyms, abbreviations, and alternate expressions map to canonical terms. They are the layer where subject matter expertise lives—the articulation of how practitioners in a domain understand and name the entities and relationships they work with.

## Bee taxonomy

Two vocabulary structures appear in knowledge graph architectures. A taxonomy organizes concepts into a strict hierarchy of broader and narrower relationships and classifies concepts to define that this thing is a kind of that thing. A thesaurus extends the taxonomy with associative relationships between terms that are not hierarchical, as well as preferred labels, alternate labels, and scope notes that govern how each term may be used in practice. Together, the taxonomy and thesaurus constitute the controlled vocabulary infrastructure that supports consistent, unambiguous description of domain entities.

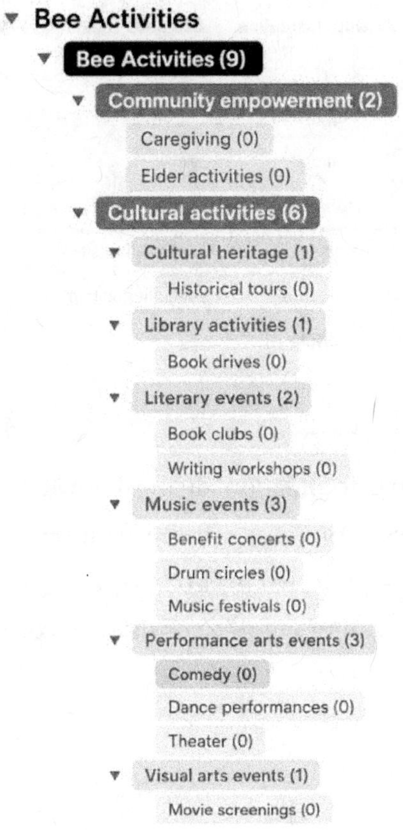


Figure 96: Bee activities.

SKOS—the Simple Knowledge Organization System—is the W3C standard for representing taxonomies, thesauri, and other controlled vocabularies in RDF.[22] SKOS provides skos:broader and skos:narrower for hierarchical relationships, skos:related for associative relationships, and a full label vocabulary for term management. ISO 25964, the international standard for thesauri and their interoperability, provides the institutional governance framework within which SKOS is applied in professional information environments.[23]

---

[22] World Wide Web Consortium. (2009). SKOS Simple Knowledge Organization System Reference. W3C Recommendation. https://www.w3.org/TR/skos-reference/.

[23] International Organization for Standardization. (2011). ISO 25964-1: Information and Documentation—Thesauri and Interoperability with Other Vocabularies.

| Concepts | Labels & Notation | Documentation | Semantic Relations | Mapping Properties | Collections |
|---|---|---|---|---|---|
| Concept | prefLabel | note | broader | broadMatch | Collection |
| ConceptScheme | altLabel | changeNote | narrower | narrowMatch | orderedCollection |
| inScheme | hiddenLabel | definition | related | relatedMatch | member |
| hasTopConcept | notation | editorialNote | broaderTransitive | closeMatch | memberList |
| topConceptOf | | example | narrowerTransitive | exactMatch | |
| | | historyNote | semanticRelation | mappingRelation | |
| | | scopeNote | | | |

Figure 97: SKOS vocabulary organized by theme.

The vocabulary is the conceptual foundation of the knowledge graph. It is, however, not the reasoning infrastructure. A SKOS taxonomy or thesaurus specifies that one concept is broader than another and that certain terms are preferred over others. It does not encode logical rules. It cannot derive new facts by inference. It cannot enforce consistency constraints over asserted data. Those functions belong to the ontology.

---

## The ontology: Formal logic and reasoning

The ontology is the formal logical model of the domain. Where the vocabulary provides the conceptual models—what things exist and what they are called—the ontology provides the reasoning model, the formal axioms, class definitions, property restrictions, and logical constraints that govern how knowledge about those things may be structured, validated, and computationally reasoned over. The ontology enables a machine to derive new facts from existing ones and detect inconsistencies in the data.

---

## NTWF workflow ontology

OWL 2—the W3C Web Ontology Language—is the primary formal language for ontology expression in RDF-based knowledge graph architectures. OWL 2 provides the machinery of description logic—class equivalence, property transitivity, cardinality restrictions, disjointness constraints, and the closed- and open-world reasoning semantics that determine how the graph responds to the absence of a fact.[24] OWL 2 offers three profiles calibrated to the trade-off between expressivity and computational cost: OWL 2 EL for large biomedical ontologies requiring polynomial-time reasoning, OWL 2 QL for conjunctive query rewriting over relational sources, and OWL 2 RL for scalable rule-based inference.

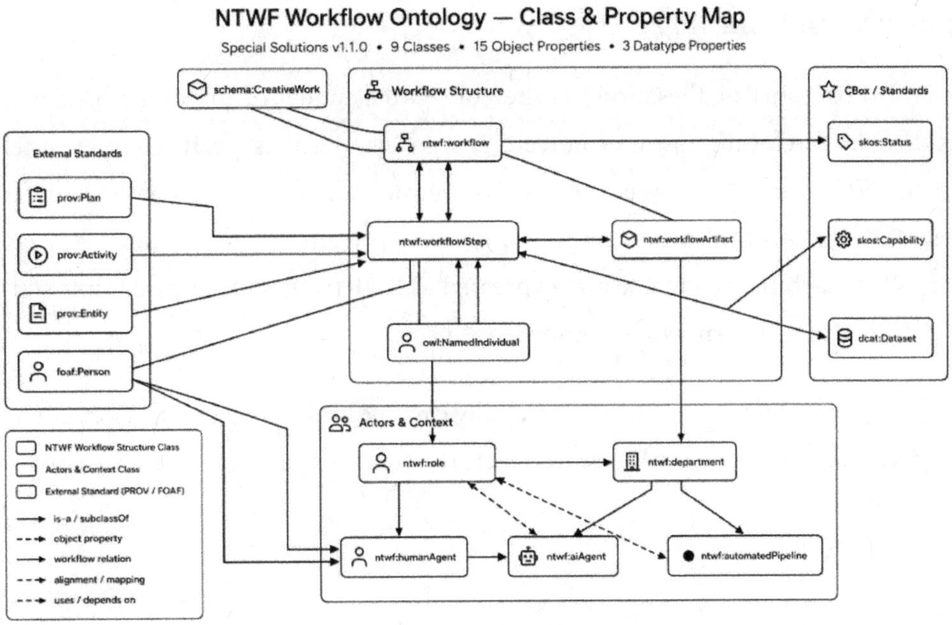


Figure 98: Workflow ontology.

The relationship between vocabulary and ontology is complementary, and a well-designed knowledge graph has both. The vocabulary provides the labels, terminology, and conceptual organization. The ontology provides the logical structure that makes terms and data formally meaningful to a reasoning system.

Using the NTWF workflow taxonomy and ontology as our example, the conceptual model exists as a SKOS taxonomy and thesaurus. The taxonomy reveals that "Code Review" is narrower than

[24] World Wide Web Consortium. (2012). OWL 2 Web Ontology Language Profiles, Second Edition. W3C Recommendation. https://www.w3.org/TR/owl2-profiles/.

"Quality Assurance Activity." The ontology adds depth in meaning by encoding that any work item with a completed review step and a passing test record is logically classified as a member of the class ReleasableArtifact—an inference the system can derive without explicit assertion. These are different kinds of knowledge serving distinct functions.

---

## Vocabulary versus ontology

A vocabulary (taxonomy or thesaurus) is the conceptual model of the domain. It names things, organizes them hierarchically and associatively, and governs term usage. It is human-intelligible and expressed in SKOS. An ontology is the formal logical model of the domain. It defines classes, properties, and axioms that a reasoning engine can process to derive new facts and enforce consistency. It is machine-executable and expressed as RDF triple statements. Triple statements are stored in a triple store, also known as a knowledge base.

Vocabularies and ontologies are required for a fully capable knowledge graph. They are not the same artifact and conflating them produces architectures that can look complete visually but cannot reason.

---

## Ontologies, neural networks, and AI

The current AI landscape is dominated by large language models and neural networks, systems that excel at pattern recognition across vast corpora but operate largely as statistical black boxes. They cannot guarantee logical consistency, nor can they explain their reasoning in terms that are human-verifiable. They struggle to generalize reliably in low-data domains and hallucinate facts when the training distribution provides no grounding signal. These are known limitations of the neural paradigm.

Ontologies are the structural complement to what neural networks lack. Where a neural network perceives, an ontology reasons. When a language model generates plausible text, an ontology enforces formal constraints on what may be asserted. When domain ontologies serve as the symbolic backbone of a neural system, the paradigm is called neurosymbolic AI. Ontologies provide the symbolic and LLMs contribute the neuro.

Ontologies make model outputs interpretable by connecting predictions to human-understandable classes, properties, and relations, thereby reducing data requirements. By encoding prior domain knowledge, the model does not need to learn from scratch. The neurosymbolic approach enables formal inference, a capability that statistical approaches cannot perform on their own.

Knowledge graph architectures ground LLMs in a well-formed ontology, enabling the retrieval of formally typed, encoded facts with provenance. The graph constrains what the model can assert. The ontology ensures that constraints are coherent, while the vocabulary provides labels and supports tasks such as indexing, decision trees, natural language processing, and search. Ultimately, these components of the bedrock knowledge graph architecture are not optional. For AI deployments, these are the foundational infrastructure elements that help instantiate AI systems that are reliable, auditable, and capable of reasoning and inference.

*Where a neural network perceives, an ontology reasons.*
*The graph constrains what the model can assert.*
*The ontology ensures those constraints are coherent.*

## The knowledge base

The knowledge base is the store of asserted facts—the instance data that populates the ontology's logical model. In the formal terminology of description logics, the ontology defines the TBox (terminological box): the classes, properties, and axioms that constitute the schema. The knowledge base is the ABox (assertional box): the individual entities and their relationships. If the ontology is the DDL, the knowledge base is the data that conforms to it. A knowledge graph without an ontology is a graph of facts with no formal model. An ontology without a knowledge base is a logical schema with nothing to reason over.

In RDF-based architectures, the knowledge base is a triple store, a database optimized for storing and querying subject-predicate-object triples. Leading triple stores include Apache Jena TDB2, Ontotext GraphDB, Stardog, Amazon Neptune (in RDF mode), and Virtuoso. SPARQL is the W3C standard query language for these systems, operating over both the TBox and ABox layers.

In property graph architectures, the knowledge base is a labeled property graph (LPG) database. Neo4j, Amazon Neptune (in Gremlin mode), and TigerGraph are all examples of LPG databases, where nodes and edges carry key-value property maps and are traversed using GQL, Cypher, or Gremlin. LPG databases typically operate under the closed-world assumption, and don't offer support for ontological reasoning. LPGs fall short in query language expressivity, federation capability, reasoning support, and performance characteristics as compared to ontology-based knowledge graphs. These primary differentiators will be elaborated upon later in this chapter.

*The vocabulary, the ontology, and the knowledge base form the irreducible core of a knowledge graph.*

The vocabulary names and organizes concepts. The ontology defines the logical commitments—the classes, properties, constraints, and axioms—that govern what those concepts mean and how they relate. The knowledge base stores the asserted facts that the ontology makes it possible to reason over. Remove any one of the three, and what remains may be a useful data structure, but it is not a knowledge graph.

## Metadata schemas

Every entity in a knowledge graph was asserted by someone, at some point in time, from some source, under some authority. Metadata schemas capture this context. They are the infrastructure of provenance and description that allows the graph to answer not just "what" but "when," "by whom," "from which source," and "under what license." Without metadata, assertions in the graph are floating claims with no grounding in facts.

Several W3C and community standards govern metadata in knowledge graph contexts, all of which use RDF to express metadata. The Dublin Core Metadata Terms provide basic descriptive metadata: title, creator, subject, date, and rights.[25]

DCAT, the Data Catalog Vocabulary, describes datasets and data services within a catalog structure, enabling discovery across multiple graph deployments.[26] PROV-O, the W3C Provenance Ontology, provides the formal vocabulary for asserting who generated what, from which inputs, through which process, at what time.[27] Schema.org offers a widely adopted lightweight vocabulary for entity description, readable by web crawlers and search engines. These standards are not mutually exclusive; knowledge graphs often use different elements from RDF metadata models to form cohesive knowledge graph-ready metadata schemas.

---

## The reasoner

A reasoner is a software component that applies the formal axioms in the ontology to derive new facts from existing assertions in the knowledge base. Given an ontology axiom stating that every Person who holds an employment relationship with a Company is an Employee, a reasoner will automatically classify any individual with that relationship as an instance of Employee—without the assertion being made explicitly. This is inference over the logical model: the derivation of implicit truths from explicit ones.

Widely deployed OWL reasoners include Pellet (integrated into Stardog), HermiT, and ELK. ELK is designed for OWL 2 EL ontologies such as the Gene Ontology, where hundreds of thousands of classes are reasoned over in biomedical informatics environments.[28] The choice of reasoner is constrained by the OWL 2 profile of the ontology and the scale of the knowledge base. Reasoning is

25 Dublin Core Metadata Initiative. (2020). DCMI Metadata Terms. https://www.dublincore.org/specifications/dublin-core/dcmi-terms/.

26 World Wide Web Consortium. (2020). Data Catalog Vocabulary (DCAT)—Version 2. W3C Recommendation. https://www.w3.org/TR/vocab-dcat-2/.

27 World Wide Web Consortium. (2013). PROV-O: The PROV Ontology. W3C Recommendation. https://www.w3.org/TR/prov-o/.

28 Kazakov, Y., Krötzsch, M., & Simancik, F. (2014). The incredible ELK: From polynomial procedures to efficient reasoning with EL ontologies. Journal of Automated Reasoning, 53(1), 1–61.

computationally expensive; many operational architectures materialize inferred facts at load time rather than computing them at query time, trading storage overhead for query latency.

**Mandatory elements**:

- **Accession (also known as Unique Identifier):** Every term has a GO ID, a unique seven-digit identifier prefixed by GO; e.g., GO:0005739, GO:1904659, or GO:0016597.
- **Term name:** Every term has a human-readable term name—e.g. mitochondrion, D-glucose transmembrane transport, or amino acid binding.
- **Ontology (also known as Aspect):** Denotes which of the three sub-ontologies the term belongs to. Written as molecular_function (MF), biological_process (BP), and cellular_component (CC).
- **Definition:** A textual description of what the term represents, plus reference(s) to the source of information.
- **Relationship to other terms:** How the term relates to other terms in the ontology. All terms (other than the root terms representing each aspect, above) have an is a sub-class relationship to another term. The Gene Ontology employs a number of other relations; the relations documentation page describes the relations used in the ontology.

---

## Requirements from the Gene Ontology (GO)

The reasoner operates on the ontology, not on the vocabulary. A SKOS taxonomy cannot be reasoned over in the OWL sense. Only the formal axioms of an OWL ontology provide the logical premises from which a reasoner can derive conclusions. This is why the vocabulary-ontology distinction is not merely terminological. It has direct consequences for what the knowledge graph can do.

## The validation layer

SHACL—the Shapes Constraint Language—is the W3C standard for defining and enforcing constraints over RDF graph data. Its function is categorically different from OWL reasoning and the two are frequently confused. OWL operates under open-world semantics—the absence of a fact does not imply its negation, and the reasoner derives what is logically entailed from what is asserted. SHACL operates under closed-world assumptions for validation purposes. It enforces that the data in the graph conform to defined structural requirements and reports violations when it does not.

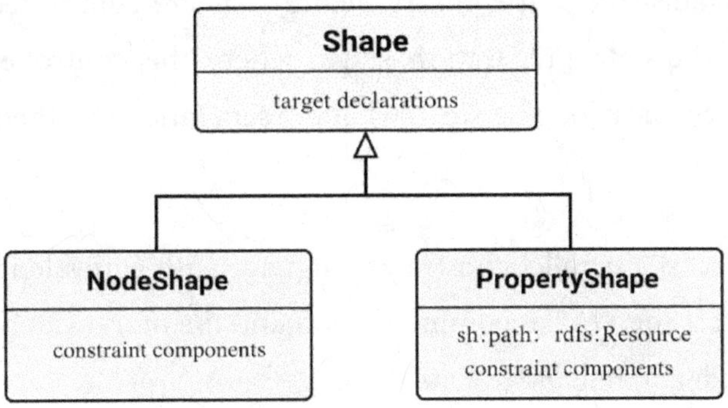


Figure 99: SHACL (Shapes Constraint Language) shapes.

### *SHACL shapes*

A SHACL shape defines a set of constraints that nodes in the graph must satisfy. A node shape might require that every instance of a workItem have exactly one assigned status value drawn from a defined vocabulary, that the value be of type xsd:string, and that a created timestamp be present and parseable as a date. If data in the graph violates any of these constraints, SHACL reports a validation result—a typed, structured account of what failed, against which constraint(s), and impacting which node(s). The graph is not corrected automatically. The validation result is a signal to the data pipeline or the human data steward that an assertion has been made that does not conform to the required shape.

This can be viewed as gates and checks for a knowledge graph architecture. OWL provides the logical, formal model that can be reasoned over, while SHACL tells you whether the data looks the way it is required to look. Both are necessary in production knowledge graphs, and neither substitutes for the other. An ontology with tight cardinality constraints and disjointness axioms will detect logical inconsistencies through a reasoner. It will not detect that a required property is missing from an instance, that a literal value falls outside the expected datatype range, or that a relationship target is of an unexpected class—the kinds of data quality failures that SHACL is designed to catch before they propagate downstream.

In the Ontology Pipeline, SHACL validation is the enforcement mechanism at the knowledge base stage. Once the vocabulary, taxonomy, thesaurus, and ontology are in place, SHACL shapes codify the structural expectations derived from the ontology into executable validation logic. Every data load can be validated against the shape library before facts are committed to the graph. SHACL reports travel back to the data preparation stage, where the controlled vocabulary was first disciplined, closing the feedback loop between what the semantic model requires and what the data contains.

Shape Expressions (ShEx) is a parallel constraint language with equivalent expressive scope and a different syntax. SHACL is the W3C recommendation and the more widely implemented standard in enterprise and research graph deployments.

---

## The query layer

SPARQL is the W3C standard query language for RDF-based knowledge graphs—the mechanism through which the vocabulary, ontology, and knowledge base are interrogated at runtime. It is the operational infrastructure through which the graph's semantic content becomes accessible.

SPARQL 1.1 supports four query forms: SELECT for tabular result retrieval, CONSTRUCT for building new RDF graphs from query results, ASK for Boolean existence tests, and DESCRIBE for returning descriptions of named resources. SPARQL UPDATE adds write operations. The SPARQL 1.1 Federated Query specification introduces the SERVICE keyword, enabling a single query to retrieve and join data across multiple remote SPARQL endpoints—a capability that has no equivalent in other graph query languages and that makes SPARQL the correct choice for linked data architectures where data is distributed across independently maintained graphs.

### *Example SPARQL query*

The critical capability that distinguishes SPARQL from alternative query layers is its integration with the inference model. When a SPARQL query is executed against a reasoner-enabled triple store, it can be directed to run over the inferred graph—the full set of facts the ontology entails, not just the explicitly asserted facts. A query for all instances of Employee will return every individual the reasoner has classified as an Employee via formal axioms, including those that were never explicitly typed as such. No other graph query language provides this capability because no other graph query language was designed to operate over a formal ontological model.

Semantic middleware platforms, including TopBraid EDG and Stardog, offer GraphQL and Cypher query interfaces alongside SPARQL. This is a developer accessibility decision, rather than an architectural equivalence.

GraphQL is a client-server query protocol designed for hierarchical data retrieval over APIs. It returns tree-shaped results against a defined schema. In a knowledge graph context, this means it operates over a surface projection of the graph that the schema the platform exposes, rather than over the underlying triple model and its inferred extensions. Federation is not available with GraphQL. Inference integration is at best partial and platform-dependent. SPARQL CONSTRUCT queries, which build new graph structures from existing ones, have no GraphQL equivalent.

Cypher is a graph traversal language designed for labeled property graphs, where nodes and edges carry key-value property maps. It excels at path traversal and pattern matching over graph topology. It does not operate on RDF triples, does not have a standard mechanism for integration with OWL reasoning, and does not support federated queries across remote endpoints. When Stardog surfaces a Cypher interface, it translates Cypher patterns into underlying RDF queries, a convenient translation that sacrifices the full expressive surface of SPARQL for developer familiarity.

An organization that builds an ontology-based knowledge graph and queries it exclusively through GraphQL or Cypher has paid the full cost of the semantic architecture and recovered only a fraction of its capabilities. Inference-derived facts may be inaccessible or incomplete, and federation may be unavailable. CONSTRUCT-based graph augmentation—a standard pattern for enriching the knowledge base—requires SPARQL. The query language choice is important because it determines what parts of the architecture are reachable at runtime.

## Natural Language Processing (NLP)

Most organizational knowledge exists in unstructured text. Natural Language Processing (NLP) pipelines extract entities, relationships, and events from that text and link them to the knowledge graph's vocabulary and knowledge base. Named entity recognition (NER) identifies mentions of domain entities within documents. Entity linking maps those mentions to specific nodes in the knowledge base, resolving that "MSFT," "Microsoft Corporation," and "Microsoft" all refer to the same entity with a canonical identifier.[29] Relation extraction identifies the predicate connecting two entity mentions in a sentence and populates the knowledge base with a new typed, ontology-aligned edge.

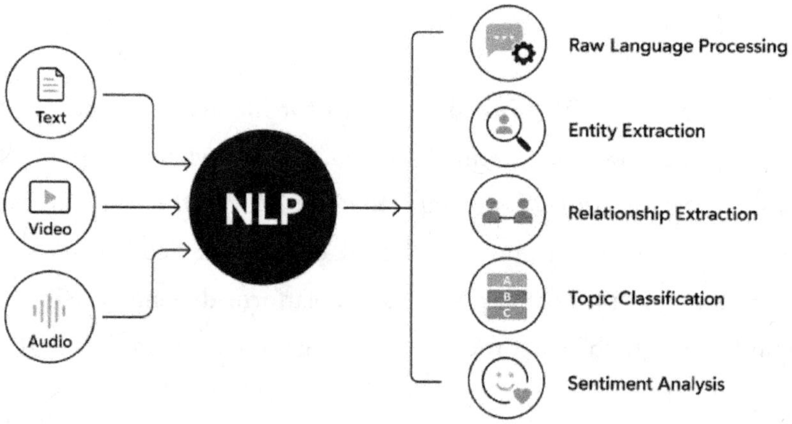


Figure 100: NLP.

The quality of NLP extraction is bound by the quality of the vocabulary and ontology that define the target entity types and relationship types. NLP extracts what the text contains. The vocabulary determines the naming conventions of the extracted text. The ontology determines whether it is correctly typed and produces logically coherent assertions. A knowledge graph with a weak vocabulary and no ontology will produce an NLP-populated knowledge base full of entities that cannot be reasoned over consistently.

---

[29] Shen, W., Wang, J., & Han, J. (2015). Entity linking with a knowledge base: Issues, techniques, and solutions. IEEE Transactions on Knowledge and Data Engineering, 27(2), 443–460.

## Vector databases

A vector database stores high-dimensional numeric embeddings of content—text passages, entity descriptions, document chunks—encoded by a machine learning model and supports approximate nearest-neighbor search over those embeddings. This is a type of semantic similarity retrieval: finding what is conceptually proximate to a query in embedding space, rather than what is an exact or rule-based match.

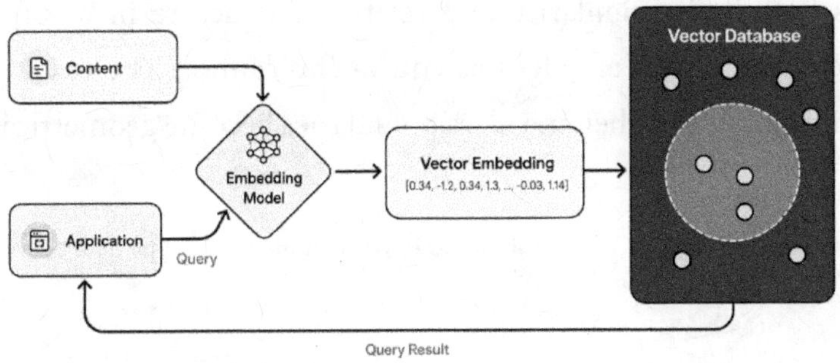


Figure 101: Vector database.

Vector databases are not knowledge graphs, and they do not replace knowledge graphs. They are a complementary retrieval layer for the similarity-based access pattern that structured graph queries cannot serve. A knowledge graph query returns what is formally true according to the vocabulary, ontology, and knowledge base. A vector similarity search returns items that are numerically proximate in embedding space. Both are useful but answer different questions.[30]

## Knowledge graph embeddings

A knowledge graph embedding is a translation of a symbolic graph structure into numerical representations. A knowledge graph stores meaning as explicit facts that say, "This entity relates to that entity in this specific way." An embedding model takes that same information and learns to

[30] Lewis, P., Perez, E., Piktus, A., Petroni, F., Karpukhin, V., Goyal, N., Küttler, H., Lewis, M., Yih, W.-t., Rocktäschel, T., Riedel, S., & Kiela, D. (2020). Retrieval-augmented generation for knowledge-intensive NLP tasks. Advances in Neural Information Processing Systems, 33, 9459–9474.

represent every entity and every relationship as a list of numbers—a vector—so that closely related entities are assigned similar numbers. In contrast, unrelated entities are assigned very different numbers. The result is a version of the knowledge graph that machine learning models can work with directly, leveraging the numbers to understand symbolic facts.[31]

The dominant RDF-native approach is RDF2Vec, which generates random walks across the RDF graph to discover sequences of alternating entities and predicates, then feeds the sequences into a Word2Vec model.[32] Because RDF graphs carry typed edges (predicates with formal semantics), RDF2Vec captures both entity similarity and relational structure in a way that generic graph embedding methods–which treat all edges as equivalent–cannot. The result is a vector space in which similar entities cluster together and class boundaries become geometrically separable.

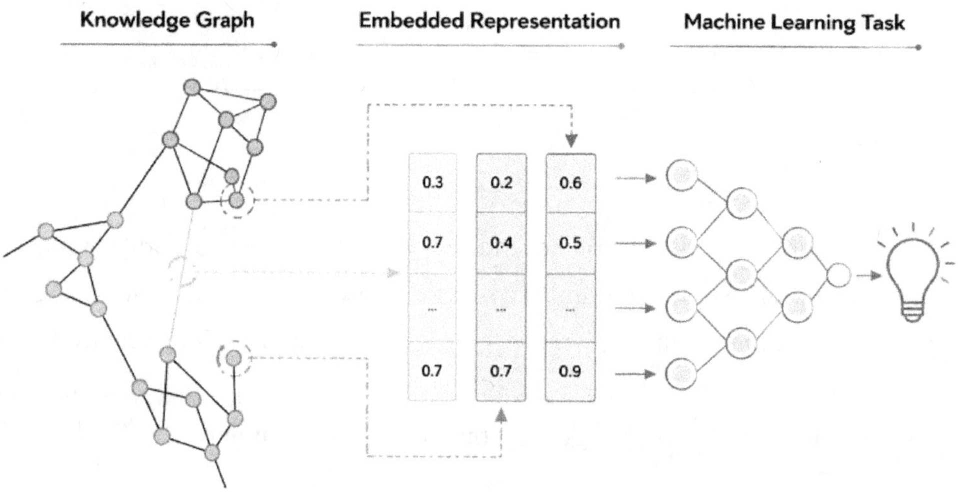


Figure 102: A vector space in which similar entities cluster together and class boundaries become geometrically separable. (EdoardoRamalli - Own work, CC BY-SA 4.0).

[31] Wang, Q. et al. "Knowledge Graph Embedding: A Survey of Approaches and Applications." *IEEE Transactions on Knowledge and Data Engineering*, 29(12), 2017.

[32] Ristoski, P. and Paulheim, H. "RDF2Vec: RDF Graph Embeddings for Data Mining." *Proceedings of the 15th International Semantic Web Conference (ISWC)*, 2016. See also rdf2vec.org for implementations and extensions.

An alternative family of approaches (TransE, RotatE, ComplEx, and their variants) optimizes directly for link prediction, treating each relation as a geometric operation from subject to object.[33] These models are useful where predicting missing triples is the primary task, but they are trained on relation patterns rather than the full structure of the RDF graph.

Embeddings are a downstream inference layer, not a replacement for the symbolic architecture beneath them. The ontology defines the classes, properties, and constraints that give the graph's triples consistent meaning. The knowledge base populates that schema with instances. The embedding model then learns over the populated graph, producing representations that support tasks the symbolic layer cannot perform, such as link prediction, entity resolution, and similarity search.[34]

What the embedding learns is only as coherent as the structure it learns from. A well-architected approach treats the RDF graph and its embedding models as complementary data sources—the former providing explicit, reliable statements about entities, and the latter encoding implicit relations that can be queried alongside the graph through federated SPARQL.[35]

Without an ontological backbone providing consistent class semantics and relation definitions, the embedding model will learn from conflated entities and structurally undifferentiated data. The resulting vector space will usually reflect that noise. To be clear, the ontology is not a preprocessing step for embeddings, but rather the condition under which the embedding space becomes meaningful.

---

[33] Bordes, A. et al. "Translating Embeddings for Modeling Multi-relational Data" (TransE), *NeurIPS*, 2013; Sun, Z. et al. "RotatE: Knowledge Graph Embedding by Relational Rotation in Complex Space," *ICLR*, 2019; Trouillon, T. et al. "Complex Embeddings for Simple Link Prediction" (ComplEx), *ICML*, 2016.

[34] Alshahrani, M. et al. "Application and Evaluation of Knowledge Graph Embeddings in Biomedical Data." *PeerJ Computer Science*, 7:e 341, 2021. https://doi.org/10.7717/peerj-cs.341.

[35] Nikolov, A. et al. "Combining RDF Graph Data and Embedding Models for an Augmented Knowledge Graph." *WWW '18 Companion*, Lyon, France, 2018. https://doi.org/10.1145/3184558.3191527.

## Graph algorithms

At its core, an RDF knowledge graph is a network of connected facts. Graph algorithms are computational methods that operate on networks—finding paths between entities, identifying the most connected nodes, detecting clusters of related resources, and comparing datasets for consistency. SPARQL, the standard query language for RDF, is excellent at retrieving specific facts from a graph, but it was not built for the kind of network-wide analysis that graph algorithms perform.[36] Think of SPARQL as a precise lookup tool, and graph algorithms as the methods for understanding the shape and structure of the network itself. In practice, running graph algorithms over RDF data often means first converting it into a property graph format—the model used by databases like Neo4j and Amazon Neptune—where mature algorithm libraries are readily available. A framework called G2GML automates this conversion, translating RDF data into a form these engines can process without losing the underlying ontological structure.[37]

The same approach works for relational databases. RDF graph algorithms can surface relationships hidden across normalized tables—join paths, implied hierarchies, structural patterns—that would otherwise take significant hand-coding to find, making them a useful tool for anyone working with legacy data systems.

The W3C's RDF Dataset Canonicalization standard (2024) provides a deterministic algorithm for producing a stable fingerprint of an RDF dataset, enabling cryptographic signing and reliable comparison across systems.[38] Finally, large language models can themselves be thought of as a kind of learned graph algorithm. Rather than traversing a graph by explicit rules, they encode relational patterns in their weights and can generate SPARQL queries, identify relevant subgraphs, and navigate knowledge graph structure, complementing traditional methods.[39]

---

[36] Matsumoto, S., Yamanaka, R., and Chiba, H. "Mapping RDF Graphs to Property Graphs." arXiv:1812.01801, 2018.

[37] Ibid. G2GML implementation at https://g2gml.readthedocs.io.

[38] Longley, D. and Kellogg, G. "RDF Dataset Canonicalization." W3C Recommendation, 21 May 2024. https://www.w3.org/TR/rdf-canon/.

[39] He, X. et al. "G-Retriever: Retrieval-Augmented Generation for Textual Graph Understanding and Question Answering." arXiv:2402.07630, 2024.

*The vocabulary names the world.*
*The ontology defines the logic for reasoning about it.*
*The knowledge base stores what is known.*
*Each layer has a distinct function, and none substitutes for another.*

## Knowledge graph component summary

The following table summarizes the component categories of a knowledge graph architecture and details the required components: vocabulary, ontology, and knowledge base. The other optional components are architectural decisions driven by the business's needs, the domain being modeled, and the technical environment in which the knowledge graph resides.

| Graph Component | Status and Role | Common Technologies |
|---|---|---|
| Vocabulary (taxonomy and thesaurus) | Required—the conceptual model of the domain | SKOS, ISO 25964, ANSI Z39.19 controlled vocabularies |
| Ontology | Required—formal logic and reasoning rules | OWL 2 (EL, QL, RL), RDF Schema |
| Knowledge Base | Required—store of asserted facts | Triple store, labeled property graph DB |
| Metadata Schema | Optional but common—provenance and description | Dublin Core, DCAT, PROV-O, Schema.org |
| Reasoner | Optional—derives inferred facts from ontology axioms | Pellet, HermiT, ELK, FACT++JCEL |
| NLP Pipeline | Optional—entity and relation extraction from text | spaCy, Stanford NLP, Hugging Face |
| Vector Database | Optional—embedding-based similarity retrieval | Weviate, Qdrant, pgvector, Pinecone |
| Graph Embeddings | Optional—learned vector representations of entities and relations supporting link prediction, entity resolution, and similarity search | TransE, RotatE, DistMult, ComplEx |
| Graph Algorithms | Optional — structural and network analytics | Neo4j GDS, NetworkX, Spark GraphX |

Table 16: Knowledge graph components.

A knowledge graph is only as good as its architecture. And understanding each of its component sets, both optional and required, is essential for any intentional knowledge graph architecture.

The Ontology Pipeline was developed in direct response to a persistent organizational state in which teams attempt to build knowledge graphs without the prerequisite design and build processes in place. The result is predictable and painful to observe. Ontologies built on messy, undefined vocabularies proliferate logical errors because the underlying data lacks data quality and therefore cannot be logically structured. Knowledge graphs assembled without a formal ontology produce queryable data stores that cannot reason. AI systems grounded in such graphs retrieve facts that lack consistency and coherence, and the ungoverned output compounds in unpredictable ways downstream.

The Pipeline's contribution is to deliver an iterative process for building a knowledge graph, where each stage prepares the way for the next. When an organization can see that a knowledge graph requires a thesaurus, that a thesaurus requires a taxonomy, that a taxonomy requires clean controlled vocabularies, and that controlled vocabularies require a disciplined data preparation process, the investment can be measured in time and money. The scope of each phase can be estimated because it has a clear beginning and end, and each phase delivers a valuable semantic data structure. The sequencing, therefore, becomes defensible. The deliverables at each stage become measurable milestones, each with its own value and utility.

*Without the Ontology Pipeline, organizations struggle to understand the level of effort and investment needed, let alone how to derive metrics to measure benefits, system performance, and returns on investment.*

## The Ontology Pipeline stages at a glance

The Ontology Pipeline also serves to clarify semantic investment to organizational stakeholders. When the stages are named, sequenced, and associated with concrete deliverables and standards, leadership can understand what is being built, why each stage is necessary, and the measurable outcomes of each stage. Without this visibility, SKMS programs are routinely underfunded, prematurely terminated, or scoped in ways that produce fragmentation rather than a proper semantic system. The Pipeline can therefore be framed as a communication framework, the vocabulary through which semantic engineers and organizational decision makers can find common ground on what it means to build knowledge infrastructure that works.

**The Ontology Pipeline Stages at a Glance**

| Stage | Function | Key Standards |
|---|---|---|
| **Controlled Vocabulary** | Deduplicates and defines every term. Resolves synonyms and abbreviations. Establishes the clean, shared lexicon from which all downstream structures are built. | SKOS, ANSI/NISO Z39.19, ISO 25964 |
| **Metadata Schema** | Assigns fields to facts — who, what, when, from which source. Creates the structural frame that vocabulary values populate. Enables entity reconciliation and validation. | Dublin Core, DCAT, Schema.org |
| **Taxonomy** | Organizes the clean vocabulary into a strict parent–child hierarchy. Introduces the first formal relationships. The skeleton of the domain model. | SKOS, ANSI/NISO Z39.19, ISO 25964-1 |
| **Thesaurus** | Extends the taxonomy with associative (non-hierarchical) relationships, preferred labels, alternate labels, and scope notes. Encodes near-synonymy and related-term logic at scale. | SKOS-XL, ANSI/NISO Z39.19, ISO 25964-2 |
| **Ontology** | Adds the formal logical model: classes, properties, axioms, cardinality constraints, disjointness. Enables machine reasoning and inference over asserted facts. | OWL 2 (EL / QL / RL), RDF, RDFS |
| **Knowledge Graph** | Synthesizes all prior stages into a queryable, semantically rich graph. The vocabulary names. The ontology reasons. The graph stores, connects, and surfaces. | Vocabulary (taxonomy, thesaurus), Knowledge Base, SPARQL, SHACL, Vector Database, Graph Embeddings, Graph Algorithms, NLP, Reasoner |

Table 17: Ontology Pipeline stages.

## The landscape of architectures

Before scoping to a specific set of architectures, it is worth acknowledging the diversity of the knowledge graph landscape. The term encompasses an array of technical patterns whose variation reflects decades of parallel development across the Semantic Web community, the commercial graph database industry, the enterprise data management world, and, most recently, the AI infrastructure market. It is therefore difficult to prescribe a specific graph architecture without knowing a little more about an organization and its use cases.

Practitioners routinely disagree about which architectural components qualify as knowledge graphs in the fullest sense, and commercial incentives can create market confusion when the label is applied to less rigorously defined systems.

At the most formal end of the spectrum sit ontology-driven RDF architectures descended from the W3C Semantic Web vision. RDF graphs are fully axiomatized, SPARQL queryable, reasoner-enabled, and aligned with international controlled vocabulary standards. Adjacent to these are linked data architectures built on RDF that emphasize web-scale federation and open publication over organizational enclosure. Property graph architectures, built on systems such as Neo4j and TigerGraph, are the dominant commercial pattern in enterprise environments where traversal performance and developer accessibility outweigh the need for formal logical inference. Semantic property graph architectures aim to hybridize the two paradigms by adding ontological semantics to a property graph backend.

The landscape extends further still. Document-centric knowledge graphs organize semi-structured content around entity types without a formal OWL ontology. Temporal knowledge graphs treat the evolution of facts over time as a first-class architectural concern, modeling not just what is true, but when it was true and when it ceased to be. Domain-specific knowledge graphs are purpose-built for a single industry or regulatory context, such as clinical genomics, financial instrument classification, or legal entity identification. They are often aligned with externally published controlled vocabularies and ontologies maintained by standards bodies.

Data fabric and data mesh architectures incorporate knowledge graphs as the semantic layer governing meaning across distributed data products. And graph-augmented AI architectures—the pattern that has received the most attention since 2023—combine any of the above with a vector database and an LLM inference layer, using the graph to ground generative AI outputs in formally asserted, provenance-tracked facts.

Each of these patterns makes different tradeoffs. Some prioritize semantic expressivity and the long-term interoperability that formal standards confer. Others prioritize throughput, developer experience, or integration with existing data pipelines. Some are built to last decades and federate with external knowledge systems. Others are built to solve a specific operational problem quickly and well. None is universally superior, and all reflect legitimate architectural responses to real domain and use-case requirements.

This breadth is exactly why we must refine the scope to three selected knowledge graph architecture patterns. The overarching goal is to help practitioners understand the nuances of knowledge graph components and their alignment with use cases. Breadth at the expense of depth produces exactly the kind of summary-level familiarity that leads organizations to make poor architectural choices.

*The knowledge graph landscape is wide enough that two systems called knowledge graphs can differ from each other more than either differs from systems that carry a different name entirely.*

## Three common RDF architectures

The three architectures are all built on the RDF standards stack. This is a deliberate choice, not a dismissal of the property graph and AI-first patterns. The RDF stack represents the most semantically complete knowledge graph paradigm, and the one in which the vocabulary-ontology-knowledge base distinction is most clearly articulated and applied. Understanding RDF architectures well is the foundation for understanding the benefits and tradeoffs.

Architectural variation can be significant within the RDF paradigm. Three patterns account for most RDF knowledge graph deployments in enterprise and research contexts, and they differ in how they configure the component layers described earlier.

The first pattern is the enterprise knowledge graph, a broad-scope, multi-domain RDF architecture designed to serve as the semantic backbone of an organization's data infrastructure. The second is the domain knowledge graph, a deep, narrow-scope architecture purpose-built for a specific domain, typically aligned to an external published ontology and controlled vocabulary. The third is the linked data knowledge graph, an architecture designed for web-scale publication and federation, where open world interoperability with external knowledge systems takes precedence over organizational enclosure and operational performance.

Let's look at each in turn, describing characteristic components, explaining the nuances of how those components are configured in practice, mapping it to the use cases it serves best, and examining the conditions under which it is the right architectural choice. The goal is to convey the kind of understanding that allows practitioners to make intentional architectural decisions.

---

## The enterprise knowledge graph

The Enterprise Knowledge Graph is a broad-scope, multi-domain RDF architecture designed to serve as the semantic backbone of an organization's data infrastructure. Its primary functions are entity resolution, master data management, and cross-system integration. It is a system whose value extends beyond any individual dataset to encompass semantic connections across all datasets.

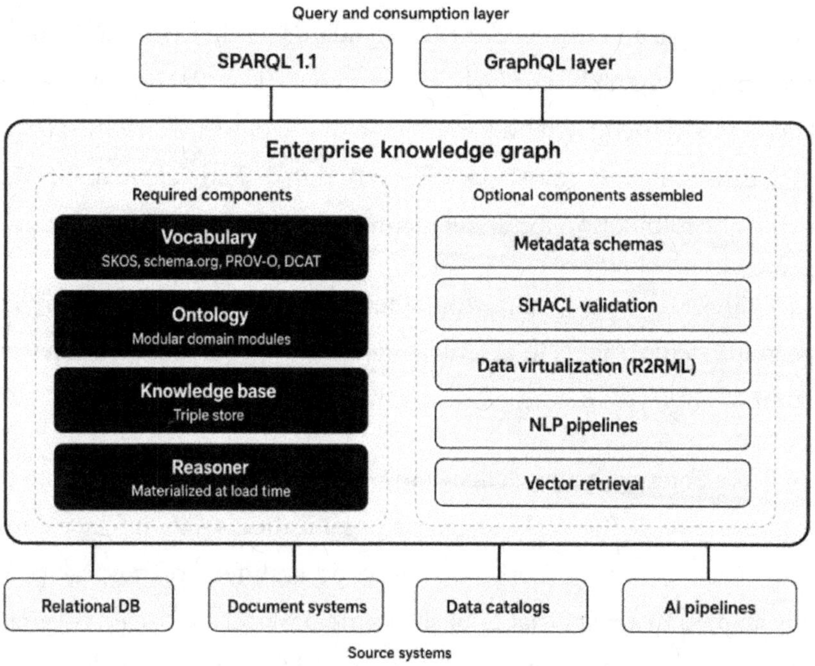


Table 18: Query and consumption layer.

This is the architecture for organizations whose primary problem is fragmentation—when the same entity appears across a dozen systems, with no single source of truth to determine which version of that entity is correct. The enterprise graph does not model a single domain in depth. It connects knowledge across domains that are currently siloed in separate systems, vocabularies, and teams.

## *Required components*

### Vocabulary

The enterprise knowledge graph requires the broadest vocabulary of the three patterns. It must name and organize concepts across every business domain the graph touches, and those domains routinely use the same words to mean different things. The controlled vocabulary infrastructure is typically a federated set of SKOS concept schemes, one per business domain, with cross-domain alignment properties connecting terms that refer to the same or related concepts across schemes. The vocabulary stack layers schema.org for general entity types, SKOS for business taxonomies, PROV-O for data lineage, DCAT for dataset cataloging, and the W3C ORG ontology for organizational structures.

### Ontology

The enterprise ontology is intentionally thin and modular. Rather than a single monolithic model, the architecture assembles domain-specific ontology modules that share an upper-level alignment: a workflow ontology, a product ontology, and a compliance ontology. The NTWF workflow ontology developed throughout the Ontology series is an example of such an ontology. Class hierarchies are typically derived from existing relational database schemas, semantic layers, and data catalogs, with properties aligned to business objects. The design philosophy is to implement a schema that is just expressive enough to support the priority use cases, then extend it as new requirements emerge. It is advised that initial implementations be conservative, as it's much easier to scale an ontology than to shrink one.

### Knowledge base

The enterprise knowledge base is enormous, containing millions, maybe billions of triples. The knowledge base is heterogeneous and continuously updated from multiple source systems. Data arrives from operational databases, content management systems, data catalogs, HR systems, engineering platforms, and AI pipelines. The triple store must handle high write throughput alongside complex read queries. The distinction between instance data operations and ontology governance is critical at enterprise scale. Conflating the two is how enterprise knowledge graph programs stall.

### *Optional components assembled*

The enterprise pattern requires the assemblage of multiple components, more than any of the three architectures, because integration at this scale demands a robust support stratum to operationalize the graph effectively. Because reconciliation of datasets, vocabulary alignment, and disambiguation are core functions of an enterprise knowledge graph, modules are assembled to support them. In addition, the enterprise knowledge graph will stretch across team boundaries.

Query support and knowledge graph access must address different user types—those who may query via GraphQL and those who may query via SPARQL. Finally, the enterprise knowledge graph must maintain freshness, with strategies and components that support integrating new data and data types at the speed of the business.

#### Metadata schemas

Every entity must carry provenance: who asserted it, when, and from which source system. Dublin Core, DCAT, and PROV-O are RDF ontology schemas, perfectly positioned to provide the metadata infrastructure. The metadata layer functions as the primary integration surface with existing organizational systems, as detailed in the metadata phase, in addition to the ontology phase of the pipeline.

#### Validation layer

SHACL is essential because data arrives from multiple sources with varying quality. The shape library codifies the structural expectations derived from the ontology, and every data load is validated before triples are committed to the graph. This is the feedback loop between what the semantic model requires and what the data contains.

### Data virtualization

Most organizations that build enterprise knowledge graphs are not starting from scratch. They have decades of operational data in relational databases, including customer records, transaction histories, product catalogs, and HR systems. Migrating this data into a triple store is neither practical nor desirable. The data is live and changes continuously. Existing systems govern it with their own access controls, update cadences, and compliance requirements. Extracting it, transforming it into RDF, and loading it into a separate store creates a copy that is stale the moment it lands.

Data virtualization solves this by leaving the data where it is. Instead of moving relational data into the graph, the graph retrieves relational data at query time and projects relational rows as RDF triples on the fly. The relational database remains the system of record. The knowledge graph provides the semantic layer that makes it queryable alongside native graph data.

R2RML—the W3C standard RDF mapping language—is the mechanism that makes this work. An R2RML mapping defines how relational tables, columns, and joins project into RDF classes, properties, and relationships. A row in a customer's table becomes an instance of a class. A foreign key join between customers and orders becomes a typed property linking two graph individuals or classes. The mapping is declarative, specifying the correspondence between the relational and graph structures without procedural transformation code.

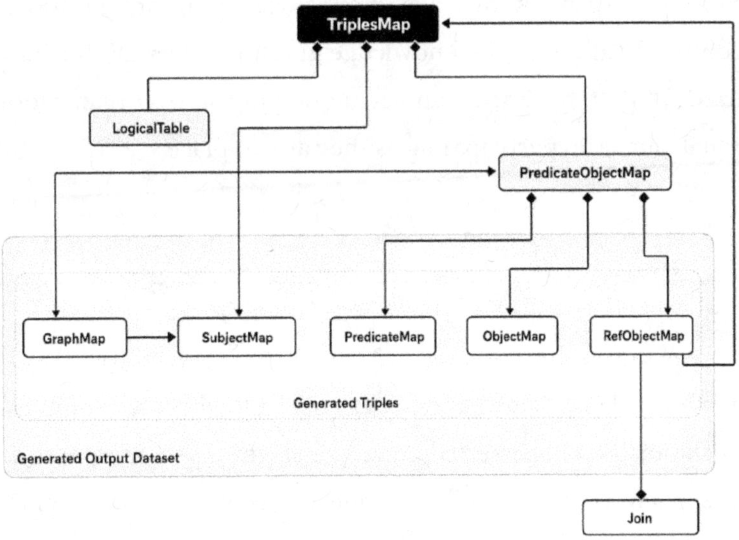


Figure 103: W3C standard RDF mapping language.

## R2RML overview

This decision is architecturally significant because a single SPARQL query can traverse both native graph triples stored in the triple store and virtualized triples projected from relational sources in the same query execution. An analyst querying the enterprise knowledge graph does not need to know whether a particular fact lives natively in the graph or is being projected from a relational database at query time. The semantic layer is unified, while the storage is not.

The tradeoff is query performance. Virtualized queries are slower than queries over materialized triples because the triple store must translate SPARQL patterns into SQL, execute them against the relational database, transform the results into RDF, and join them with native graph data—all at query time.

This latency may be unacceptable for high-throughput operational queries. The common architectural response is a hybrid, where virtualized data that changes frequently and must remain authoritative in its source system materializes into data stable enough to replicate into the triple store without governance risk. The R2RML mappings support both patterns; the same mapping can drive either virtualization or periodic materialization, depending on the data source's operational requirements.

This capability makes enterprise knowledge graphs viable in organizations with established relational infrastructures. Without it, the knowledge graph requires a full data migration before it can be operationalized. With it, the graph can begin querying across organizational systems on day one, with the relational databases participating as they are, in place.

## Reasoning

Reasoning typically materializes when the reasoner runs at load time, computes all inferred triples from the ontology's axioms and the asserted data, and stores those inferences directly in the triple store alongside the explicit assertions. When a query executes, it runs against the full graph—

asserted and inferred—without the need to invoke the reasoner. This trades storage overhead for query latency, the correct tradeoff for operational deployments where response time matters.

A SPARQL query that returns in milliseconds over materialized inferences might take seconds or longer if the reasoner had to derive those inferences at query time across billions of triples. The cost is that materialized inferences must be recomputed whenever the ontology changes or significant new data is loaded, a batch process that enterprise architectures typically schedule during off-peak windows.

---

## NLP pipelines

Enterprise graphs frequently use NLP to extract entities and relationships from unstructured organizational text, such as documents, emails, support tickets, and meeting transcripts, and link them to the knowledge base. Named entity recognition identifies mentions of domain entities within text. Entity linking resolves those mentions to specific nodes in the graph—determining that "MSFT," "Microsoft Corporation," and "Microsoft" all refer to the same canonical entity. Relation extraction identifies the predicates connecting two entity mentions and adds a new typed edge to the knowledge base.

The quality of the vocabulary and ontology bounds the quality of NLP extraction. NLP extracts what the text contains, but the vocabulary determines the naming conventions, and the ontology determines whether the extraction is typed correctly and produces logically coherent assertions.

---

## Query layer

SPARQL is the primary query language, but enterprise graphs often expose GraphQL convenience layers for application developers who are fluent in REST and JSON but not yet in the standards stack. Query language choice has consequences, as an organization that queries exclusively through GraphQL recovers only a fraction of the architecture's capability.

GraphQL returns tree-shaped results against a defined schema, meaning it operates over a surface projection of the graph rather than the underlying triple model and its inferred extensions. Inference-derived facts may be inaccessible or incomplete. Federation across remote endpoints is unavailable. CONSTRUCT queries—which build new graph structures from existing ones, a standard pattern for enriching the knowledge base—have no GraphQL equivalent. The convenience layer supports adoption, while SPARQL supports the architecture.

---

## Deployments

Google's Knowledge Graph, announced in 2012 under the "things not strings" framing, powers knowledge panels across Search, YouTube, and Cloud APIs. Industry-scale experience at Google, Microsoft, Facebook, eBay, and IBM Watson has identified knowledge graphs as providing a shared substrate of knowledge, enabling different products and applications to use similar vocabularies and reuse definitions.[40]

Amazon's Product Knowledge Graph uses automated knowledge collection to build an authoritative product graph, increasing facts in the consumables product graph by approximately 200 percent at 87.7 percent accuracy.[41] Siemens deployed industrial knowledge graphs for gas turbine maintenance, building automation digital twins and spare parts management, saving 1,500 hours of manual processing in the first year at Siemens Energy and approximately $10M annually.[42] Thomson Reuters (now LSEG Refinitiv) released the first major Knowledge Graph Feed for financial services, reusing the FIBO Entities' ontology for company data.[43]

---

[40] Noy, N., Gao, Y., Jain, A., Narayanan, A., Patterson, A., & Taylor, J. (2019). Industry-scale knowledge graphs: Lessons and challenges. *Communications of the ACM*, 62(8), 36–43.

[41] Dong, X. L., et al. (2020). AutoKnow: Self-driving knowledge collection for products of thousands of types. *Proceedings of the 26th ACM SIGKDD International Conference on Knowledge Discovery & Data Mining*. DOI: 10.1145/3394486.3403323.

[42] Biletskiy, Y., & Rankin, J. (2018). Use cases of the industrial knowledge graph at Siemens. *Proceedings of the ISWC 2018 Posters & Demonstrations*. CEUR-WS Vol. 2180.

[43] Popov, P. (2025, November 12). *The power of ontologies and knowledge graphs: practical examples from the financial industry.* https://www.ontotext.com/. https://www.ontotext.com/blog/the-power-of-ontologies-and-knowledge-graphs-for-the-financial-industry/.

## The enterprise pattern's tradeoff

The enterprise pattern commits to breadth over depth—integration over formalism. The schema is relatively simple, but instance data is typically enormous—billions of triples spanning customers, transactions, products, and organizational entities. A second structural tradeoff is developer accessibility. RDF and SPARQL skills are rarer than SQL, which has led to GraphQL convenience layers in many deployments. The convenience layer serves developers. It is not a substitute for the standards stack itself.

The enterprise knowledge graph's defining commitment is to breadth. Its schema is thin enough to span the organizations. Its instance data or data graph is virtualized, maintaining alignment to relational database systems.

## The domain knowledge graph

The domain knowledge graph inverts the enterprise pattern's priorities. Where the enterprise graph goes wide, the domain graph goes deep, modeling a single field with rich axiomatization aligned to externally published ontologies and controlled vocabularies maintained by standards bodies and expert communities.

This is the architecture for organizations whose primary need is precision and domain knowledge, where competency questions require formal inference to align with established external vocabularies and ontologies. A domain graph architecture relies upon domain experts as graph users, who will evaluate graph results against expert standards.

### *Required components*

#### Vocabulary

The vocabulary in a domain knowledge graph is typically aligned with, and often governed by, an externally published controlled vocabulary maintained by a standards body or domain consortium. Examples include financial domain graphs aligned with FIBO, legal domain graphs aligned with jurisdictional classification schemes, and industrial domain graphs aligned with ISO standards for engineering specifications and product lifecycle management. The domain graph does not invent its vocabulary from scratch. It adopts what the domain's expert community has already standardized and extends only where the organizational use case requires concepts the standard does not cover, following the standards survey methodology.

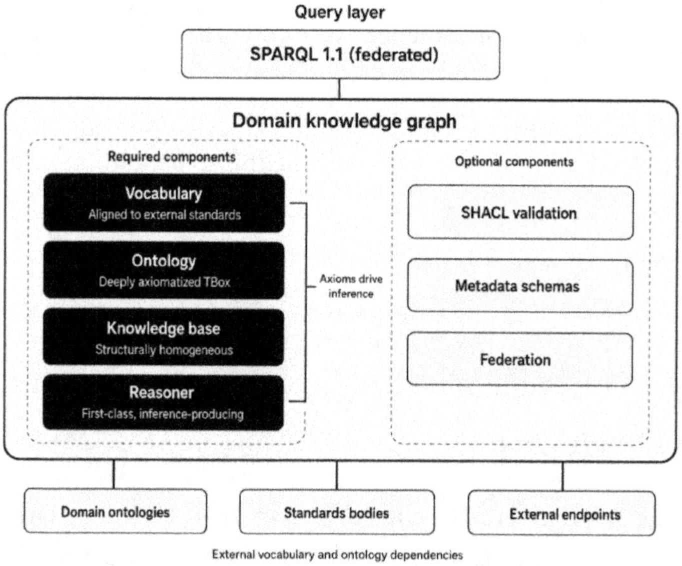


Figure 104: Query layer.

These external dependencies are sometimes legally mandated. Regulatory frameworks in financial services, legal compliance, and government reporting frequently dictate which vocabularies and classification schemes must be used. Domain knowledge graph architects often do not choose their vocabulary; the standards body chooses it for them, and the architect's job is alignment, extension, and operational deployment.

### Ontology

The ontology is the primary intellectual asset of a domain knowledge graph. Where the enterprise ontology is intentionally thin, the domain ontology is deeply axiomatized—rich class hierarchies, formal property constraints, and logical rules that enable machines to derive new facts from existing assertions. FIBO for financial instruments, LKIF Core for legal concepts, and the OBO Foundry ontologies for life sciences are all examples of domain ontologies that serve as the terminological backbone for their respective knowledge graphs.

**Knowledge base**

The knowledge base in a domain knowledge graph is often large but structurally homogeneous, comprising millions or tens of millions of triples that all conform to a single, deeply axiomatized schema. The data is specialized and typically curated by domain experts or extracted from authoritative sources through carefully governed pipelines.

Unlike the enterprise pattern, where data arrives from dozens of heterogeneous source systems in varying quality, the domain knowledge base draws from a narrow set of authoritative sources—regulatory filings, peer-reviewed annotations, standards body publications, institutional registries—where the domain community establishes the provenance and curation standards before the data enters the graph. Deep reasoning is tractable due to structural homogeneity. Reliable inference is possible because the reasoner operates over a knowledge base in which every triple conforms to the same axiomatized schema.

### *Optional components assembled*

The domain pattern assembles fewer optional components than the enterprise pattern, but the components it does assemble carry more weight, particularly the reasoner.

**Reasoner**

In the enterprise pattern, the reasoner operates in the background and materializes at load time. In the domain pattern, the reasoner is on center stage. The entire architecture exists to enable formal inference with a level of rigor that expert communities can trust. In many domain deployments, the reasoner produces more triples than were explicitly asserted classifications entailed by axioms and asserted relationships, never manually assigned. The defining capability of the domain knowledge graph is that the ontology does not just organize knowledge; it produces new knowledge through formal inference.

**Validation layer**

SHACL enforces constraints that the ontology's open-world semantics cannot express, such as structural requirements like mandatory properties, value ranges, and reference integrity. Both the ontology and the validation layer are necessary. Neither substitutes for the other, as they operate in concert.

**Federation**

Domain knowledge graphs frequently federate with external domain endpoints and support querying across independently maintained graphs in a single SPARQL request. A financial domain graph can federate with FIBO endpoints maintained by the EDM Council. A life sciences graph can join its internal annotations with UniProt's protein data and ChEMBL's compound data in a single query. The data never leaves its authoritative source, and the query spans organizational boundaries to return a unified result set. This is architecturally differentiated from the enterprise pattern's data virtualization, which reaches into internal relational databases. Domain federation extends outward to the published endpoints of other domain participants. This federation capability makes SPARQL non-negotiable in domain deployments as no other query language supports the SERVICE keyword that makes cross-endpoint queries possible.

**SPARQL 1.1 Federated Query Extension**

*The SERVICE keyword instructs a federated query processor to invoke a portion of a SPARQL query against a remote SPARQL endpoint.*

This section presents examples of how to use the SERVICE keyword. The following sections define the syntax and semantics of this extension.

*From SPARQL 1.1 SERVICE keyword*

## *Deployments*

There are several examples of deep domain knowledge graphs and their SPARQL endpoints, all of which capture regulated industries where domain vocabulary alignment is high-stakes. The OBO

Foundry ecosystem governs 150+ active ontologies formalized in accordance with community principles. FIBO, developed by the EDM Council and standardized by the OMG, is deployed across major financial institutions for instrument classification, regulatory reporting, and entity resolution.[44] LKIF Core, developed under the EU ESTRELLA project, provides the formal legal ontology used in computational legal reasoning systems across European jurisdictions.[45] The EBI RDF Platform integrates multiple life sciences databases with federated SPARQL queries across all endpoints. UniProt's RDF knowledge graph contains 232+ billion triples served via a public SPARQL endpoint.[46]

### *The domain pattern's trade-off*

The domain pattern trades breadth for depth, flexibility for standardization, and speed-to-deploy for long-term interoperability. Adding new concepts to a domain standard requires submission and review through the governing body. The reward for this overhead is a high level of semantic precision that is unmatched in enterprise and linked data graphs.

The domain knowledge graph's defining commitment is to precision. Its ontology is its primary intellectual asset. Its instance data is secondary to the ontological structure that governs it.

---

## The linked data knowledge graph

The Linked Data Knowledge Graph follows Tim Berners-Lee's four principles:

1. Use URIs as names for things.
2. Use HTTP URIs so people can look up those names.
3. Provide useful information using RDF when someone looks up a URI.
4. Include links to other URIs so that agents can discover more.

---

[44] EDM Council. (n.d.). *FIBO: Financial Industry Business Ontology*. https://spec.edmcouncil.org/. Retrieved April 8, 2026, from https://spec.edmcouncil.org/fibo/.

[45] Hoekstra, R., Breuker, J., Di Bello, M., & Boer, A. (2007). The LKIF Core ontology of basic legal concepts. *Proceedings of LOAIT 2007*.

[46] UniProt Consortium. (2021). UniProt: The universal protein knowledgebase in 2021. *Nucleic Acids Research*, 49(D1), D480–D489.

This architecture descends directly from the Semantic Web vision discussed earlier.

Where the enterprise graph connects knowledge within an organization, and the domain graph models a single field in depth, the linked data knowledge graph connects knowledge across organizations and to the outside world of linked data graphs. Federation is the architecture's reason for being.

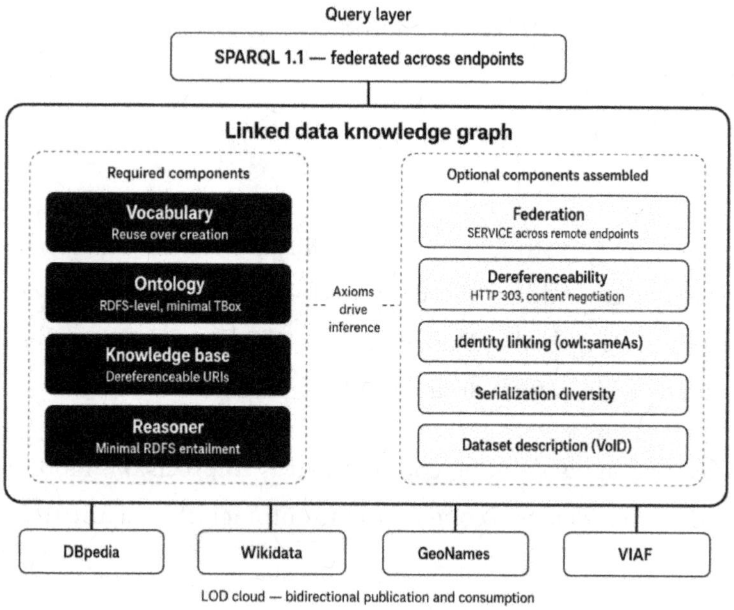


Figure 105: Query layer.

## *Required components*

### Vocabulary

Vocabulary reuse takes precedence over ontology creation. The linked data graph assembles its vocabulary from published standards rather than building custom terms. The schemas and vocabularies typically leveraged are Dublin Core Metadata Terms (dcterms) for descriptive metadata, FOAF for people and social relations, SKOS for concept schemes, schema.org for general-purpose entity types, VoID for dataset description, and DCAT for catalog metadata. This is the inverse of the enterprise and domain patterns, where custom vocabularies and ontologies are built to represent organizational or domain-specific knowledge.

The linked data pattern's vocabulary strategy is intentional. Every published standard term or concept serves as a bridge to every other dataset that uses it. A **foaf:Person** in one graph is recognizable to any system that understands FOAF, without custom mapping or vocabulary negotiation. Custom terms are introduced only when no published vocabulary covers the concept. Custom terms are normally represented by **rdfs:label** alongside **rdfs:comment**. Alignment properties connect custom terms to the nearest published equivalent so that consuming systems can interpret them without prior knowledge of the publisher's vocabulary.

Linked data vocabularies must be structured to be highly interoperable, in order to capitalize off of the goodness encoded in other linked data graphs.

### Ontology

The ontology in a linked data knowledge graph is expressed primarily through rdfs:Class and **rdfs:subClassOf** hierarchies, **rdfs:domain**, and **rdfs:range** declarations on properties, and **rdfs:subPropertyOf** chains. These are the building blocks—class membership and property structure that an RDFS-aware processor can infer over. If a resource is typed as **foaf:Person** and **foaf:Person** is declared **rdfs:subClassOf foaf:Agent**, any consuming system infers the resource is also a **foaf:Agent**. Inference is therefore enabled through the TBox or RDF class—subclass hierarchical structure.

Full OWL axiomatization—disjointness, cardinality restrictions, class constructors—are architecturally incompatible with this pattern because linked data graphs federate across independently maintained endpoints. A disjointness axiom asserted by one publisher may contradict the class definitions of another, and a federated query that encounters conflicting axioms produces unpredictable reasoning results.

The linked data pattern avoids this by keeping ontological commitments within the bounds of what RDFS can express, mainly hierarchies and property constraints. Property relations such as **owl:sameAs** are used to identify linking rather than to encode deep logical machinery. The priority is not inferencing depth, but interoperability breadth. Any system that understands RDFS can consume and reason over any linked data graph without needing to negotiate OWL profiles.

**Knowledge base**

The knowledge base is designed to support publication and discovery. Data is published at dereferenceable HTTP URIs. When a client requests a URI, the server returns RDF, describing that resource. Content negotiation enables the server to return Turtle, JSON-LD, RDF/XML, or HTML based on the client's request headers. This turns every entity in the knowledge base into a discoverable, machine-readable resource on the web.

### *Optional components assembled*

The linked data pattern assembles the fewest optional components of the three architectures. Its architectural investment goes into publication infrastructure and federation rather than reasoning or validation.

**Federation**

SPARQL 1.1's SERVICE keyword enables a single query to retrieve and join data from multiple remote SPARQL endpoints. A query that retrieves a local organization's project metadata and enriches it with geographic data from GeoNames, classification data from a VIAF source library, and Subject Headings and entity data from Wikidata—all in a single SPARQL query—is a federation pattern that no other graph query language supports. This is what SPARQL enables: the ability to query across multiple RDF sources.

**Dereferenceability infrastructure**

When a client performs HTTP GET on a URI identifying a non-information resource, the server returns either an HTTP 303 redirect to an RDF document or uses hash URIs to serve multiple identifiers from a single document. The Accept header enables content negotiation—HTML for browsers and Turtle or JSON-LD for machines—from the same URI. This mechanism renders the web of data browsable for both human and machine agents.

## Dereferenceable

To dereference is to access a value or object located in a memory location stored in a pointer—the pointer directs you to the stored value. In the context of Linked Data (LD), dereferencing is used in relation to Uniform Resource Identifiers (URIs) and whether they are dereferenceable. A dereferenceable URI is one that resolves to a webpage: it can turn from an abstract reference into something more concrete, namely a web resource. If you can put a URI into the address bar of a browser and access a webpage through that address, then it is dereferenceable.

*From LINCS Portal*

**Identity linking**

Identity linking is the mechanism that turns independently published datasets into a connected web of knowledge. When two datasets describe the same entity—same person, place, or organization—an owl:sameAs triple declares that the URI in one dataset and the URI in the other refer to the same thing. A consuming system encountering that declaration can merge everything known about both URIs into a single entity view. This is the architectural primitive that enables cross-dataset traversal.

In practice, identity linking is harder than it sounds. The owl:sameAs predicate carries strong formal semantics—it asserts complete identity, meaning everything true of one URI is true of the other. That assertion is powerful when it is correct. When it lacks precision—when two URIs refer to things that are similar but not identical, or that overlap in some contexts but not others—the owl:sameAs link propagates incorrect inferences across every system that consumes it. A geographic entity in GeoNames and a geographic entity in Wikidata may share a name and a coordinate but have different administrative boundaries, population figures, and temporal scopes. Declaring them owl:sameAs flattens those differences.

This is why LODStats analysis found owl:sameAs present in only approximately 9.4 percent of LOD dataset dumps. Publishers are correct to be cautious about asserting full identity across datasets they do not control. The LOD cloud is less densely interlinked at the identity level than its visual diagram suggests, and the sparse interlinking is as much a quality signal as it is a gap. Careless owl:sameAs assertions degrade the graph faster than missing ones do.

Alternative predicates have emerged to address this. SKOS mapping relations provide skos:exactMatch and skos:closeMatch for vocabulary alignment, where full identity is too strong a claim. Schema.org provides schema:sameAs with weaker formal semantics. Some linked data publishers use rdfs:seeAlso to point to related resources without asserting identity at all. The architectural decision about which identity predicate to use and how aggressively to assert cross-dataset links is a critical choice in a linked data knowledge graph, as it determines the quality of federation query results.

### Serialization diversity

The linked data pattern supports more serialization formats than any other graph architecture because the same data must be consumable by different kinds of clients. RDF/XML provides legacy compatibility with systems built during the early era of the Semantic Web. Turtle (TTL) offers human-readable, compact syntax and is the format most ontology engineers write and read directly. N-Triples supports streaming and bulk processing, where each line is a self-contained triple that can be parsed without context. JSON-LD bridges RDF to mainstream web development, giving JavaScript developers a familiar JSON structure that is simultaneously also valid RDF.

RDFa embeds structured data directly in HTML pages, making web content machine-readable without a separate data endpoint. HDT provides compressed binary storage for massive datasets. For example, LOD-a-lot stores 28 billion triples in 524 GB using HDT. The choice of serialization determines who can consume the data and how. A linked data knowledge graph that publishes in only one format excludes every client that uses a different interoperable format.

---

## Deployments

The LOD Cloud grew from 203 datasets and approximately 25 billion triples in September 2010 to 1,658 datasets in December 2024.[47] DBpedia serves as the historical hub, with approximately 438 million triples extracted from Wikipedia infoboxes. Wikidata has become the dominant node, with 100+ million items and billions of RDF triples.

The BBC's Dynamic Semantic Publishing architecture generates 800+ dynamic aggregation pages via SPARQL queries across a suite of domain ontologies that includes Programmes, Sport,

---

[47] Pellegrino, M. A., Rula, A., & Tuozzo, M. (2026). Lost in LOD. *ACM Journal of Data and Information Quality*. DOI: 10.1145/3786331.

CoreConcepts, Storyline, and Curriculum, using MusicBrainz URIs for 50 million artists rather than minting its own identifiers. Europeana publishes open metadata on 17+ million cultural heritage items from 1,500+ European institutions using the Europeana Data Model built on Dublin Core Terms, SKOS, and OAI-ORE. The Library of Congress's BIBFRAME initiative replaces MARC format for bibliographic records with a linked data vocabulary for bibliographic description.

---

## Infrastructure and availability

The linked data pattern's central reliability problem is countered with endpoint availability. The Triple Pattern Fragments framework addresses the reliability problem by offering linked data fragments that match single triple patterns rather than full SPARQL query evaluation. The client then decomposes SPARQL queries into triple-pattern requests to achieve higher accuracy. DBpedia's TPF server achieved 99.99 percent availability over 16.8 million requests with a 43 percent cache hit rate, compared with the frequent outages of traditional SPARQL endpoints. Pellegrino's, Rula's, and Tuozzo's 2026 analysis of the December 2024 LOD Cloud snapshot found that many earlier issues persist: datasets still lack consistency in metadata structure, licenses, and distribution format.[48]

---

## The linked data pattern's tradeoff

The linked data pattern trades control for openness, performance for interoperability, and semantic richness for participation. The value proposition favors external connectivity over internal accuracy to support an agent's ability to follow a chain of RDF links between datasets. The main objective is to discover knowledge that no single organization could curate and populate in isolation.

The defining commitment of the linked data knowledge graph is openness. Its value lies not in internal precision but in external connectivity. The knowledge that emerges from following links across datasets helps with category discovery, trend analysis, knowledge curation, and context

48 Ibid.

retrieval. A linked data knowledge graph is best positioned as a reliable alternative to web scraping and vector databases, connecting knowledge from sources such as Wikidata, VIAF, DBpedia, the Getty, and the EU Knowledge Graph.

| Dimension | Enterprise | Domain | Linked Data KG |
|---|---|---|---|
| **Scope** | broad: multiple business domains | Narrow: single domain, maximum depth | Variable: always connectable |
| **Vocabulary** | federated SKOS schemes schema.org PROV-O DCAT | externally governed domain standards | Published standard vocabularies as primary vocabulary |
| **Ontology** | Thin, modular, incremental | Deep, axiomatized, formally governed | RDFS-level, minimal commitment |
| **Knowledge Base** | billions of triples, heterogeneous sources | millions of triples, structurally homogeneous | Massive, distributed across the web |
| **Key Optional Components** | Metadata SHACL, data virtualization NLP, materialized reasoning | reasoner (first-class) SHACL federation | federation dereferenceability infrastructure identity linking |
| **Key Examples** | Google KG, Amazon Product KG, Siemens | FIBO, LKIF CORE, OBO Foundry, UniProt | DBpedia, Wikidata, Europeana, BBC DSP, LoC BIBFRAME |
| **Primary Tradeoff** | Breadth over depth; integration over formalism | Depth over breadth; precision over speed-to-deploy | Openness over control; interop over performance |

Table 19: Comparative summary.

---

## Architecture as commitment

A product ships with a feature set. An architecture ships with a set of decisions and their consequences.

These three patterns are not interchangeable. Selecting an architecture means selecting a set of commitments that determine a knowledge graph's expressivity, openness, and where intelligence lives in the stack. Where the enterprise pattern commits to breadth and operational pragmatism, the domain pattern commits to precision and community alignment, and the linked data pattern commits to openness and decentralization.

Individually, each graph architecture type has variances in configuration, the optional components assembled, the weights each carries, and the resulting architecture it is optimized to produce. The configuration defines the architecture and graph type. While there are tools and vendors in the knowledge graph space, you most likely cannot purchase the architecture. A knowledge graph is something you design, build, and maintain.

The technical decisions—which triple store, OWL profile, and serialization format—are important, but they are downstream of organizational decisions. Most knowledge graph literature treats the sociotechnical aspects of knowledge graph work either superficially or entirely. Which domain does the graph serve first? Who staffs it? How does a pilot become a production system? What happens when the domain changes and the ontology must change with it? These are the difficult questions and conversations that make or break a knowledge graph program.

*Most knowledge graphs stall or fail in the gaps between architecture and practice.*

Typically, an organization selects a pattern, acquires tooling, and hires or contracts for semantic engineering capabilities, only to discover that the hardest problems lie not in the technology stack but in the organizational seams. This is where friction and conflict emerge: competing vocabularies owned by different teams, data governance structures designed for relational databases that cannot accommodate graph-structured knowledge, and AI pipelines that consume the graph with no mechanism for feeding corrections back into it. These are solvable problems, but they are not automatically resolved by selecting the right architecture.

Below, we'll examine how a specific architecture is scoped given domain constraints, how it is staffed, the implementation phases from pilot to production, and how to maintain semantic integrity as domains and organizations evolve. The goal is not to prescribe a single methodology, but to surface the decisions every knowledge graph program must navigate, regardless of pattern, vendor, or industry.

## Scoping the graph

Every knowledge graph begins with scoping and decisions. A knowledge graph that is scoped too broadly will take years to build and even longer to deliver value; it also risks collapse under its own integration weight. Scoped too narrowly, and the system built may work beautifully for a single function, but it will not justify the investment required to maintain it.

Scoping is not the same as requirements gathering. Requirements gathering asks what the system should do. Scoping asks which slice of the world the system needs to represent to deliver value. A knowledge graph's determined scope is critical because it charts the course for the vocabulary, ontology, data sources, validation rules, and–ultimately–its cost structure. Every commitment translates into classes, properties, and relations that must be represented, defined, populated, validated, governed, and maintained.

Scope is cost.

---

## Competency questions as the scoping device

Competency questions, first formalized by Grüninger and Fox in the context of enterprise modeling, are the primary mechanism for scoping a knowledge graph.

A competency question is a natural-language question that the knowledge graph must be able to answer. It is not a vague business objective or a KPI. It is a question with a definite answer that the graph either can or cannot return. "Which suppliers have delivered components that failed quality inspection in the past 12 months and which product lines were affected?" is a competency question. "Improve supply chain visibility" is not a competency question.

> *The discipline of writing competency questions forces precision at the earliest stage, when precision is cheapest.*

Each question implies classes, properties, and relationships, as well as logical, temporal, and spatial constraints. The union of all competency questions defines the minimum viable scope of the graph. Any class, property, or relationship not required by at least one competency question is a candidate for deferral or omission.

Competency questions also function as acceptance criteria. A knowledge graph that cannot answer its own competency questions has failed, regardless of how elegant its ontology is or how many triples it contains. Wisniewski et al. demonstrated that competency questions can be formalized as SPARQL-OWL queries, providing a direct bridge between the scoping device and the query layer.[49]

## Scoping by pattern

The three graph patterns each have different scoping constraints. These constraints flow directly from each pattern's architectural commitment.

## Enterprise knowledge graph

The enterprise graph's commitment to breadth creates a scoping paradox: its value increases with every system integration. However, each additional system will multiply the vocabulary alignment work, present new data quality challenges, and increase the surface area for governance. The scoping discipline for an enterprise graph is to identify the smallest set of cross-system integration points that deliver measurable, meaningful value.

In practice, this means starting with entity resolution, the problem of determining that the same entity, such as customer, product, location, or organizational unit, appears across multiple systems under different namespaces and identifiers. Entity resolution is the enterprise graph's natural first scope because it addresses existing operational pain points while delivering measurable results, such as reduced duplicate entities, improved match rates, and query consolidation. This body of work requires a vocabulary and ontology that are broad enough to span the systems involved without modeling any single system too deeply.[50]

---

[49] Wiśniewski, D., Potoniec, J., Świetlik, R., & Lawrynowicz, A. (2019). Competency questions and SPARQL-OWL queries dataset and analysis. Data in Brief, 27, 104641. DOI: 10.1016/j.dib.2019.104641.

[50] Sequeda, J., & Lassila, O. (2021). Designing and building enterprise knowledge graphs. Morgan & Claypool. DOI: 10.2200/S01105ED1V01Y202105DSK020.

The scoping question for an enterprise graph is founded upon enterprise-wide connections. Competency questions for enterprise graphs tend to be cross-system, such as "Is the customer in the CRM the same entity as the account holder in the billing system?" or "Which product in the catalog corresponds to which SKU in the warehouse system?" Each competency question identifies a seam between systems, and each seam implies vocabulary alignment and relative ontological commitments.

---

## Domain knowledge graph

The domain graph's commitment to depth creates the opposite scoping challenge, abating the temptation to go too deep in modeling and architectural decisions. A domain ontology can always scale to accommodate more axioms, property constraints, and class distinctions. The focus here is to determine whether additional expressiveness serves the competency questions or satisfies an intellectual appetite not shared by organizational needs or production.

Scoping a domain graph begins with the published standard. If the domain has an authoritative domain or industry ontology such as FIBO for financial instruments, OBO Foundry ontologies for life sciences, or LKIF Core for legal concepts, the scoping question is not what to model, but how much of an existing standard to adopt.[51] As an example, full adoption of a domain standard like FIBO is rarely justified for an initial deployment, as the standard is designed to cover the entire domain. The organization's competency questions will likely cover a slice of the domain. The scoping discipline is to identify that slice, adopt the classes and properties required, and defer the rest, with the knowledge that the standard's architecture supports incremental scaling and expansion.

Competency questions for domain graphs tend to require inference. A question like, "Given the reported adverse events for this compound, which other compounds sharing the same mechanism of action should be flagged for review?" implies that data, inference, and reasoning will be required, thereby helping to scope both the ontology and the graph architecture. This type of question will

---

[51] OBO Foundry. (2024). OBO Foundry Principles. https://obofoundry.org/principles/fp-000-summary.html—Community governance principles for 150+ active domain ontologies in the life sciences.

require a class hierarchy deep enough to support inference, a property structure rich enough to connect compounds to mechanisms, and a reasoner configured to derive the entailment. The scope of the domain graph is all about supporting the scope of the descriptive and logical components of the graph.

## Linked data knowledge graph

The linked data graph's commitment to openness constrains scope differently. The graph's value stems from its connectivity to external datasets, which means its scope is partly determined by the availability of desired connections. A linked data graph scoped around cultural heritage artifacts can connect to Wikidata, the Getty vocabularies, VIAF, and Europeana linked data knowledge graphs. A linked data graph scoped around proprietary financial instruments has fewer external datasets to federate with and may be better served by the domain pattern.

The scoping question for a linked data graph may be something like, "What external datasets exist for this domain, and what entity types do they expose?" The answer determines the graph's vocabulary because linked data graphs prioritize vocabulary reuse over custom term creation. The ontology's RDFS-level commitments must align with the endpoints it federates over, and its identity linking strategy will have to consider the quality of owl:sameAs and skos:exactMatch linked data assertions. These design decisions and implementation details determine the quality of federated query results. The patterns of a linked data graph are distinct and will guide the scope.

## Staffing the graph

A knowledge graph amounts to knowledge infrastructure. This means that staffing for the work will be guided by the skills required to build and maintain a knowledge graph. These skill sets overlap with, but are not identical to, the skills required for software engineering, data engineering, or data science. Organizations that staff knowledge graph programs exclusively with software engineers discover that the engineering is competent, but the semantics are hollow. Organizations that staff exclusively with ontologists discover that the model is elegant, but the system does not integrate with anything. Staffing decisions will center on assembling a team with diverse, specialized skills, able to focus on and prioritize specific tasks, jobs, and workflows.

---

## Core roles

### *Ontologist*

The ontologist is the person who designs and builds the ontology. The ontologists determine what the graph represents and how things are logically defined. Where the ontology engineer builds the systems that operationalize formal models, the ontologist designs the models themselves: the class hierarchies, property constraints, classification structures, and semantic commitments that determine what the graph can say about the world and what it cannot. This is knowledge design work rooted in information science, library science, philosophy, and linguistics.

The ontologist works closely with the ontology engineer and the reasoner to operationalize ontologies. The roles are complementary and not interchangeable. Amazon, the largest employer of ontologists globally, requires that ontologists have formal education in Library Science, Information Systems, or Linguistics—not Computer Science—and specifies requirements for prior experience in ontology and taxonomy roles. The ontologist leads the effort to develop competency questions and carries that thread throughout the lifecycle of both the ontology and the knowledge graph. She sits with domain experts and asks the questions that determine whether the graph's formal commitments match the domain's actual structure throughout the design, build, and operationalize stages.

### *Taxonomist or vocabulary manager*

The taxonomist governs the controlled vocabularies that feed the ontology and semantic layers and populate the graph. In the Ontology Pipeline framework, the vocabulary is the conceptual model—the controlled vocabulary, taxonomy, and thesaurus expressed in SKOS that defines the domain's concepts and their relationships. The ontology is the formal, logical reasoning model expressed in

RDFS and OWL that governs what the system can infer. The taxonomist ensures that the conceptual model is accurate, current, aligned with the domain's language, and consistent with what practitioners and stakeholders use.

This role is particularly critical in domain and enterprise deployments where vocabulary governance has organizational implications. When a financial services firm aligns its internal terminology to FIBO, or a healthcare organization maps its clinical terms to SNOMED CT, the taxonomist is the person responsible for ensuring the alignment is correct and maintained. Managing term deprecation, vocabulary evolution, and coordinating changes with standard release cycles are core taxonomist responsibilities—operational complexities that disappear when taxonomy work is handed to teams unfamiliar with the discipline.

### *Ontology engineer or semantic engineer*

The ontology engineer is the architect of the semantic layer, the person responsible for the formal model that determines what the graph can represent and how to support what inferences. This role requires intimate knowledge of OWL, RDFS, SKOS, and SHACL, as well as the ability to translate domain expertise into formal class hierarchies and property constraints. The ontology engineer must exercise judgment to determine which level of axiomatization is required for each use case and where additional expressiveness will add cost without capabilities.

In enterprise deployments, the ontology engineer works at the intersection of every business domain the graph touches, which means the role is as much diplomatic as it is technical. Vocabulary alignment across business units requires the ability to surface and resolve terminological conflicts that have been invisible for years because the conflicting systems never needed to interoperate. The ontology engineer is frequently the first person in the organization to make the call on whether two terms used by different teams refer to the same thing—and to absorb the organizational consequences of that determination.

### *Knowledge engineer or knowledge graph data engineer*

The knowledge engineer builds and operates the graph as a data system. This includes extraction from source systems, transformation into RDF, validation against SHACL shapes, loading into the triple store, query optimization, and increasingly, integration with AI and RAG pipelines. In enterprise deployments, this role overlaps substantially with data engineering, with the difference being that the knowledge engineer must understand the semantic model well enough to ensure that instance data conforms to structural requirements and ontological commitments. A data engineer loads data that passes a schema check. A knowledge engineer loads data that is semantically coherent with the ontology it instantiates.

This is the broadest and most actively hired role in the knowledge graph labor market. It is also the role most visibly shaped by the GraphRAG wave; roughly 40% of current job listings require experience integrating knowledge graphs with large language models. The knowledge engineer is becoming the person who ensures that when an LLM retrieves context from a graph, it retrieves the right context, with the right provenance, structured in a way the model can reason over. This is knowledge engineering applied to a new consumption layer.

### *SPARQL developer or graph database administrator*

The SPARQL developer or graph database administrator is responsible for the performance, reliability, and operational integrity of the graph's storage and query infrastructure. This role ensures the triple store handles the read and write patterns the use case demands, that queries execute within defined service levels, that indexing strategies are appropriate for the access patterns, and that backup, recovery, and all high-availability requirements are met.

In practice, this role splits into two tracks that share graph data modeling as common ground but diverge in everything else. The Semantic Web track works with SPARQL, RDF4J, Apache Jena, and triple stores such as GraphDB, Stardog, and Blazegraph—the infrastructure that makes formal ontologies computationally useful.

The property graph track works with Neo4j, Cypher, and labeled property graph operations—the infrastructure that serves application-layer graph analytics. The most capable practitioners work across both paradigms and can articulate when one serves the use case better than the other. This role is essential but frequently understaffed in production knowledge graph deployments—organizations invest in ontology engineering and data integration while treating graph infrastructure as something that will take care of itself. But it does not; it needs management at multiple levels.

### *Domain expert*

The domain expert is not a technology role; it is an essential staffing commitment. No ontology engineer, however skilled, can model a domain without sustained access to people who work in that domain every day. Domain experts serve as the source of truth for competency questions, the validators for class hierarchies and property constraints, and the first testers of query results. In domain graph deployments, the domain expert is often the primary user of the graph: a researcher querying a life sciences graph, an analyst querying a financial compliance graph, a legal professional querying a regulatory graph, or an AI domain research system.

The most common organizational mistake is to treat domain expertise as a consultative input, something extracted in a few workshops and then encoded by engineers. Domain expertise is a continuous requirement. Domains have deep, specialized knowledge requirements, with evolving vocabularies and competency questions. The domain expert must be embedded in the program rather than interviewed at the start of the project for input and later released.[52]

### *Knowledge graph product manager*

The knowledge graph product manager owns the knowledge graph strategy and its connection to AI investment. This is not a technical role in the engineering sense, but it does require technical fluency: the ability to evaluate architectural trade-offs, understand what an ontology change means for downstream queries, and articulate the business case for graph infrastructure investment to audiences that have never heard of SPARQL.

The risk in this role is the same as in any product management function that governs a deeply technical system. A product manager who understands GraphRAG but not ontology design will build a roadmap that optimizes for retrieval performance without ensuring the retrieved knowledge is semantically coherent. The organizations that staff this role most effectively—Bloomberg, Capital

[52] Grüninger, M., & Fox, M. S. (1995). The role of competency questions in enterprise engineering. In Proceedings of the IFIP WG5.7 Workshop on Benchmarking—Theory and Practice. IFIP Advances in Information and Communication Technology.

One, Salesforce—require their KG product managers to have direct experience with W3C semantic standards. The organizations that do not impose this requirement may discover the cost of omission downstream, when the product roadmap and the semantic architecture diverge in ways that only someone fluent in both would have caught early enough to prevent.

---

## Staffing by pattern

The three patterns require different staffing emphases, reflecting their different architectural commitments.

### *Enterprise knowledge graph*

Data engineering and integration specialists dominate the team with the enterprise knowledge graph. Ontology engineering is present but constrained to thin, modular schemas. The vocabulary manager role is critical because terminology conflicts across business units are the primary source of integration friction. A dedicated SHACL engineer may be warranted, given the volume and heterogeneity of incoming data.

### *Domain knowledge graph*

Taxonomists, ontologists, and ontology engineering are the primary investments for the domain knowledge graph. The ontology is the intellectual asset, and its quality determines the graph's reasoning capability. Domain experts carry more weight than in any other pattern because the graph's users are domain experts evaluating results against professional standards. Knowledge graph data engineering is present but secondary to model engineering.

### *Linked data knowledge graph*

Publication infrastructure and federation engineering dominate the linked data knowledge graph. The ontology commitment is deliberately light, staying at the SKOS and RDFS levels, so the ontology engineer's role shifts toward vocabulary alignment and identity linking strategies. The critical skill is the ability to assess external datasets for quality, coverage, and linkability.

## Phases of implementation

Knowledge graph programs fail when they attempt to deliver a production architecture in a single phase. The technical and organizational complexity is too high, with excessively long feedback loops, risking investment in the wrong scope. Every successful knowledge graph deployment, including Google's Knowledge Graph, the BBC's semantic publishing architecture, and the OBO Foundry ecosystem, evolved through phases. None shipped in one swoop, as a finished system.

The phased approach is an engineering strategy that recognizes that the quality of a knowledge graph depends on feedback that can only be obtained from operating the graph against real data and queries. In other words, the vocabularies and ontology cannot be validated in isolation. The competency questions cannot be confirmed as answered until the graph is queryable. Phases exist to create those feedback loops as early and as cheaply as possible.

### *Phase 1: Proof of concept*

The proof of concept will confirm if the proposed architecture can successfully answer the priority competency questions with real data. Not sample data, synthetic data, or hand-curated demo data. *Real data*, from the source systems and the production graph. The scope is deliberately narrow and will typically be primed to answer three to five competency questions from a single source system or two. The vocabulary and ontology will be just large enough to support those questions. The triple store can be a local instance and the validation layer can be minimal. The query interface may be raw SPARQL. Nothing needs to be production-grade, but everything needs to work.

The proof of concept (POC) validates the semantic model. The validation matrices will ensure that the ontology's class hierarchy supports the inferences required by the competency. Vocabulary alignment with source system(s) and coverage for entity types are also critical validation points for the POC. A POC moves beyond whiteboard modeling and is query intensive.

**Proof of Concept deliverables:**

- A set of 3–5 competency questions with corresponding SPARQL queries that return correct results.

- A minimal vocabulary (SKOS concept scheme) and ontology (RDFS/OWL) sufficient to support those queries.
- A populated triple store with data from at least one production source system.
- A documented gap analysis that covers what the competency questions revealed about the data, the vocabulary, and the model.

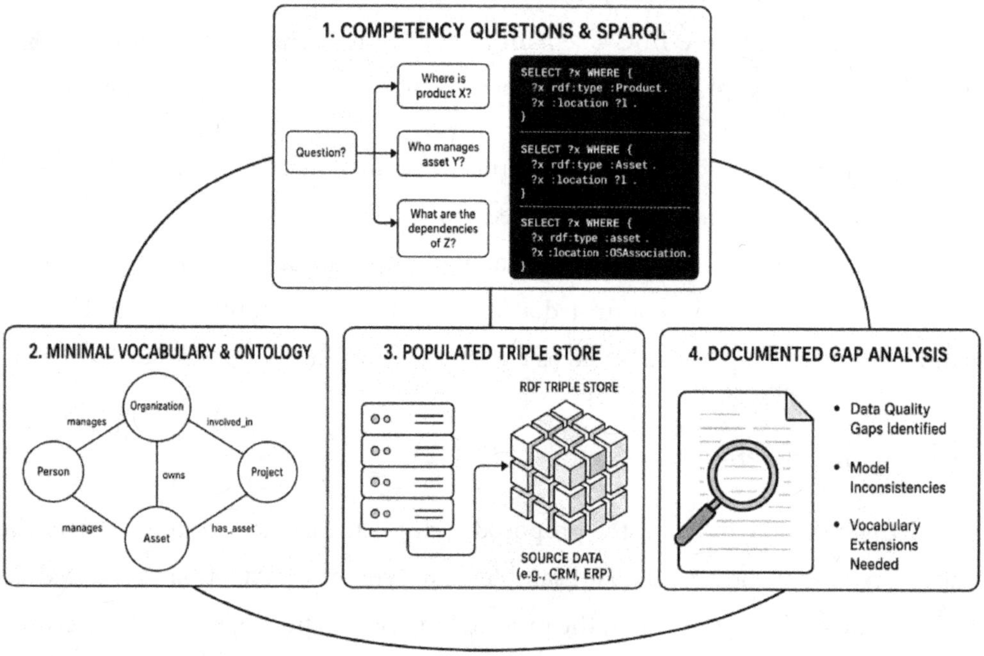


Figure 106: Proof of concept deliverables.

## *Phase 2: Pilot*

The pilot extends the POC into a system for real users to evaluate. The scope expands to cover the full set of priority competency questions, typically 10 to 20, and integrates additional source systems. The ontology matures from a minimal model into a governed artifact with documented design decisions, and the validation layer becomes operational with SHACL shapes enforcing data quality on every load.

The pilot's defining characteristic is that it introduces real users to the graph. In an enterprise deployment, this means analysts running queries against cross-system data they have never been able to join. In a domain deployment, this looks like domain experts evaluating whether the reasoner's inferred triples are correct and whether the entailments the ontology produces match the domain's encoded semantics. In a linked data deployment, this means testing federation queries against external endpoints and evaluating whether the identity links produce coherent results.

User feedback during the pilot is the most valuable input the program will receive, because it exposes semantic errors that engineering reviews cannot catch. A domain expert may discover that the inferred classification is wrong and that two things described as closely coupled are not actually related. In this case, the domain expert has identified an ontological error that would have propagated through every inference in the production graph. The pilot exists to surface those errors while correction is still cheap. Think of the pilot as an opportunity to fine-tune the components of the graph and dial in the general and specific details of the knowledge graph architecture.

The pilot also validates the organizational model. Can the vocabulary governance process keep pace with the data integration schedule? Does the ontology change management workflow function when multiple stakeholders propose conflicting extensions? Are the domain experts engaged enough to provide timely feedback on query results? These questions are answered throughout a pilot, as it requires a system bolstered with enough scope and users to appropriately stress the governance model.[53]

### *Phase 3: Production*

Production is not a launch. It is the point at which the graph transitions from a project with a delivery date to an infrastructure with an operational cadence. The transition to production requires three shifts: from project funding to operational funding, from delivery milestones to quality metrics, and from staging a build team to codifying the operational team.

The operational team may be smaller than the build team, but it must include semantic engineering capability—not just system administration. A production knowledge graph without an ontology engineer is like a production database without a DBA. It will run until something changes. When it breaks, the graph will need semantic experts, such as ontologists and taxonomists, to assess, diagnose, and fix breaking changes.

---

[53] Noy, N. F., Gao, Y., Jain, A., Narayanan, A., Patterson, A., & Taylor, J. (2019). Industry-scale knowledge graphs: Lessons and challenges. Communications of the ACM, 62(8), 36–43. DOI: 10.1145/3331166.

And then there are pragmatics. The production phase moves the knowledge graph past the pilot phase, as most knowledge graph programs are funded and managed as projects with a start, a delivery milestone, and an implied end. Continual maintenance is required to prevent degradation once a knowledge graph is delivered. Vocabularies will drift from their source standards; ontological commitments will become inconsistent as the domain evolves, and data quality can erode as source system schemas change without corresponding updates to the SHACL shapes. The graph becomes a stale snapshot of a world that has moved on.

The transition to production requires three shifts. First is the shift from project funding to operational funding; second, from delivery milestones to quality metrics; and third, from a build team to an operational team. The operational team may be smaller than the build team, but it must include semantic engineering capability, not just system administration. A production knowledge graph without an ontology engineer is like a production database without a database administrator (DBA). It will run until something changes, and then it will break in ways that only semantic expertise can diagnose.

---

## Production infrastructure

The production triple store must handle the read and write patterns demanded by use cases. Enterprise graphs with high write throughput from continuous source system integration have different triple store requirements than domain graphs with periodic batch loads and complex reasoning queries. The validation layer must be automated—SHACL shapes executed on every data load, with violations routed to a triage workflow rather than ignored or accepted. The query layer must be monitored to ensure performance meets defined service levels.

For enterprise deployments, R2RML mappings and data virtualization must be operationally monitored. A mapping that was correct when written against a relational schema six months ago will most likely break when that schema is updated, producing virtualized triples that are structurally valid but semantically wrong.[54] Production knowledge graph operations include semantic monitoring and observability—not just "Is the system up?", but "Are the triples still correct?"

## Production governance

Governance in a production knowledge graph has two dimensions. One is data governance; the other is semantic governance. Data governance asks who can add, modify, or remove triples from the knowledge base. Semantic governance oversees who can change the ontology—add a class, modify a property's domain or range, introduce a new axiom—and what the change management process is for modifications that affect downstream queries and inferences.

The separation between instance data operations and ontology governance is essential in production. Knowledge graph programs stall or fail when these two facets are conflated. An ontology change that adds a disjointness axiom can invalidate existing instance data. A property range change can break downstream SPARQL queries. Semantic changes have semantic consequences that require governance processes that include impact analysis before changes are committed.[55]

## Maintaining semantic integrity

A knowledge graph is a living system. The domain it represents changes as new entity types emerge, existing relationships are redefined, regulatory frameworks are updated, and organizational structures are reconfigured. The source systems that feed the graph change as schemas are updated, fields are deprecated, and new data sources come online. The users of the graph change as new competency questions emerge when the organization discovers the graph's capabilities, pushing the boundaries of what could not be done before.

---

[54] World Wide Web Consortium. (2012). R2RML: RDB to RDF Mapping Language. W3C Recommendation. https://www.w3.org/TR/r2rml/.

[55] Hogan, A., et al. (2021). Knowledge graphs. ACM Computing Surveys, 54(4), Article 71. DOI: 10.1145/3447772.—Section 5 addresses knowledge graph lifecycle, maintenance, and change management.

Maintaining semantic integrity means ensuring that the graph's semantic commitments (ontology, vocabulary, and validation rules) remain accurate as things change and evolve. This is the long-term engineering challenge that differentiates a knowledge graph from a data warehouse or a search index. A data warehouse can tolerate schema drift because its queries are typically written against specific tables and columns. A knowledge graph cannot tolerate ontological drift because its inferences are derived from the formal model, and a change in the model propagates through all inferences supported by the architecture and model.

## Ontology evolution

Ontology evolution is the controlled process of modifying an ontology in response to changes in the domain, use cases, or the organizational context. The challenge is that ontology changes are not local. In a relational database, adding a column to a table affects the queries that reference that table. In a knowledge graph, adding a class or modifying a property's characteristics can trigger new inferences, invalidate existing ones, and change the results of queries that do not directly reference the modified elements.[56]

Ontology evolution requires a change management process that includes several components. Impact analysis must determine which inferences are affected by the proposed change. This is where the reasoner serves as both an engineering tool and an inference engine. By running the reasoner against proposed modifications and comparing the inferred triples, the before and after reveal the semantic consequences of proposed changes before they reach production. In addition, versioning must track the ontology's state over time, so that downstream systems can reference a specific version and migrate to new versions on their own schedule. The ontology is not a library that can be wholesale updated under consuming systems.

Backward compatibility analysis must determine whether the proposed change breaks existing SPARQL queries, SHACL shapes, or R2RML mappings. A class rename, a property domain change,

[56] Zablith, F., Antoniou, G., d'Aquin, M., Flouris, G., Kondylakis, H., Motta, E., Plexousakis, D., & Sabou, M. (2015). Ontology evolution: A process-centric survey. The Knowledge Engineering Review, 30(1), 45–75. DOI: 10.1017/S0269888913000349.

or a new disjointness axiom can each break downstream consumers in different ways. The ontology engineer must understand these dependencies before committing any change.[57]

## Vocabulary maintenance

The vocabulary—the conceptual model expressed in SKOS—evolves at a different cadence than the ontology. Vocabularies track the language of the domain to capture new emerging terms, shifts in meaning for existing terms, and synonyms or near-synonyms that proliferate throughout an organization as different communities adopt different naming conventions. The taxonomist's ongoing responsibility is to ensure that the controlled vocabulary remains aligned with the domain's actual usage while maintaining the structural integrity on which the ontology relies.

For domain graphs aligned to external standards, vocabulary maintenance includes tracking the standard's release cycle. When FIBO publishes a new version, or when an OBO Foundry ontology introduces new terms and deprecates old ones, the domain graph's vocabulary must be assessed for alignment. Each change must be evaluated for its impact on the existing graph. Do new terms replace terms the graph already uses? Do deprecated terms appear in existing RDF triples that must be migrated? Does the alignment between the graph's internal vocabulary and the external standard still hold true?

Vocabulary maintenance is complicated by organizational change for enterprise graphs. Mergers, acquisitions, reorganizations, and product line changes all produce vocabulary disruptions. Terms that were unambiguous within a single business unit become ambiguous when two business units merge, or terms that refer to the same concept diverge as organizational structures separate. The taxonomist must monitor these organizational shifts and update the controlled vocabularies before the semantic layer becomes inconsistent with the organizational reality it represents.

[57] Khattak, A. M., Pervez, Z., Khan, W. A., Khan, A. M., Latif, K., & Lee, S. Y. (2013). Mapping evolution of modular ontologies using extended SPARQL syntax. Knowledge-Based Systems, 39, 211–220. DOI: 10.1016/j.knosys.2012.10.016.

## Validation as continuous assurance

SHACL validation is not a one-time quality gate. In a production knowledge graph, validation is continuous assurance, a system that confirms, on every data load and at scheduled intervals, that the knowledge base conforms to the semantic model's structural expectations. The SHACL shape library evolves alongside the ontology so that when a new class is added, shapes that define its mandatory properties and value constraints are added at the same time. When a property's range is modified, the corresponding shape must be updated before the next data load.

Validation drift—the condition where the SHACL shapes no longer reflect the current ontology—is one of the subtler failure modes in knowledge graph operations. The graph continues to accept data and the data passes validation. But the shapes are validating against an ontological structure that no longer matches the production ontology, so the validation provides false assurance. Preventing this requires coupling the ontology change management process to the validation layer so that no ontology change is complete until the corresponding SHACL shapes have been updated and tested.[58]

## The AI feedback loop

Knowledge graphs increasingly serve as the structured, descriptive, semantic knowledge layer for AI systems, providing entity resolution for NLP pipelines, domain context for retrieval-augmented generation (RAG), and formal reasoning that statistical probabilistic models struggle to perform independently. This creates a feedback loop. AI systems consume the graph and/or query it. The knowledge graph system must capture this feedback when gaps are observed or queries fail.

An NLP pipeline that extracts entities from unstructured text and links them to the knowledge base will inevitably encounter entities that the graph does not represent, relationships the ontology has not modeled, and classification ambiguities that the vocabulary cannot resolve. Each of these

---

[58] Knublauch, H., & Kontokostas, D. (2017). Shapes Constraint Language (SHACL). W3C Recommendation. https://www.w3.org/TR/shacl/.

encounters is a welcome signal, a domain evolution event that the semantic infrastructure must process, evaluate, and either incorporate or explicitly defer.[59]

The operational challenge is building the feedback mechanism. In most current deployments, the path from AI output to ontology modification is manual and slow. An NLP extraction pipeline produces candidate entities, which a knowledge engineer reviews. For vocabulary evolution, a taxonomist determines whether new terms are needed. An ontology engineer evaluates whether the model requires extension. The cycle can take weeks, during which the graph is out of step with the AI system's operational reality.

Neurosymbolic architectures—where the ontology serves as the symbolic backbone of a neural system—intensify this feedback requirement. When the ontology makes predictions interpretable, it thereby reduces data requirements through encoded prior knowledge while enabling formal reasoning for statistical models. The ontology's accuracy directly determines the AI system's reliability. An ontological error becomes a reasoning error that propagates through system predictions and is evident in AI output.

---

*Strengthening methodologies for capturing AI feedback is essential across all aspects of AI implementations.*

---

Neurosymbolic AI is especially primed for capturing and recording feedback, as the ontology and AI work as a coordinated system; the codependency is based upon one part prediction and one part reasoning.

---

## The cost of semantic debt

Software engineering has the concept of technical debt: shortcuts taken during development that must be repaid later, with interest, in the form of refactoring, bug fixes, and architectural

[59] Ristoski, P., & Paulheim, H. (2016). Semantic Web in data mining and knowledge discovery: A comprehensive survey. Journal of Web Semantics, 36, 1–22. DOI: 10.1016/j.websem.2016.01.001.

remediation. Knowledge graphs accumulate a parallel form of debt, known as semantic debt, that is less visible.

Semantic debt accrues when the semantic infrastructure—the vocabulary, ontology, and validation layer—falls behind the domain, data, or use case it was built to serve. A vocabulary that has not been updated to reflect a domain's current terminology carries semantic debt. So does an ontology that models an organizational structure from two reorganizations ago. Semantic debt shows up in a SHACL shape library that validates against an ontology version the production system has already moved past.

Unlike technical debt, semantic debt is often invisible to the engineering team because the system continues to function and all seems fine. Queries return results; the triple store is active, and data loads are complete. But the results are subtly wrong, such as when inferences derived from an ontology no longer reflect the domain, or when vocabulary-based entity resolution no longer matches the source systems. Validation may provide assurance against a model that no longer governs the production graph. The system won't necessarily fail. Rather, it will degrade, and the degradation will only be detectable by people who understand both the domain and the semantic model deeply enough to recognize that the results are no longer trustworthy.

*Semantic debt is the gap between what the graph's model commits to and what is required by the domain. It accrues silently and compounds through inference.*

In a relational database, a stale schema can produce incorrect results for queries that reference those elements. In a knowledge graph, a stale ontology produces incorrect inferences that propagate through every query, including queries that do not directly reference the stale elements. A single unresolved disjointness conflict can cascade through the reasoner, affecting classifications across the entire graph. The interest rate on semantic debt is higher than on technical debt, because semantic errors extend through the reasoning layer in ways that structural errors in a relational system do not.

However, the remedy is the same as for technical debt. Budget for it. Allocate ongoing ontology engineering capacity, schedule vocabulary reviews with a cadence that matches the domain's rate of change and maintain the SHACL shape library as a first-class engineering artifact, not an afterthought. Treat the semantic infrastructure with the same operational seriousness as the data infrastructure. A knowledge graph is not a sideshow or an ancillary artifact. It is a type of data architecture and system and should be treated as such.

---

## Architecture is a practice

A knowledge graph is an architecture, not a product, with a purposeful arrangement of components assembled in relationship to one another, in service of what the organization needs to represent, reason over, and query. We've defined those components, some required and some optional, establishing the irreducible core as the vocabulary, ontology, and knowledge base. We've also examined three common RDF-based patterns and the architectural commitments that distinguish them. We've addressed how the architecture is scoped to a domain, staffed with the right expertise, phased from proof of concept through production, and maintained as the domain and the organization evolve.

The thread that runs through a knowledge graph is that the architecture is not a one-and-done decision. A knowledge graph architecture is a practice, an ongoing discipline of aligning the semantic model with the domain it represents, the data it governs, and the systems it serves. The enterprise graph architecture must align vocabularies across business units, evaluate and test competency questions, and maintain ontological commitments that withstand changes and organizational demands. The ontology engineer who runs the reasoner against a proposed modification and analyzes the inferential consequences before committing the change to production is practicing in accordance with the graph architecture.

Architecture requires maintenance, governance, and the organizational commitment to treat semantics and knowledge as infrastructure, with the same operational cadence, staffing continuity, and institutional seriousness as the data pipelines, application services, and AI systems it supports.

The current moment in industry discourse treats knowledge graphs as a technology choice with a box on a diagram, a vendor to select, or a product to acquire. I have reframed that discourse to shift the conversation and approach.

---

*A knowledge graph is not something you buy.*
*It is something you design, build, and maintain.*

---

The architecture represents a system design that relies on decisions, discipline, and practice. Because a knowledge graph is dimensional, it must evolve to keep pace with the rate of change in the world it represents. A knowledge graph is not static but dynamic, much like humans and nature.

## Conclusion

The knowledge graph landscape is wide. Property graph architectures, linked data architectures, domain-specific semantic graphs, graph-augmented AI systems, temporal knowledge graphs, and semantic layers in data fabric deployments all carry the knowledge graph name and all represent legitimate engineering patterns. We've focused here on the three most common RDF-based architectures because the RDF paradigm provides the clearest articulation of the component distinctions—vocabulary, ontology, knowledge base, reasoning—that matter across all knowledge graph patterns.

# The Pipeline Is a Practice

*The end of the Ontology Pipeline is the beginning of the work.*

We have reached the end of the Ontology Pipeline. We began with a controlled vocabulary, a flat and disciplined list of terms, each one defined and disambiguated, each one earning its place. We grew that list into a taxonomy, giving it hierarchy and the power of inheritance. We matured the taxonomy into a thesaurus, adding the associative and equivalent relations that let concepts extend beyond the confines of a hierarchy. We lifted the thesaurus into an ontology, where classes, properties, relations, and axioms let a machine reason over what we know and derive new facts. And we connected that ontology to the world as a knowledge graph, where real entities and the facts about them become a living, queryable semantic network. Stage by stage, we moved from loose words to structured meaning.

That is the whole arc of the book, and it looks, laid out this way, like a straight line with a destination at the end. It is not. The end of the Pipeline is a vantage point, not a finish line. From here you can see the shape of the terrain and realize that the path loops back on itself. A new term surfaces in the vocabulary and asks to be placed in the taxonomy. A taxonomy branch grows heavy and reveals an associative link to be modeled. You run a reasoner over the ontology, and one of its inferences exposes a definition that was never quite right. The knowledge graph meets the messy world and sends you back to refine a concept three stages upstream. The Pipeline is iterative by nature. You do not finish it; Rather, the process laid out by the Ontology Pipeline is iterative.

The Ontology Pipeline is not a project with a single delivery date. It is a discipline and a practice—a sustained muscle you build and keep using, the way an athlete keeps training long after the first race is won. The value is in the discipline of returning: revising concepts and definitions when the domain shifts, reconciling duplicates when two teams describe the same thing two ways, re-running the reasoner when new axioms arrive. Each pass matures and evolves the structures, leaving knowledge assets sharper and more trustworthy. And with the iterations, new knowledge is captured and old knowledge preserved, ultimately giving way to a reliable and persistent knowledge infrastructure.

What that Ontology Pipeline builds is durable and resilient, in a way many technologies are not. Systems are replaced and platforms are deprecated. Models are retrained and superseded, sometimes multiple times within a quarter. A knowledge infrastructure built with intention outlives system and product lifecycles, because it is anchored in meaning rather than in any single tool. A concept with a stable URI, a clear definition, and logical relationships can be exported, imported, mapped, and reused across systems, free from vendor obligations. That is what resilience looks like in knowledge work: not the absence of change, but the ability to survive it intact. Persistence is the goal—meaning that endures, that can be inherited and shared, that does not evaporate when the software underneath it does.

It is worth saying, at the close of a book written in the age of artificial intelligence, that this work stands on its own, with or without AI. AI is the most enthusiastic beneficiary of a well-built knowledge infrastructure. A clean vocabulary sharpens retrieval; a sound taxonomy grounds classification; a rich thesaurus feeds context to a language model and pulls it back from hallucination. Those gains are authentic, as I have demonstrated throughout these chapters. But they are gains, not the reason. The reason is older and larger.

Human beings have always needed to organize what they know so that it can be found, trusted, shared, and preserved. That is what makes us human. Libraries organize with metadata, catalogs, taxonomies, and ontologies. Scholars with indexes and scholarly communication. Institutions with records and archives. We are doing it now with semantic data models so that knowledge does not scatter. If every AI system went dark tomorrow, a well-made ontology would still be worth having, because it captures how a community agreed to understand its own world. AI makes the work more visible and more valuable. It does not make it more necessary. It was always necessary.

This is the grander vision the pipeline serves. It is a stance toward knowledge management and knowledge preservation—treating the meaning an organization carries as an asset worth curating, not a byproduct to be scraped and discarded. It is a way of working: deliberate, incremental, honest about ambiguity, patient with iteration. It is, in the end, what I mean by intentional arrangement. Nothing in a good knowledge infrastructure happens by accident. Every concept is chosen, every relationship is asserted on purpose, every definition is the result of someone deciding what a word means in a domain, and for a community. That intentionality is the whole craft. The tools will keep changing but the intention is what carries.

So we are at the end, which is really the beginning. You now have the full Ontology Pipeline—vocabulary, metadata schemas, taxonomy, thesaurus, ontology, knowledge graph—and, more than the stages themselves, you have the practice that connects them. The next time a model or mandate or merger forces a change, you will have the structure and the reflexes to absorb it without losing what you know and have the tools to integrate new knowledge as an organization evolves.

**Go build something that lasts. Then keep building it.**

# Ontology Glossary

**ABox (Assertional Box):** The ABox (Assertion Box) is the section of your knowledge base that contains your actual data instances, facts, or "individuals." While the TBox provides the structural blueprint and rules (e.g., defining the category Musician), the ABox holds the specific statements that populate that structure (e.g., asserting that "Jimi Hendrix is a Musician").

- Contains facts about specific individuals
- Answers: "What specific things exist? What are their properties?"
- Data-level; changes as you add/remove data

**Attribute:** Often used interchangeably with "property," but sometimes specifically refers to datatype properties—characteristics whose values are data (strings, numbers, dates) rather than other entities. In practice, "Attribute" tends to emphasize intrinsic characteristics; "property" is the broader RDF term.

**Examples of attributes (datatype properties):**

```
:Sarah :hasName "Sarah Smith"
:Sarah :hasEmail "sarah@example.org"
:Sarah :dateOfBirth "1985-03-15"^^xsd:date
```

**Examples of relational properties (object properties):**

```
:Sarah :worksAt :Acme
:Sarah :hasFriend :John
:Sarah :authorOf :SomeBook
```

**Axiom:** A formal statement that defines constraints, relationships, or facts in an ontology. Axioms are the logical assertions from which inferences can be drawn.

**CBox (Concept Box or Category Box):** While not a strict mathematical division like the TBox or ABox, the CBox (Concept Box or Category Box) is a practical term used to describe a conceptual model, taxonomy, or thesaurus. It is most commonly built using the Simple Knowledge Organization System (SKOS) vocabulary. When you build this "CBox" using SKOS, you rely on two main W3C standard components:

- skos:ConceptScheme: The container representing your overall taxonomy, vocabulary, or classification scheme.
- skos:Concept: The actual categories, themes, or units of thought contained within that scheme.

What makes SKOS so useful for this is that it models these categories as individuals (ABox data) rather than strict logical classes (TBox rules). This allows you to easily link and organize categories—like declaring that "Rock" is broader than "Psychedelic Rock"—without triggering the strict logical constraints of an OWL ontology.

**Class:** A category or grouping of entities that share common characteristics. Classes define kinds of things. In RDF/RDFS: Defined using rdfs:Class or owl:Class. Classes live in the TBox (terminological knowledge). In description logic: Also called a "concept." Examples include:

```
:Person  rdf:type rdfs:Class
:Organization rdf:type rdfs:Class
:Book   rdf:type rdfs:Class
```

**Closed World Assumption (CWA):** The closed world assumption is a principle commonly used in traditional database systems. Under this assumption, if a piece of information is not explicitly found in the system, it is automatically assumed to be false. This is the exact opposite of the Semantic Web's open world assumption, which treats missing data as simply unknown rather than false. In data modeling, the closed-world assumption allows you to enforce strict integrity constraints, which is typical of traditional database systems. Because the system assumes it contains all relevant facts, any missing information is treated as definitively false rather than just unknown. This means your data model can be very rigid—for example, it can safely reject a record or trigger a rule if a specific piece of data is absent. This is quite different from Semantic Web models (such as SKOS or OWL), which have fewer strict constraints because they must account for data distributed across the Web.

**Concept:** In knowledge organization systems (SKOS, thesauri), a "concept" is a unit of thought—an abstract idea independent of how it's labeled. In description logic: Often used interchangeably with "class."

**Datatype Property:** A Datatype Property (formally **owl:DatatypeProperty**) is a relationship that links a resource to a literal data value rather than to another resource. These values are textually expressed, such as strings, numbers, or dates, and can be tagged with a specific language or formal data type. For example, if you wanted to state a musician's birth year, you would use a Datatype Property to link the musician to the number "1942."

**Domain:** In the Semantic Web, a domain (formally, rdfs:domain) is a rule that specifies which class of resources can serve as the subject of a specific property. For example, if you set the domain of the property hasAuthor to the class Book, a reasoner will understand that anytime a resource uses the hasAuthor property, that resource must logically be a Book. This rule states that any resource that acts as the subject (the sender) of the writes property must logically be a Person:

```
@prefix rdfs: <http://www.w3.org/2000/01/rdf-schema#> .
@prefix ex: <http://example.org/> .
ex:writes rdfs:domain ex:Person.
```

**Entity:** The broadest term—anything that exists or can be identified. Physical objects, abstract ideas, events, people, organizations—all are entities. In RDF, the specification notes that "resource" is synonymous with "entity." Anything denoted by an IRI or literal is an entity. For example:

The Library of Congress (an organization)
The concept of "sustainability" (an abstract idea)
ISBN 978-0-06-112008-4 (a specific book)
The 2024 Paris Olympics (an event)

**Functional Property owl:FunctionalProperty:** Declares that a property can have at most one value for any given subject. If a property is functional, a reasoner that finds two different objects for the same subject and property will not flag an error; instead, it will infer that the two objects must be the same thing. This is the open-world assumption at work: The reasoner assumes the data is consistent and draws the strongest conclusion available.

**Instance:** A specific, individual member of a class. Also called an "individual" (OWL) or "member." In RDF, instances are connected to classes via rdf:type. Instances live in the ABox (assertional knowledge). **In description logic,** concept assertions like Person(Sarah) place individuals in classes. Examples include:

```
:Sarah rdf:type: Person
```

```
:Acme rdf:type :Organization
:ToKillAMockingbird rdf:type :Book
```

**Knowledge Graph:** A knowledge graph is a system that represents information as a network of interconnected data points, typically built on the RDF graph structure. In practical enterprise architectures, a knowledge graph integrates different layers of information to make data highly organized and searchable:

- **TBox (Terminological Box):** The formal ontology, rules, and schema.
- **ABox (Assertional Box):** The individual instances, facts, and relationships.
- **CBox (Categorical Box):** The taxonomies and controlled vocabularies that bridge the formal ontology with the user-facing data.
- **Reasoner:** An ontology reasoner is a system that evaluates the formal rules defined in your ontology to automatically make logical inferences.

**Linked Data:** Linked Data refers to the practice of publishing and interlinking structured data across the web using RDF. It allows people and automated processes to follow links between different datasets, creating a massive, decentralized network of interconnected information. Because the data is formally structured and linked, it can be easily aggregated and searched using query languages like SPARQL. The primary benefit of Linked Data is that it allows information scattered across the Web to be easily connected, merged, and searched as if it were a single global database. This drastically increases the discoverability of data and enables a decentralized approach, allowing anyone to publish and link their information to existing concepts worldwide. AI and other software agents can easily read Linked Data. In fact, Linked Data is explicitly designed to be processed by machines rather than humans. Because the data uses formal, machine-readable structures (like RDF and OWL), AI applications can automatically process the underlying meaning of the information, aggregate it from multiple sources, and even use "reasoners" to draw logical inferences.

**Namespace:** A namespace is a mechanism for grouping related vocabulary terms (such as classes and properties) under a common, globally unique identifier, typically a base URI. In RDF and the Semantic Web, namespaces are often paired with prefixes to abbreviate long URIs, making your data much easier to read and write. For example, instead of writing out the full URI **http://xmlns.com/foaf/0.1/Person** every time, you can define foaf: as the namespace prefix and simply write **foaf:Person.**

**Object Property:** An Object Property (formally **owl:ObjectProperty**) is a relationship that links one resource directly to another resource. While the Datatype Property links a resource to a literal value (like a text string or a number), an Object Property connects two distinct entities. For example, "knows" is an Object Property that links the person "Bob" to the person "Alice."

**Ontology:** An ontology is a formal, explicit description of a domain of knowledge—a shared vocabulary that defines what kinds of things exist in a given area and how they relate to each other. The word comes from philosophy, where "ontology" means the study of being and existence. In knowledge engineering and the Semantic Web, it takes on a more practical meaning: a structured model that a computer can reason over.

**OWL (Web Ontology Language):** While RDFS allows you to categorize resources into basic classes and properties, **OWL (Web Ontology Language)** provides a more powerful, formal data modeling language to frame your ontology. Its primary purpose is to add expressivity, define constraints, and establish integrity conditions that allow systems to detect logical inconsistencies in the data. Because OWL is an RDF vocabulary, it seamlessly layers directly on top of your existing RDFS structure.

**Open World Assumption (OWA):** The open world assumption is the principle that you cannot assume the data you have is completely exhaustive. Because systems like the Semantic Web are widely distributed, it is practically impossible to know where all the data is located. Therefore, if information appears to be missing, you must assume it might exist somewhere else. This means you cannot draw logical conclusions solely from the absence of data, and removing a piece of data will never render the remaining data logically inconsistent.

**Property:** A characteristic, attribute, or relationship that can be asserted about entities. Properties are the "verbs" of your ontology—they describe what can be said about things. In RDF, properties are URIs/IRIs used in the predicate position of triples. The RDF spec states: "The predicate itself is a URI or IRI and denotes a property, that is, a resource that can be thought of as a binary relation."

**Range:** In the Semantic Web, the range (formally rdfs:range) does the exact opposite of the domain: it specifies what class of resources can act as the object (or value) of a specific property. If the domain restricts the "sender" of a relationship, the range restricts the "receiver". For example, if you set the range of the property hasAuthor to the class Person, a reasoner will understand that whatever resource is on the receiving end of that hasAuthor link must logically be a Person. This rule states that any resource that acts as the object (the receiver) of the writes property must logically be a Document:

```
@prefix rdfs: <http://www.w3.org/2000/01/rdf-schema#> .
@prefix ex: <http://example.org/> .
ex:writes rdfs:range ex:Document .
```

**RDF (Resource Description Framework):** The Resource Description Framework (RDF) is a standard framework for expressing information about resources (like documents, people, or abstract concepts) on the web. It is specifically designed so that information can be easily exchanged and processed by computer applications, rather than just being displayed to people. RDF is the foundational data model and W3C standard that describes and relates data using the triple structure. An RDF triple creates a statement.

**RDF Graph:** An RDF graph is a set of RDF triples. If you visualize these triples as a map, the subjects and objects become the "nodes" (the dots), and the predicates become the "arcs" (the directional lines connecting the dots). Because the exact same resource can act as the object in one triple and the subject in another, they naturally link together to form a web, or graph, of data.

**Reasoner (Ontology Reasoner):** An ontology reasoner is a system that evaluates the formal rules defined in your ontology to automatically make logical inferences. When you feed it a set of input data (triples), a reasoner analyzes the relationships and can deduce new facts that must logically also be true. Additionally, reasoners are used for validation; they can automatically detect if your input data contradicts the rules of the ontology and flag those logical inconsistencies.

**Relation (Relationship):** A connection between two or more entities. In RDF, relations are expressed as properties connecting a subject to an object. In RDF, every triple expresses a relation: subject --predicate--> object. In description logic, role assertions like worksAt(Sarah,Acme) express relations.

**SHACL (Shapes Constraint Language):** A W3C standard used as a syntactic validation tool. It allows you to define specific profiles or constraints to automatically verify that your RDF data is correctly structured and conforms to your expected rules. SHACL is a syntactic validation tool. It often operates more like a traditional database, using a closed-world assumption. Instead of creating new facts, it strictly checks your data against predefined "shapes" to catch errors, ensuring the data perfectly conforms to your expected structure.

**SPARQL:** The standard query language for searching, retrieving, and interacting with RDF data. Much like how SQL is used for traditional relational databases, SPARQL allows you to ask specific questions and extract information from interconnected knowledge graphs. Here is an example of a basic SPARQL query that searches a dataset for the names and addresses of museums in New York City:

```
SELECT ?name ?housenumber ?street
WHERE {
      ?museum osmt:addr:city "New York";
            osmt:tourism "museum";
            osmt:name ?name ;
            osmt:addr:housenumber ?housenumber ;
            osmt:addr:street ?street .
}
```

**Taxonomy:** A taxonomy is a type of knowledge organization system used to classify, group, and tag information. A taxonomy is a hierarchical model that represents concepts in parent-child or broader-narrower relations. In the context of knowledge graphs, taxonomies are maintained within the **CBox** (Categorical Box). They act as a bridge between your formal, abstract schema **(TBox)** and your actual, raw data instances (ABox). Because taxonomies are often more volatile than a formal ontology but more stable than daily transaction data, they are usually built using the SKOS standard we discussed earlier.

**TBox (Terminological Box):** The TBox (Terminological Box) is the part of your knowledge base that defines the "schema" or vocabulary for your domain. It contains the definitions of your categories (classes) and relationships (properties), as well as the logical rules that govern them. For example, when you use OWL or RDFS to declare that Musician is a subclass of Person, or define a playsInstrument property, you are building the TBox.

**Thesaurus:** A thesaurus is another type of knowledge organization system, very similar to the taxonomies. While a taxonomy focuses heavily on hierarchical classification, a thesaurus organizes distinct concepts using natural language labels and maps out a rich network of relationships—

specifically indicating which terms are "broader," "narrower," or "related" to one another. Just like taxonomies, thesauri belong in the **CBox** of your knowledge graph and are typically modeled using the **SKOS** standard.

**Triple:** A triple is the fundamental building block of RDF, used to make a simple statement about a resource. It always consists of exactly three parts:

- **Subject:** The resource you are describing
- **Predicate (Property)**: The specific relationship or characteristic you are defining
- **Object:** The value or the other resource it is related to

Because these statements are always structured with these three elements, they are simply called "triples." For example, in the statement **<the Mona Lisa> <was created by> <Leonardo da Vinci>**, the Mona Lisa is the subject, "was created by" is the predicate, and Leonardo da Vinci is the object.

**Turtle:** "Turtle" is the name of the syntax used to write out RDF data in a human-readable way, while **.ttl** is simply the standard file extension used when saving a document written in the Turtle format. Whenever you see a file ending in **.ttl** or hear someone refer to a "TTL serialization," it just means the RDF triples inside that document are written using Turtle.

**Type:** The class(es) to which an instance belongs. Typing classifies individuals. In RDF, the predicate rdf:type asserts that a resource is an instance of a class. For example:

```
:Sarah rdf:type :Person Sarah's type is Person
:Sarah rdf:type :Employee Sarah also has type Employee
:Sarah rdf:type :Author Multiple types are permitted
```

**URI (Uniform Resource Identifier):** A Uniform Resource Identifier (URI) is a compact sequence of characters that identifies an abstract or physical resource. By providing a globally unique identifier, a URI distinguishes a specific resource from all other things within its scope. For example, **mailto:John.Doe@example.com** and **https://www.rfc-editor.org/rfc/rfc3986.html** are both URIs.

**W3C:** The W3C (World Wide Web Consortium) is the primary international organization that develops and maintains standards for the Web. They are responsible for creating the foundational specifications for the Semantic Web that we've been discussing, such as RDF, OWL, SKOS, and SPARQL.

# Index